A New Look
at
Biblical Crime

A New Look
at
Biblical Crime

Ralph W. Scott

Dorset Press
New York

To Harriet

Quotations from *The Interpreter's Bible,* Vol. I. Copyright 1952 by Pierce and Smith (Abingdon Press). Used by permission.

Quotations from *The Interpreter's Bible,* Vol II. Copyright 1953 by Pierce and Washabaugh (Abingdon Press). Used by permission.

The foregoing acknowledgment and copyright notice covering Volume I and/or Volume II of *The Interpreter's Bible* is incorporated by reference, as though set out in full, into all citations of quotations from said Volume I or Volume II, as the case may be, wherever such quotations are duplicated in this book.

First published by Nelson-Hall Inc., 1979

This edition published by Dorset Press,
a division of Marboro Books Corporation,
by arrangement with Nelson-Hall Inc.,
1987 Dorset Press

ISBN 0-88029-134-6

Printed in the United States of America

M   9   8   7   6   5   4   3   2   1

Contents

Foreword/*The Reverend Stanley R. Sinclair, M. Div.*   vii
Preface   xi
Acknowledgments   xiii
Explanatory Notes   xiv

Part 1   Homicide   1
  1   Cain Reconsidered   3
  2   Jephthah's Daughter   7
  3   The Case Against Samuel   14
  4   The Impulsive Prophets   22
  5   The Female of the Species   30
  6   Cloak and Dagger Act   54
  7   War Crimes   58
  8   Kill or Be Killed   77

Part 2   Sex   99
  9   Lot and His Daughters   101
  10   The Maltreatment of Sarah   110
  11   Lady of the Bath   121
  12   The Rape of Tamar   133
  13   The Levite's Concubine   140
  14   Dinah and Shechem   151

Part 3   Miscellaneous Offenses   161
  15   Daniel Out of the Lions' Den   163
  16   Noah's Nudity   170
  17   Pottage and Pothunting   177
  18   Susanna and the Elders   192

Bibliography   201
Index   206

Foreword

The Reverend Stanley R. Sinclair, M.Div.*

Many people read the Bible, if the staggering sales of contemporary versions are any indication of use; but I suspect that more people would read that revered text, or read it to greater purpose, if they could first recognize its principal figures as real, flesh-and-blood human beings. Because of their remoteness in time, there is a tendency to regard the patriarchs, prophets, and princes of the Old Testment with such awe that they are reduced to lifeless statuary or to the pious phoniness of characters in a De Mille scriptural extravaganza. Yet the Bible is uncompromising in its presentation of human subjects with warts and all—or at least it gives us an honest portrayal which makes it possible for us to draw our own conclusions about them. Ralph Scott has done just that, and he brings the tools of his legal trade to his unique inquiry.

What the author terms "biblical criminology" has not been covered in English theological writing to any great extent, but it may be preferable to have the subject treated by a lawyer rather than by a theologian. Bible students who also

*Dean of Wascana (Regina, Saakatchewan); Anglican Church of Canada; Associate Editor, *Saskatchewan Anglican*.

enjoy mystery and detective fiction and courtroom drama will be fascinated by the way the author brings together religion and crime in a lawyer's view of biblical behavior.

Law is order, and without order no polity is possible. Furthermore, law is a sacred sanction commanding what is right and prohibiting all wrong. This is a much-overlooked truth in this era, when theologians and moral philosophers tend to discount the *legal* aspects of ethics and morals in their concern for a personalistic approach to the relationship of man to God, and of people to each other, within the framework of religion. Yet here is a part of the *Corpus Juris* for all time, all ages, since the regulation of society began.

Law occupies a place of unquestioned importance in both Old and New Testaments. And even though the Christian Gospel stresses the Grace of God above the Mosaic Law, it does not alter the spirit of that Law as Christ interpreted it, and St. Paul explained the inter-relationship of the two. An intelligent examination of the legal questions raised by the biblical narrative adds still another dimension to our knowledge of Scripture.

Dorothy Sayers, mystery writer-turned-theologian, remarked that she was not so much concerned with whether people accepted the Christian faith as she was that they know what it really is. Faith in unquestionably a deeper matter than the accumulation of religious knowledge—"even the Devil quotes scripture." But everyone, avowedly "religious" or not, should consider education incomplete without a thorough acquaintance with the fundamental literary document of our culture and civilization. This book is a help in broadening that acquaintance. The Bible is a comprehensive resource to handling practically all known occasions of human stress. Behavior patterns are not new, and perhaps the Bible best handles them because it "got there first"! At any rate even the agnostic or atheist can hardly fail to respond to the human drama of Cain slaying Abel, of the confrontation between Elijah and Jezebel, or to the complex personalities of Moses and David.

The author does not always exonerate these heroes and heroines for their crimes, but this poses no threat to Judeo-

Christian faith. The Old and New Testaments set forth the glory and holiness of *God*, not its human characters, and clearly show the need for his holy influence amid the violence, the vagaries, the moral blindness of the human species. Nor should we be concerned because Old Testament writers attribute to God some arbitrary, sometimes horrifying actions or attitudes. Jesus has given the Christian a lofty and loving conception of the Divine character, which makes it possible for us to discern the difference between supernatural truth and mere human interpretation.

Scott does not claim to solve all the problems presented in the text, and leaves us free to disagree with some of his findings. But laymen, lawyers, clergy, biblical *literati,* "all sorts and conditions" should enjoy this book and will be sent back to their Bibles for another reading of many passages which they thought had been "wrung dry" of meaning. *A New Look at Biblical Crime* lives up to its title, and I commend it to every reader for its insights, wealth of information, and, not to be despised, its ability to keep us absorbed and entertained.

Preface

This book is a critical analysis and specialized treatment of the offenses of Old Testament stalwarts from which they may be judged not only on the basis of their own laws but also in the light of present day concepts of justice and fair play. It is recognized that many of these ancients believed their behavior was justified by time and circumstance. Hence it may be suggested that they were not criminals, in a true sense, when judged by the standards of their time. But as we of the twentieth century subscribe to much of their philosophy, you are asked to resolve for yourself, if sitting as a juror, whether you would acquit or convict and whether you would accept free and clear the words of wisdom which fell from the lips of some. "Thou shalt not kill," said Moses.[1] Yet Moses himself was guilty of homicide.[2]

You are not asked to agree with any opinion expressed in this book. Please draw your own conclusions. You will note,

---

1. 20 Ex. 13; 5 Deut. 17; 9 Gen. 6.
2. 2 Ex. 11, 12. After looking "this way and that way" to be sure he was unobserved, Moses killed an Egyptian who was chastising a Jew. Moses fled from Egypt to save his own life.

however, a marked tendency on the part of the clergy and other commentators to palliate the offenses of Old Testament characters on the ground that they should not be judged by Gospel standards. Instead, it is urged that these people should be viewed in the framework of the age in which they lived. This contention would carry considerable weight if those portions of the Old Testament which recount the violations of Mosaic, Levitical, and Deuteronomic laws were regarded merely as history and not as sacred literature. However, the Old Testament has been canonized throughout western history and its heroes should stand the test of time if we are to cover them with an aureate mantle of piousness.

This book is based on the facts stated in the King James Version. It is assumed that this Version is a correct translation of the Bible and that the English words used therein must be given their ordinary meaning. This may conflict with the views of those biblical scholars who say the Good Book should not be construed literally. But such contentions can hardly apply to the acts and words of Old Testament characters because there is no reason to ascribe inerrancy to the Scriptures in such respects. Therefore you will be more objective if you resist the temptation to weave an orthodox interpretation of the Old Testament into the structure of this book.

For all that the Bible has been circulated, year in and year out, it is possible there are still millions of people, all over the world, upon whom it does not score a direct hit. The Bible has been extolled as a guide for life; it has been lauded as literature; it has been rewritten throughout the ages. But it does not appear ever to have been examined intelligently as it touches the strictly legal aspects of crime and criminology. Consequently, it is hoped that a discussion of some of the offenses recorded in the Bible will activate your interest in the Good Book, cause you to peruse it from cover to cover, absorb the wheat, and disregard whatever you may consider chaff. Jesus himself distinguished "between significant and negligible elements" of the Old Testament.[3] So can you.

---

3. Fosdick (1) 92.

Acknowledgments

Grateful acknowledgment is made of the courtesy and consideration extended to me by (1) the library staffs of the Pacific School of Religion, the Graduate Theological Union, and the San Francisco Theological Seminary, all of the San Francisco Bay Area, (2) the staffs of the public libraries in the California cities of San Francisco, Oakland, Stockton, and Sacramento, (3) the staff of the Mechanics' Institute Library of San Francisco, (4) Mr. John Adams of the Los Angeles Public Library, (5) the Reverend Stanley R. Sinclair for his Introduction to this book, and by (6) the late D. E. F. Easton, M.D., of San Francisco for his views on the subject of male sexual response.

Explanatory Notes

1. Except as otherwise noted, all biblical quotations, references, and dates are taken from the King James or Authorized Version. Variations in the Rheims-Douay, Revised Standard, or other versions of the Bible are recorded when substantially different from the text of the King James Version.

2. The conversations and utterances of biblical characters are quoted in this book exactly as they appear in the King James Version unless otherwise noted.

3. To make reading easier references to chapter and verse numbers of the Bible are separated by the name of the book. Thus the twenty-first verse of the fifteenth chapter of the First Book of Samuel is written 15 I Sam. 21 in lieu of I Sam. 15:21.

4. Similarly the volume and page numbers of references to encyclopedias, dictionaries, commentations, and other texts are separated by the abbreviated names set forth in the Bibliography. To illustrate, a reference to volume 5, page 100, of *The Jewish Encyclopedia* is written 5 Singer 100. Works of one volume are cited by the abbreviated name followed by the page number. Thus a reference to page 101 of Piercy's *Bible Dictionary* is cited as Piercy 101.

5. The dates assigned to the events discussed in this book are taken from The Scofield Reference Bible (King James Version) which, in turn, appear to be derived from the computations of Archbishop James Ussher in his *Annales Veteris et Novi Testamenti*. These dates may not agree with other versions such as the Septuagint, Massoretic, or the Samaritan recension. Their importance here is to show the time differential between succeeding episodes. Cf. *The Interpreter's Dictionary of the Bible,* vol. 1, page 580 et seq. Abingdon Press, 1962).

Part 1

Homicide

1
Cain Reconsidered

WE ARE TAUGHT from infancy that crime does not pay. Yet an act which has been called the world's first murder paid the culprit handsome dividends. It lifted Cain out of the doldrums of dirt farming and set him up as the builder of a city "east of Eden"[1] where he became one of its influential and wealthy citizens. From this it follows that either Cain did not commit a crime in disposing of Abel, or that crime does pay. Take your choice. You must reach one conclusion or the other because there is no middle ground. A closer look at the facts, however, forces the conclusion that while the killing of Abel was morally wrong, it was not a crime. Certainly it was not murder or manslaughter because there was no law prohibiting such acts at the time.

Cain was a farmer by trade, and his brother Abel was a sheepherder.[2] Because of their respective occupations Abel had a lamb to offer to the Lord while Cain only had a product of the soil.[3] The Lord had "respect"[4] for Abel's offering but none

---

1. 4 Gen. 16.
2. 4 Gen. 2.
3. 4 Gen. 3, 4.
4. 4 Gen. 4.

whatever for Cain's. No reason is given in the Bible for this discrimination,[5] although some commentators say that Cain's offering was too little, too late, and did not come from the heart.[6] When Jehovah rejected the offering, Cain's "countenance fell," and he became "very wroth."[7]

"Why art thou wroth? and why is thy countenance fallen?" asked the Lord. "If thou doest well, shalt thou not be accepted? and if thou doest not well, sin lieth at the door. And unto thee shall be his desire, and thou shalt rule over him."[8]

Cain was not swayed by this encouragement and advice. According to Septuagint, the Greek version of the Bible, he invited his brother to meet him in a field. This indicates that either homicide or a lesser assault on the person of Abel may have been premeditated. Arriving at the appointed place, the jealous Cain "rose up against Abel his brother, and slew him."[9] On the other hand, homicide may not have been intended, because it is possible that Cain struck Abel in a fit of anger without meaning to kill him.[10]

When Jehovah inquired of Abel's whereabouts, Cain tried to dodge the issue by asking if he was his "brother's keeper."[11] But the Lord learned the truth from the "voice" of Abel's "blood . . . from the ground."[12] Jehovah did not invoke the law of retribution (an eye for an eye) and punish Cain with death. He merely banished Cain from his native land and denied him the right to pursue his calling as a farmer.[13] This was the best thing that ever happened to Cain; it marked the

---

5. Concise 343; cf. also Jerome 14 where it is said the matter was "the Lord's concern."
6. The "ground of the divine displeasure (of Cain's offering) has commonly been sought in the tardiness of the offering, or in its comparative worthlessness . . . either because he witheld his best, or because of the insufficiency of a sacrifice without blood; . . ." 1 Hastings (1) 338, parenthesis added.
7. 4 Gen. 5.
8, 4 Gen. 6, 7.
9. 4 Gen. 8.
10. Cf. 1 Cook 56; 1 I.B. 516, 517.
11. 4 Gen. 9.
12. 4 Gen. 10.
13. 4 Gen. 12.

turning point in his life. Thereafter he was quite successful. He went to the land of Nod where he built Enoch, the first city recorded in the Bible, and raised a sizable family.[14] As one of the founding fathers of the city he became one of its leading citizens.

The exact location of the land of Nod is unknown. Some say the expression represents merely a nomadic existence.[15] On the other hand the building of a city is inconsistent with the life of a wanderer, even though Enoch may not compare in size with a modern city.[16] Without any explanation in the Bible we find that Cain gives up "his unsettled life, and advances further in civilisation than before. He builds a 'city.' This is not to be explained by the ingenious remark that even nomad tribes in Arabia have central market stations ... for a 'city' is evidently used as a general term; Cain is as much a city-builder as Nimrod.... How are these inconsistent statements to be reconciled? Every possible way has been tried and has failed."[17]

The death of Abel occurred in the year 3875 B.C. and has been classified as murder by authors of the chapter headnotes in different versions of the Bible.[18] It has also been designated as manslaughter. Actually Cain did not commit murder, manslaughter, or any other crime when he liquidated Abel. A crime is an act or omission which is prohibited by law with a prescribed penalty for a violation.[19] A moral wrong is not necessarily a crime, and no act is punishable as a crime unless first prohibited by law.[20] Except for the injunction against eating fruit from the "tree of ... knowledge,"[21] *there was no law or edict prohibiting anything at the time of Abel's death.* Cain was under no restrictions other than the dictates of his own con-

---

14. 4 Gen. 16 et seq.
15. Cf. Gore 45; Douglas 175; Jerome 13.
16. 1 Cook 56.
17. 1 Cheyne 621. Nimrod built Ninevah on the Euphrates River, a city of about 175,000 people. 3 Cheyne 3421.
18. 1 Cook 55; 2 McClintock 12; Tuck 137; Douglas 2; 1 Vincent 220.
19. 21 Am. Jur. 2d 84; 22 C.J.S. 2; Tuck 137.
20. 22 C.J.S. 54 et seq.; 21 Am. Jur 2d 95 at seq.; Tuck 137.
21. 2 Gen. 17.

science. He could not have known that centuries later his assault on Abel would be classified as a crime involving moral
turpitude. More than 1500 years passed before the Lord denounced homicide for the first time and fixed a penalty.[22] This
occurred after the Deluge of 2348 B.C. when He admonished
Noah and his progeny to refrain from committing homicide
and other immoral acts.[23] These laws were called the Seven
Commandments of Noah.[24] The well-known Ten Commandments were not announced by Moses until 1491 B.C.[25] which
was 2384 years after Abel's death.

If the banishment of Cain from his native land is regarded
as a punishment, then it would be illegal today because it was
ex post facto,[26] that is, it was punishment for homicide before
homicide was ever denounced as a crime. Penalties of this kind
have no force in law, and if the case were reviewed by the
courts of today's enlightened governments, it is likely that
Jehovah's judgment would be reversed, thus clearing Cain of
all criminal culpability. This would not, of course, remove
the stigma of immorality from his name.

Some biblical scholars say the unhappy affair did not occur
at all, but is merely symbolic of the reward for good conduct
and the penalty from wrongdoing.[27] This idea is hard to follow
to a logical conclusion. Cain was rewarded for wrongdoing and
was protected by the Lord from a homicidal attack by an
enraged populace.[28] All that Abel got for good conduct was
death.

---

22. 9 Gen. 6.
23. 9 Gen. 1 et seq.
24. 8 Jackson 184.
25. 20 Ex. 1 et seq.; 5 Deut. 6-21.
26. Broadly speaking an *ex post facto* law is one that has retroactive
    effect. More specifically in point here, it is one that punishes as a
    crime an act done before the enactment of the prohibitory law making
    such an act a crime. Convictions based on *ex post facto* laws are sub-
    ject to reversal. Cf. 16 Am. Jur. 2d 734 et seq.; 16A C.J.S. 90 et seq.;
    Calder v. Bull, 3 U.S. (Dallas) 385; Black 662; Blackstone's Commen-
    taries, vol. 1 #46.
27. Cf. 1 Hastings (1) 5, 338, 339; Gore 45.
28. 4 Gen. 15.

2
Jephthah's Daughter

ONE OF THE MOST pathetic stories of the Bible is the account of Jephthah's sacrifice of his own daughter as a burnt offering to the Lord. The poor girl was the victim of her father's rashness and also of his cowardice in not risking the consequences of a broken vow. Jephthah might have thrown himself on the mercy of the Lord[1] and asked to be relieved from a vow, the terms of which had become distorted by circumstances beyond his control. But he preferred not to hazard the Lord's displeasure, and so the young lady was sacrificed. Whether she was burned alive or first killed and then cremated is not revealed in the biblical text. However, one commentator believes "her flesh charred and her veins burst and her bones calcined in the sacrificial flame,"[2] and some Catholics accept the idea that she was offered in a "holocaust."[3]

The hideous affair was aggravated by a two-month respite which the girl begged from her father before submitting her-

---

1. The Lord was merciful at times. 21 I Chron. 13; 1 II Chron. 11; 7 II Chron. 3; 44 Isa. 21, 22. At other times He was revengeful and jealous. 1 Nahum 2; 47 Isa. 3; 63 Isa. 4, 5, 6; 65 Isa. 12; 5 Jere. 29; 7 Jere. 20.
2. Lofts 37.
3. Jerome 158.

self for the kill. What were her thoughts during the sixty-day period? And how many agonizing hours did she endure before the end? Surely there must have been times when the law of self-preservation became dominant, and feelings of despair engulfed her.[4]

One phase of the case has been overlooked entirely by the clerical commentators, expositors, and exegetes. Assuming the King James Version of the story is correct, Jephthah could have complied with the vow without sacrificing his daughter. The same if true is we accept literally the Greek, Latin, Hebrew, or Aramaic versions as well as the Revised Standard Version of today. Jephthah was either poorly advised or he had no advice at all. He needed a Portia to construe the language of the vow correctly.[5]

Here are the facts.

Jephthah was a swashbuckling Israelite who came to the rescue of his people when they were threatened by the Ammonites in 1143 B.C.[6] The illegitimate son of Gilead and an unknown harlot, he was driven out of the family circle by his father's wife and her progeny.[7] He fled to the land of Tob[8] where he assembled a strong and warlike band of discontents like himself.[9]

About that time the Ammonites were determined to recover some of the lands seized by the Israelites many years before. When hostilities became imminent, the elders of Gilead solicited Jephthah's aid. They stipulated he could become the "head over all the inhabitants of Gilead"[10] if he would lead

---

4. Lofts 63.
5. Cf. Shakespeare's "Merchant of Venice" in which Portia, a lawyer, construed Shylock's contract calling for a pound of flesh to mean flesh only and not flesh and blood, thereby saving her client's life.
6. 11 Judg. 1 et seq.
7. 11 Judg. 1, 2; cf. Wood 285.
8. Tob is probably located on the east side of the Sea of Galilee.
9. 4 Hastings (1) 785. Concise 406.
10. 11 Judg. 8. In addition to being the name of a man, Gilead was also the name of a tribe.

them in the coming fight. Jephthah accepted their terms. Just before the battle he uttered his historic vow to the Lord, "If thou shalt without fail deliver the children of Ammon into mine hands, Then it shall be, that *whatsoever* cometh forth of the doors of my house to meet me, when I return in peace from the children of Amon, shall surely be the Lord's, and I will offer *it* up for a burnt offering."[11]

The Ammonites were routed by Jephthah's forces. He returned triumphantly from battle and was about to enter his own house when "his daughter came out to meet him with timbrels and with dances."[12] Jephthah was dumbfounded.

"Alas," he exclaimed to the girl, "thou has brought me very low, and thou art one of them that trouble me: for I have opened my mouth unto the Lord, and I cannot go back."[13]

"My father," she replied, "if thou hast opened thy mouth unto the Lord, do to me according to that which hath proceeded out of thy mouth."[14]

The girl then requested two months of grace "that I may go up and down upon the mountains, and bewail my virginity, I and my fellows."[15] When she returned sixty days later, Jephthah "did with her according to his vow which he had vowed; and she knew no man."[16]

In Jephthah's time a vow was a vow, not to be taken lightly but to be fulfilled, especially when made to the Lord.[17] With many people the same is true today. Nevertheless it is difficult to believe that if any devout person of this day and age should find himself in a predicament similar to Jephthah's, he would go to such extremes. Most men would bear the con-

---

11. 11 Judg. 30, 31, emphasis added. 2 Cook 184.
12. 11 Judg. 34.
13. 11 Judg. 35.
14. 11 Judg. 36. This discussion between Jephthah and his daughter may be the origin of today's well known admonition to keep your mouth shut if you are not sure of what you're talking about.
15. 11 Judg. 37.
16. 11 Judg. 39.
17. 30 Num. 2; 23 Deut. 21.

sequences of their own folly rather than allow an innocent child to suffer, let alone be put to death. Had Jephthah lived in the twentieth century, it is not unlikely that a jury of his peers would have terminated his carrer at the end of a rope.

According to the Reverend William Piercy, some historians, such as Kimchi, Konig, and Edersheim, contend that the girl was not sacrificed but was only denied the right to marry.[18] Reliance is placed on the words in verses 37 to 39 of the eleventh chapter of Judges which say that during the period of grace she went to "bewail (her) virginity" and in the execution of the vow "she knew no man." These historians might have placed greater reliance on various provisions of Mosaic law. Through the Sixth Commandment the Lord Jehovah issued His fiat against homicide. He was unalterably opposed to human sacrifice and ordered the Israelites to refrain from such practice.[19] In these respects, as in all others, the Lord must have meant what He said. Consequently it may be asserted with much force that to offer the life of a human being as payment for good fortune in war would be an insult to Jehovah's intelligence. Had the Lord believed that Jephthah intended human sacrifice, He would have handed the Israelites a defeat instead of victory. If it were otherwise, the author of the Book of Judges places Jehovah in a very awkward position. Even the Lord, without being inconsistent, cannot oppose human sacrifice and, at the same time, accept such a sacrifice for success in battle.

Other commentators share the view that Jephthah's daughter was not sacrificed as a burnt offering. The Reverend John McClintock and Reverend James Strong say the notion that the girl was put to death "is inconsistent with the first principles of Mosaic law."[20] Dr. Adam Clarke is of a similar mind,

---

18. Piercy 392. The historians referred to are probably David Kimchi, also spelled Kimhi, a French exegete (1160-1235 A.D.), Johann Konig, a German Protestant theologian (1619-1664), and Alfred Edersheim, a Christian theologian and missionary to the Jews (1825-1889). Cf. also 2 Vincent 606 and Wood 290 et seq.

19. 12 Deut. 29-32; 18 Deut. 9-14.

20. 4 McClintock 819. Cf. also Wood 290 et seq.

calling attention to the fact that Jehovah rejected the Canaanites because of that savage custom.[21] Moreover, Clarke thinks Jephthah was actuated by a benign spirit at the time, and in that frame of mind he could not possibly sacrifice anybody.[22]

While these arguments are impressive, they lose their luster in the light of the plain wording of the biblical text. Taken as a whole, the story makes it clear that death was the outcome; not virginity.[23] Dr. Robert Watson thinks there is no doubt that the body of the young lady was pledged to the Lord and that Jephthah had no alternative but to kill her.[24] The idea that death was not intended by the vow is sharply criticized by the Reverend Piercy and the Reverend Samuel Fallows and by Professor George Moore also.[25] And the Reverend Robert Tuck reluctantly concedes that "the arguments in favour of an actual sacrifice decidedly predominate."[26] But he finds no hint in the Bible of divine acceptance of the dreadful offering and wonders if the Lord could have done so. Other writers share the view that the girl was killed, one stating that she was sacrificed as a "burnt-offering,"[27] while another says she was "murdered."[28]

---

21. 2 Clarke 149.
22. "Those who assert that Jepthah did sacrifice his daughter, attempt to justify the opinion from the barbarous usages of those times: but in answer to this it may be justly observed, that Jephthah was now under the influence of the Spirit of God, ver. 29; and that Spirit could not permit him to imbrue his hands in the blood of his own child; and especially under the pretense of offering a *pleasing* sacrifice to . . . God." 2 Clarke 149.
23. 2 Fallows 918; Piercy 392; Gore 209; Concise 406.
24. "She is vowed to the Lord in sacrifice. He cannot go back, Jehovah who gave the victory now claims the fulfillment of the oath." 4 Exp. Bible 248.
25. Piercy 392; 2 Fallows 918, 919. "That a human victim is intended is, in fact, as plain as words can make it; the language is inapplicable to an animal, and a vow to offer the first sheep or goat that he comes across—not to mention the possibility of an unclean animal—is trivial to absurdity." Moore 299. Cf. also Boling 209, 210.
26. Tuck 29, 32, 33.
27. Douglas 605.
28. Lofts 57.

Correctly interpreted, the King James Version of the vow contemplates neither death nor virginity, but only the burnt offering of a *thing,* that is, some animal or inanimate object. Jephthah said that *whatsoever* came out of the house to meet him, he would offer *it* for a burnt offering. The words *whatsoever* and *it* do not denote a person. If Jephthah intended to vow the sacrifice of a person, he would have said *whosoever* or *whoever.* Certainly he would not have referred to a person as *it.* Thus, one commentator believes Jephthah had a "thing" in mind and might have meant a dog, horse, tame deer, marmoset, peacock, or leopard cub.[29] On the other hand, it may be argued that a thing or inanimate object has no power of locomotion and hence could not "cometh forth"[30] to meet Jephthah. In one way that is true. But how about a spear or an arrow? And how about the timbrels which the girl carried out of the house? These questions are answered in part by one commentator who translates verse 21 as meaning "anything coming out the door of my house."[31]

In the Revised Standard Version and in the Greek, Latin, Hebrew, or Aramaic versions, neither the word *whosoever* or *whoever* is used instead of *whatsoever,* and the word *him* replaces the word *it.*[32] Assuming these translations are correct, nobody yet has come up with the idea that the word *him* means *her.* The Bible does not declare that the masculine includes the feminine and the neuter. It follows that Jephthah did not vow to sacrifice a girl. Therefore, to extend the wording of the vow to a female under most versions of the Bible forces you to play verbal leapfrog and to pile assumption on assumption until primary intent is lost in the vortex.

One other aspect of the case has been generally overlooked

---

29. Lofts 60, 61.
30. 11 Judg. 31.
31. Boling 208-210.
32. 2 I.B. 769; 4 Exp. Bible 243; Moore 299. One exception is the Rheims-Douay Version in which the vow is written, "Whosoever shall first come forth—the same will I offer as a holocaust to the Lord." This language may have been adopted to harmonize with the fact that the girl was sacrificed.

in the shuffle of commentary. Assuming that Jephthah did intend human sacrifice, it was not necessary for him to kill his daughter at all. Levitical law permitted him to redeem a vow to sacrifice a daughter by the payment of a trifling sum of money, ten to thirty shekels depending on her age.[33] Why Jephthah did not take advantage of this statute is not explained in the biblical text, although Dr. Leon Wood, a proponent of the virginity theory, thinks Jephthah passed up a monetary redemption by devoting his daughter to service in the Tabernacle.[34] On the contrary, Dr. J. D. Douglas states that female attendants in the Tabernacle did not have to be virgins, and that Jephthah "must fulfill his vow by offering her as a burnt-offering."[35] And Dr. Symon Patrick excuses Jephthah for not invoking monetary redemption because he may have been "deceived by a mistake in the sense of the law."[36]

Jephthah could have fulfilled most versions of the vow by offering the tambourines which his daughter carried from the house, and it is likely that the Lord would have been more pleased with such an offer than with the charred remains of the unfortunate girl. This assumption is supported by the fact that in 1860 B.C. the Lord saved Isaac from the sacrifical knife of Abraham[37] and also by the teachings of the prophet Micah who says that Jehovah does not "require" human sacrifice but only "to do justly, and to love mercy, and to walk humbly with thy God."[38]

It is for you to decide if you would put Jephthah in murderer's row.[39]

---

33. 27 Lev. 1 et seq.; Dummelow 100.
34. Wood 293, 294.
35. Douglas 605.
36. 2 Patrick 58.
37. 22 Gen. 9-13.
38. 6 Micah 6-8.
39. Cf. 1 Jenks 796, 797, "In this he acted conscientiously; but his conscience was erroneous. Otherwise he would not have placed his amiable daughter ... among the devoted enemies of God; much less would he have offered so detestable a sacrifice, which was most expressly forbidden as an abomination of the Lord which He hated."

3
The Case Against Samuel

THE TIME IS 1079 years before Christ, and the place is Gilgal, an ancient city in Palestine near the north end of the Dead Sea.

Before the prophet Samuel stands Agag, the captured king of the Amalekites, whose entire people within the area of battle—every man, woman, and child—had just been "utterly destroyed"[1] by King Saul of Israel in a swift war of extermination.

The two men eyed each other narrowly for a moment. Then Agag said despairingly, "Surely the bitterness of death is past."[2]

"As thy sword hath made women childless," the prophet replied, "so shall thy mother be childless among women."[3]

---

1. 15 I Sam. 21.
2. 15 I Sam. 32. The meaning of these words is obscure. Septuagint, the Greek version of the Bible, and Vulgate, the Latin version, suggest "Surely, death is bitter," thus implying that Agag was resigned to his fate. Hebrew versions of the Bible indicate that Agag was confident his life would be spared. Cf. 2 Cook 314. According to the Reverend Scott, "Agag affected the stateliness and dignity of a monarch even in his degraded and perilous circumstances, as if he would over-awe the aged prophet." 1 Scott 504. Rheims-Douay quotes Agag as saying, "Doth bitter death separate in this manner."
3. 15 I. Sam. 33.

With these few words he picked up a sword and chopped the hapless Agag into pieces. The flow of blood, the agonizing screams or moans of the victim, and his cries for mercy or for a quick deliverance from a painful death were all lost on the pitiless prophet as he hacked Agag into a gory mass of flesh and bones. Most of the clergy try to justify this brutality. Some, however, are shocked by Samuel's viciousness. "How can such a terribly act as this be justified?" asks the Reverend Tuck.[4]

Murder is generally defined as the unlawful and malicious killing of a human being. The slaughter of Agag has all the elements of this crime. Agag's life had just been spared by King Saul and also by the people.[5] Irked at this turn of events, Samuel took matters into his own hands and butchered Agag. He defied the king and the people, contending for the record that he was obedient to a divine command to "blot out the remembrance of Amalek"[6] which had been announced through Moses more than four hundred years before the gruesome scene at Gilgal.

A better understanding of Samuel's role in the tragedy may be had by reference to his past. The last of the principal judges of Israel, Samuel brought order out of chaos by welding the several warring tribes into a nation. When the Philistines threatened war he called the tribes together at Mizpeh,[7] organized them into an army, and led them into battle. The Philistines were defeated.[8] From then on Samuel was the top man in Israel. As he grew older, he realized that none of his sons was fit to succeed him. They were local judges who took bribes and "perverted judgment."[9] That blot on the family

---

4. Tuck 48. This minister also points out that attempts to relieve the affair of some of its horror by contending that Agag was delivered to an executioner should be discounted. Samuel, he says, was impelled by the "excitement of the hour." Cf. also Dummelow 190 and Edman 76.
5. 15 I Sam. 9.
6. 25 Deut. 19; 17 Ex. 14.
7. A city about thirty-five miles southeast of the Sea of Galilee.
8. 7 I Sam. 5-11.
9. 8 I Sam. 3.

escutcheon forced Samuel to look elsewhere for a successor. At the suggestion of the elders, he picked out Saul, "a choice young man, and goodly."[10] His selection was ratified by the multitude who shouted, probably for the first time in history, "God save the king."[11] Thereafter the nation prospered under the temporal leadership of Saul and the spiritual guidance of Samuel.

The Amalekites on Israel's southern flank were a threat to the security of the nation. This worried Samuel considerably and prompted him to look for an excuse for launching a preventive war. To find one, he was obliged to go back in history more than four hundred years.[12] After their exodus from Egypt, the children of Israel under Moses had been harassed during their wandering by the Amalekites who, like most aborigines, probably resented the intrusion. Though the Amalekites were defeated by Joshua at Rephidim in 1491 B.C.,[13] Moses told his people then and there to "blot out the remembrance of Amalek from under heaven; thou shalt not forget it."[14] This was all the excuse that Samuel needed.

"Now go," he told Saul, "and smite Amalek, and utterly destroy all that they have, and spare them not; but slay both man and woman, infant and suckling, ox and sheep, camel and ass."[15]

So the war was on. It terminated in the destruction of the Amalekites "with the edge of the sword"[16] together with their livestock of poor quality. The sturdy animals and King Agag were "spared"[17] and herded northward to Gilgal.

---

10. 9 I Sam. 2.
11. 10 I Sam. 24.
12. Comparable in point of time if Spain today should start a war against England because of the experience of the Spanish Armada in 1588 A.D.
13. 17 Ex. 8-13. Rephidim was a city near the end of the Sinai Peninsula.
14. 25 Deut. 19; 17 Ex. 14.
15. 15 I Sam. 3.
16. 15 I Sam. 8.
17. 15 I Sam. 9.

The prophet's attempt to justify the murder of Agag and the massacre of the Amalekites on the Mosaic command of 1491 B.C. is pathetically weak. For in 1206 B.C. (more than one hundred years before Samuel hacked Agag into pieces) the command was set aside by the Lord because He was thoroughly disgusted with the Israelites for their backsliding and worship of other gods.

"Did not I deliver you from the Egyptians, and from the Amorites," He said to them, "from the children of Ammon, and from the Philistines?

"The Zidonians also, and the *Amalekites,* and the Maonites, did oppress you; and ye cried to me, and I delivered you out of their hand.

"Yet ye have forsaken me, and served other gods; *wherefore I will deliver you no more.*"[18]

Thereafter the Amalekites and other tribes served the Lord as an instrumentality to punish the Israelites whenever they conducted themselves improperly or, as the Bible puts it, whenever they went "a whoring after other gods."[19] When the Lord "strengthened"[20] these people against Israel, He removed all doubt that they were to be killed whenever it suited the convenience of Samuel or the Israelites. Biblical commentators have overlooked this point, namely, that the Lord had rescinded the Mosaic command of 1491 B.C. upon which Samuel relied.[21] Thus, there was nothing of divine origin to justify the killing of Agag.

---

18. 10 Judg. 11-13, emphasis added.
19. 2 Judg. 17. Rheims-Douay substitutes "committing fornications" for "whoring."
20. 3 Judg. 12, 13.
21. One commentator points out that "for both Saul and Samuel, the command of the Lord was inexorable and, according to their belief, one of religious compulsion." 2 I.B. 958. The Reverend Cook erroneously calls the killing of Agag an "uncompromising obedience to the commandments of God." 2 Cook 314. While the Reverend Dummelow classfies the execution of Agag as "mere butchery," he says it was justified as a "religious necessity" and that Saul had no right to give any "quarter" Dummelow 190.

Samuel's real motive is crystal clear. He simply did not want Agag alive to serve as a rallying point for other Amalekites who had not come in contact with Saul's army.[22] This indicates premeditation, an essential element of the crime of murder. It also shows that the prophet had made up his mind to kill Agag no matter what King Saul or the rest of the Israelites thought or did about it.

The author of the First Book of Samuel furnishes indirect evidence[23] that Samuel was more concerned with eliminating Agag than with adherence to the four-hundred-year-old edict of Moses. While Samuel lost no time in clobbering Agag, there is no indication in the Bible that he destroyed the select livestock. Samuel had ordered the destruction of these animals as well as their owners.[24] This was meant to take place near the scene of the battle and not at Gilgal, because, when the victorious army returned, Samuel was astonished by the presence of the herd.

"What meaneth then this bleating of the sheep in mine ears," he asked Saul significantly, "and the lowing of the oxen which I hear? . . . Wherefore then didst thou not obey the voice of the Lord?"[25]

Fearful of Samuel's spiritual powers,[26] Saul was obliged to think rapidly.

"Yea, I have obeyed the voice of the Lord," he replied meekly, "and have gone the way which the Lord sent me, and have brought Agag the king of Amalek, and have utterly destroyed the Amalekites.

---

22. Saul's campaign extended from Havilah to Shur. 15 I Sam. 7. It is obvious he did not kill all of the Amalekites because twenty-three years later (1056 B.C.) David, who succeeded Saul, was at war with them again. 30 I Sam. 1 et seq.

23. Indirect evidence is evidence which does not tend directly to prove a controverted fact, but which establishes a state of facts, or the existence of other facts, from which the controverted fact follows as a logical conclusion. Cf. Black 913.

24. 15 I Sam. 3.

25. 15 I Sam. 14, 19.

26. 12 I Sam. 18.

"But the people took the spoil, sheep and oxen, the chief of the things which should have been utterly destroyed, to sacrifice unto the Lord thy God in Gilgal."[27]

The sincerity of Saul's explanation is open to question. Normally people do not perform idle acts, and if Saul intended to sacrifice the choice animals, there was no occasion to herd them mile after mile to Gilgal. It would have been much easier to kill them before the long trip through arid lands. The Bible is silent as to the ultimate disposition of these animals. This omission is important because it shows by inference that Samuel feared to risk the displeasure of the army, and parceled out the choice livestock as spoils of war.[28] Parenthetically, it also suggests the possibility that Samuel failed to practice what he preached.

The prophet was not impressed by Saul's excuse. He bitterly denounced him for failing to obey the divine command to "blot out the remembrance of Amalek" by killing both Agag and the good domestic animals, omitting to mention that the command had already been revoked. Shaking a bony finger at Saul, Samuel said,

"Behold, to obey is better than sacrifice, and to harken than the fat of rams.

"For rebellion is as the sin of witchcraft, and stubbornness is as iniquity and idolatry. Because thou hast rejected the word of the Lord, he hath also rejected thee from being king."[29]

Apologists for Samuel, and there are many, cite this denunciation of Saul as a "great prophetic ... which ... sets obedience" ... above sacrifice.[30] However, the "great prophetic" never materialized. The Lord did not keep Saul from being king although Samuel tried vainly to dislodge him by promot-

---

27. 15 I Sam. 20, 21. Saul spared Agag "most likely for ransom as avarice seems to have taken a strong hold on their minds, and triumph does not appear, from history, to have become an object of national pride." 2 Vincent 651.
28. "It is somewhat remarkable that nothing further is said of the fatlings and lambs which the people had brought." H. P. Smith 141.
29. 15 I Sam. 22, 23.
30. Cf. Piercy 783.

ing David for the throne.[31] This bolsters the supposition that the Lord was not displeased with Saul. He must have felt that the king was right and that Samuel was wrong. Saul remained on the throne for twenty-three years after the Gilgal tragedy. He outlived the prophet by four years, meeting death in 1056 B.C. when he fell on his sword rather than face capture by the Philistines.[32] David himself described Saul as "the Lord's anointed,"[33] a characterization hardly befitting a rejected king.

That Samuel misconstrued and misapplied the ancient admonition of Moses is also demonstrated by an earlier divine injunction not to molest the "children of Esau."[34] The Amalekites were the "children of Esau." Esau was the grandfather of Amalek, the progenitor of the tribe which bore his name.[35] Consequently, this injunction of the Lord coupled with the well-known Sixth Commandment against homicide[36] forces the conclusion that extermination of the Amalekites was never intended when Moses instructed his people to "blot out the remembrance of Amalek." Logic dictates that the Israelites were ordered to forget the Amalekites entirely and to have no truck with them. Otherwise the mandates of the Lord conflict with each other, and it is reasonable to assume that in biblical times conflicts of law were to be reconciled, if possible, just as they are today.[37]

Samuel's memory was lopsided when it came to the Amalekites. He could recall quite handily the words of Moses uttered four hundred years before his time to "blot out" all remembrance of these people, but he promptly forgot every other divine command on the same subject. This supports the conclusion that Samuel was not acting in response to divine will.

What is your verdict? Would you hold Samuel guilty of

---

31. Cf. 16 I Sam. 1 et seq.
32. 31 I Sam. 4. Cf. also 1 II Sam. 1-15.
33. 1 II Sam. 14.
34. 2 Deut. 4-6.
35. 36 Gen. 6-12.
36. 20. Ex. 13. "Thou shalt not kill."
37. Cf. 82 C.J.S. 717.

murder or manslaughter[38] when judged either by the laws of his own era or by the standards of today? The facts show that it served Samuel's personal and political purposes to kill Agag, and that he did so with premeditation, with malice, and against the wishes of the people. The evidence also shows that the prophet violated the Sixth Commandment[39] and the Lord's injunction against molesting the Amalekites. Therefore the defense of obedience to the divine command of 1491 B.C. is too flimsy to warrant serious consideration since the command itself was misconstrued and had been repealed by fair implication.

Agag's sudden and unnatural demise is not the first of its kind recorded in the Bible, nor is it the last. It appears, however, to have caused one of the first clashes in history between temporal and spiritual power.

---

38. Manslaughter is the unlawful killing of a human being without malice. Cf. 40 Am. Jur. 2d 348.
39. "Thou shalt not kill." 20 Ex. 13; 5 Deut. 17.

4
The Impulsive Prophets

Elisha

ON A HOT summer afternoon in the year 896 B.C. a group of forty-two mischievous children, perhaps better described in present-day parlance as a bunch of kids, were loitering on a road just outside the city of Bethel. Along came Elisha, one of the most revered of the prophets. He was weary after his fifteen-mile hike from Jericho, and his nerves were frayed. He had just received the prophetic mantle from Elijah and felt the burden of his responsibilities. After bestowing the mantle on his successor, Elijah ascended to Heaven in a fiery chariot.[1] This left the new prophet on his own. Unlike Elijah, he was either bald or his hair was cropped short somewhat like a crew cut.[2]

As he approached, the children yelled, "Go up, thou bald head; go up, thou bald head."[3]

---

1. 2 II Kings. 11.
2. Men of biblical times let their hair grow to considerable length. 1 Hastings (1) 693. Elisha is described as being bald-headed and comparing unfavorably to Elijah, the prophet of the flowing locks. Cf. Piercy 246.
3. 2 II Kgs. 23. It has been suggested the children meant that Elisha should also take off in a fiery chariot for Heaven. 1 Fallows 589.

Elisha couldn't take it. He lost his temper and cursed the youngsters in the name of the Lord. Immediately two bears appeared and tore them into ribbons.[4]

What the Bethel children did to Elisha was not half as provocative as what boys of today could do with a snowball or an over-ripe tomato. What the parents of the deceased children did to Elisha, if anything, is not revealed in the biblical text. They probably did not dare to lay hands on him. Neither did the king or any of the elders of Bethel. They all feared spiritual repercussions. However, it has been said that Elisha was punished for the foul deed by ill health.[5]

Elisha has been both condemned and condoned. Dr. F. W. Farrar asks who "could doom so much as a single rude boy, not to speak of forty-two, to a horrible and agonizing death for shouting after anyone?"[6] On the other hand Clarke says that the Lord is responsible because Elisha had no power to bring about the appearance of the bears.[7] The Reverend F. C. Cook blames the Bethel parents, contending that they were unworthy of having children. It follows, he says, that the parents were punished through the death of their children.[8]

Biblical scholars disagree on the authenticity of this story. Like others, Dr. James Hastings points out that the punishment of the children is out of all proportion to their "offense,"[9] if the prankish act is entitled to be called an "offense." He goes on to say that in all probability the story is merely folklore to guide "rude and naughty children."[10] At the same time, he indicates that the tale has some factual basis. The Reverend Piercy, however, accepts the story literally and excuses Elisha

---

4. 2 II Kgs. 24. "The provocation in this case does not seem to have been sufficient to call forth curses, or to require so dreadful a punishment." Tuck 131.
5. 1 Hastings (1) 694.
6. 6 Exp. Bible 28.
7. 2 Clarke 480.
8. 3 Cook 8, 9.
9. 1 Hastings (1) 694.
10. Ibid.

on the assumption that severity is a desirable attribute even if it means the death of prankish children.[11]

Elisha inherited miraculous power from Elijah.[12] If the sad story of the Bethel children is true, it follows that the use of such power adds up to forty-two murders. In an unwarranted display of irascibility, Elisha not only overlooked but disobeyed the Sixth Commandment against homicide. In fairness to him it must be said that his encounter with the children contrasts sharply with the kindliness he showed on other occasions. He has been characterized as a tolerant man,[13] and in many ways he was. He made a poison spring wholesome,[14] made poison soup palatable and harmless,[15] saved an insolvent woman from selling her sons into slavery,[16] cured the sterility of a barren woman and raised her son from the dead,[17] and induced the king to right her wrongs.[18] He also cured the Syrian king Naaman of leprosy by transferring the dreadful disease to his own servant, Gehazi.[19] While this was no kindness to Gehazi, it was a great relief to the king.

Years later we find Elisha as the man behind the scenes in two assassinations for political purposes. The first one occurred when Hazael murdered Ben-hadad,[20] and the second took place when Elisha instigated an uprising pursuant to which the idolatrous Jehu gained the throne of Israel.[21]

---

11. "He (Elisha) showed that he could be as severe as his master, and that God would support him in his severity when 'a set of boys' from the ill-famed city of Bethel made God's exaltation of the long-haired prophet a cause of mockery to him with his close-cropped locks." Piercy 246, parenthesis added.
12. Encyc. Brit. 14th ed. 361, 362.
13. 1 Hastings (1) 694.
14. 2 II Kgs. 19-21.
15. 4 II Kgs. 38-41.
16. 4 II Kgs. 1-7.
17. 4 II Kgs. 8-37.
18. 8 II Kgs. 1-6.
19. 5 II Kgs. 1-27.
20. 8 II Kgs. 7-15; cf. Kill or Be Killed, infra.
21. 9 II Kgs. 1-37; cf. Kill or Be Killed, infra. "For his political influence, however, Elisha paid a heavy penalty. He felt, and was some-

Elisha lived more than fifty years after his encounter with the Bethel children. Upon his death in 841 B.C. Joash, then King of Israel, wept over his remains and hailed him as the "chariot" and "horsemen" of Israel.[22] While he was buried with honors, there is no indication in the Bible that the townsmen of Bethel were among the mourners.

Elijah

Elijah, the older of the prophets, did not evince much respect for the Sixth Commandment either. He killed to gain his own ends as readily as did his protégé. The stories concerning these two prophets are credited with being somewhat legendary.[23] Nebulous as the tales may be, it is assumed here that the acts attributed to the two prophets occurred precisely as related in the Bible. Of the two, Elijah was the more highly regarded. He is said to have appeared with Moses centuries later at the Transfiguration of Christ,[24] and some believe that Jesus was the personification of Elijah.[25]

We first hear of Elijah about the year 910 B.C. when he became a prophet upon receipt of "the word of the Lord."[26]

---

times worsted by, the temptation to use means which his predecessor would surely have disdained. We may, indeed, on considering the relations between Samaria and Damascus, question the representations in 8:7-15 that he was largely responsible for the murder of Ben-hadad by Hazael; but he certainly was a prime mover in the revolt by which the crafty and murderous Jehu, a man with no character for religion ... seized the throne of Israel." 2 Cheyne 1278.

22. 13 II Kgs. 14. "His guiding and animating spirit had been worth many a troop to his people." 2 Cheyne 1278.

23. "In short, the Elijah stories are not genuine biography but folk tales, some of which are told of other heroes also. Behind the folk tales stands a historical person, who evidently made a deep impression upon the minds of his contemporaries, but he is shrouded in mist, and we can no longer see him clearly." 8 Encyc. Brit. 14th ed. 357, 361, 362.

24. 17 Matt. 3; 9 Mark 4; 9 Luke 30.

25. 16 Matt. 14; 4 Mal. 5 et seq. Elijah is also known as Elias.

26. 17 I Kgs. 2.

This was during the reign of King Ahab, whose chief claim to distinction rests on his marriage to the notorious Jezebel. About four years later, Elijah became embroiled in a religious dispute with the priests of Baal. Even though the priests had been sponsored by Jezebel, Elijah fearlessly challenged them to display whatever miraculous power they possessed. He threw down the gauntlet, as the saying goes, by telling the priests that if they could not perform a miracle, he would do so.[27] In this manner it would be determined which side represented the true God.

The opportunity to get rid of religious competition in Israel came to Elijah on the heels of a serious drought. After her marriage, Jezebel brought the worship of Baal with her from Phoenicia, and the cult became firmly entrenched in Israel. Baal was the god of fertility or, more specifically, the god of free love[28] and was quite popular in Israel for a time. Conditions were going from bad to worse and the drought was in full swing when Elijah gained an audience with the king. He blamed Baalism for the country's plight[29] and suggested that the priests of Baal meet him near Mt. Carmel for a test of supernatural power to settle the issue.[30] To this proposal the king readily agreed. After a large crowd gathered to witness the affair, Elijah arose and solemnly addressed the assemblage:

"How long halt ye between two opinions? If the Lord be God, follow him," he exclaimed, "but if Baal, then follow him."[31]

When nobody demurred, Elijah outlined the nature of the test. "I, even I only," he said, "remain a prophet of the Lord; but Baal's prophets are four hundred and fifty men.

"Let them therefore give us two bullocks; and let them choose one bullock for themselves, and cut it in pieces, and lay it on wood, and put no fire under: and I will dress the other bullock, and lay it on wood, and put no fire under:

---

27. 18 I Kgs. 1 et seq.
28. Cf. Tuck 267; 1 Cheyne 403, Edman 115; Concise 435; Lofts 155.
29. 18 I Kgs. 17, 18.
30. 18 I Kgs. 19.
31. 18 I Kgs. 21.

"And call ye on the name of your gods, and I will call on the name of the Lord: and the God that answereth by fire, let him be God."[32]

This proposition appealed strongly to the people. For the priests of Baal, it was a case of put up or shut up. They outnumbered Elijah 450 to 1, and they either had to produce or they were through. Elijah, of course, was in the same tactical position.

The priests were offered the first opportunity to demonstrate their supernatural power. They built an altar, dressed their bullock, and called on their god from morning until evening to set the wood on fire. All their antics, gyrations, self-mutilation, and mumbo-jumbo were to no avail.[33] To add to their misery, Elijah showed up at noon and mocked them in their frantic efforts to produce a blaze.[34] This cynicism discounts the idea that Christ was the personification of Elijah, as one cannot picture Jesus stooping to such tactics.

By evening the priests had accomplished nothing, so the prophet decided it was time for him to take over. He erected an altar of twelve stones, and put wood on the altar and his bullock on the wood.[35] He then poured water three times on the pile and called upon the Lord to ignite it. Jehovah answered his plea, and the bullock was consumed in flames.[36]

That marked the beginning of the end for the Baal priests. Seizing his opportunity, Elijah had them brought to a small stream where the blood of his intended victims would wash away quickly. There he killed the four hundred and fifty priests with his own hand.[37] Unless worshipping the wrong gods

---

32. 18 I Kgs. 22-24.
33. 18 I Kgs. 26-29.
34. 18 I Kgs. 27.
35. 18 I Kgs. 31 et seq. These rocks represented the twelve tribes of Israel.
36. 18 I Kgs. 38. The suggestion that Elijah used something like naphtha is said to detract from the story. Concise 435.
37. 18 I Kgs. 40 et seq. Tuck says this was a case of "Lynch Law" and that it was not necessary to justify Jehovah, but can be justified only on theocratic principles, that is, Moses put idolaters to death, and therefore it was permissible for Elijah to do likewise. Tuck 90.

may be regarded as a capital offense, there was no justification for these killings.

Elijah's next encounter with death on a grandiose scale came ten years later (896 B.C.) when he burned alive one-hundred-and-two innocent and unfortunate soldiers who had been ordered by their king to take him into custody. The first group comprised a captain and fifty men. They found Elijah perched on top of a hill and ordered him to come down. He responded with fire from Heaven, and the captain and his gallant crew were cremated on the spot.[38] Undaunted, the king dispatched another captain and fifty men. They suffered the same fate as the first group.[39]

A third group of fifty-one was sent out, but its members displayed more diplomacy than their predecessors. They begged Elijah to spare their lives and implored him to accompany them to the king. Elijah complied with their request, but there is no record in the Bible that any punishment was meted out to him for killing the first two groups aggregating one-hundred-and-two men.

As in the case of Elisha, we find the commentators, figuratively speaking, on both sides of the fence. Tuck contends that the cremation of the soldiers "looks like a use of miraculous power to secure the prophet's personal safety, and in such a use of his power he surely cannot be justified."[40] The Reverend Cook takes a different view of the affair and says that Elijah had no other course because the king had challenged Jehovah's power.[41] In line with this reasoning, Dr. William Jenks and his collaborators submit that the one-hundred-and-two soldiers

---

38. 1 II Kgs. 10-11.
39. 1 II Kgs. 11-12.
40. Tuck 126.
41. In short, the Lord had to be vindicated. Elijah "is, consequently, no pattern for Christian men (see Luke ix, 55); but his character is the perfection of the purely legal type. No true Christian after Pentecost would have done what he did now. But what he did, when he did it, was not sinful. It was but executing strict, stern justice." 3 Cook 3.

"deserved death"[42] because they did not follow the teachings of Jehovah. If that be true, how about the last group of fifty-one who finaly prevailed upon Elijah to submit to arrest? They were in the same religious bracket as the first two platoons. If the first two groups "deserved death," so did the last group. Conversely, if the last group deserved life, so did the first two. Moreover, how the philosophy of Elijah's supporters harmonizes with the mandate of the Sixth Commandment is hard to detect.

Would you classify any of the acts of these two prophetic gentlemen as criminal? If so, what punishment would you prescribe?

---

42. "The officers and soldiers, who were slain, not only deserved death as idolaters, but doubtless they had been the instruments of Ahab and Jezebel in persecution; and the example would have salutary effects on many in Israel." 2 Jenks 291.

5
The Female of
the Species

Esther

THE BOOK OF Esther is a mixture of plot, counterplot, and mass murder, with a smattering of sex on the side. Its authenticity and canonicity have been questioned by the clergy and other expositors on several grounds.[1] Thus, it is said that (1) the Book "breathes" selfishness, national pride, and vindictiveness, (2) the name of God is not mentioned at all, and (3) the story is so incredible as to take on the character of fiction rather than fact.[2] To support these points, it has been said that Esther could not possibly have concealed her nationality from her future husband, King Ahasuerus.[3] Moreover, it has also been noted that nothing "is more improbable than that a Hebrew maiden could become a queen of the Persian monarch, in an age when these kings only intermarried with certain noble

---

1. 1 Hastings (1) 773, 774; 3 McClintock 309; 7 Exp. Bible 355, 357; 5 Singer 236; 2 Clarke 793; Miller 174; 5 New Cath. Encyc. 557; Lofts 163; Douglas 393.
2. Ibid.
3. Ibid.

Persian families; or that the king should have taken a Jew as prime minister."[4]

Professor Walter Adeney points out that the Book does not have the pure and lofty spirit of other parts of the Bible and hence is "on a lower plane than that of the prophetic and priestly histories of Israel."[5] Dr. Hastings adds that the Book is highly regarded by the Jews but in the Christian church it "has naturally been less esteemed."[6]

The trouble started in the sixth century B.C. when Vashti, the beautiful Persian queen who was married at the time to King Ahasuerus, refused to exhibit herself in the nude at a drunken stag party thrown by his majesty.[7] Neither the King James, the Rheims-Douay, nor the Revised Standard versions of the Bible indicates that the queen was commanded to appear naked before the king's guests. But Targum, the Aramaic version, does.[8] Other commentators have caught the idea that this lovely lady was asked to disrobe and present herself before the revelers.[9] The drinking bout was in its seventh day, and Vashti had been entertaining the royal ladies of the land when she was suddenly ordered to make her entry at her husband's party.[10] It must have come as quite a surprise to Vashti and her guests. While well fortified with wine, the sensuous sovereign apparently boasted of his wife's proportions, and it may well be that his remarks were challenged, discreetly of course, by one of the inebriates. Ahasuerus either had to produce the evidence or back down. In those times a king could not retract. So the order was delivered by seven palace eunuchs to the queen in the

---

4. 2 Forlong 70. Cf. also Cath. Bib. Encyc. 336.
5. 7 Exp. Bible 355.
6. 1 Hastings (1) 773, 774.
7. 1 Est. 11, 12; Paton 147 et seq. Many believed that Ahasuerus was the Greek Xerxes or Artaxerxes. 3 Cook 475; 2 Clarke 793, Paton 147.
8. 2 Clarke 795.
9. Cf. 3 McClintock 306; Paton 147, 148. "Although women of the East never mingled with men in public, it is doubtful if Vashti was such a stickler for form as to have risked her position and her neck by refusing to obey her husband if she could have appeared fully attired." 7 Exp. Bible 361 et seq.
10. 1 Est. 9, 10.

harem.[11] According to Dr. McClintock and Dr. Strong, "she refused to submit to the indignity which a compliance with his drunken commands involved."[12] For this she warrants admiration to this day.[13] By declining to make her appearance before the king, she lost her crown and her husband,[14] although it is believed she may have been restored to the throne sometime later.[15]

The king was now without a queen. To remedy the situation all the beautiful young virgins of the realm were rounded up to compete in the king's bed for Vashti's crown.[16] The one who pleased his majesty the most would be chosen. Before the tryouts each girl was housed in the apartments of the virgins for "purification" over a twelve-month period.[17] During the year she was sprinkled with perfumes and "sweet odours."[18] But the primary purpose of "purification" was to establish her chastity to a moral certainty and beyond all doubt. In short it was to ascertain "whether she were with *child* or not, that the king might not be imposed on, and be obliged to father a spurious offspring."[19]

Esther was one of the girls selected for the contest.[20] Her

---

11. 1 Est. 10, 11.

12. 3 McClintock 306; cf. 1 Est. 12.

13. "What woman, possesing even a common share of *prudence* and *modesty*, could consent to expose herself to the view of such a group of drunken Bacchanalians? ... Hail, noble woman! Be thou a pattern to all thy sex on every similar occasion! Surely, everything considered, we have few women like Vashti; for some of the highest of the land will dress and deck themselves with the utmost splendour, even to the *selvedge* of their fortunes, to exhibit themselves at balls, plays, galas, operas, and public assemblies of all kinds (nearly half naked), ... even, to the endless reproach and broad suspicion of their honour and chastity, figure away in *masquerades!*" 2 Clarke 795.

14. 1 Est. 19-22.

15. 7 Ex. Bible 352.

16. This was the usual custom in which harems were supplied. 2 Clarke 796.

17. 2 Est. 12.

18. Ibid.

19. 2 Clarke 797.

20. 2 Est. 8.

real name was Hadassah,[21] but it was changed to suit the Persian taste and to hide the fact she was a Jewess.[22] She was a cousin of Mordecai and, upon the death of her parents, had been reared by him as a stepdaughter.[23] Unquestionably she was a woman of rare beauty and charm, although at the time of her entry into Ahasuerus' harem she is credited with having been twenty, forty, and eighty years old.[24] Common sense rules out eighty, and it is unlikely also that a girl of twenty could possess the tact and diplomacy which Esther displayed. Hence it is safer to assume that she was about forty years old. During the year of her "purification," Mordecai kept her under surveillance while she took life easy in the virgins' apartments.[25]

Before each girl was summoned to the king's bed, she was given everything she requested to add to her attractiveness.[26] Tonight was her night, and it was a case of putting her best foot forward, so to speak. By morning she was no longer a "virgin" and was escorted by the eunuchs to the house of the concubines.[27]

---

21. 2 Est. 7.
22. 2 Est. 10, 20. In Persia the name Esther signifies a star. 2 Clarke 797. The fact that Esther was a Jewess "might have prejudiced her with the king; for it was certainly no credit at the Persian court to be a Jew." 2 Clarke 797. This was probably due to the fact that the Jews were still a captive race, and no captive was highly regarded. In 3 Cook 481, it is said: "The Persians had no special contempt for the Jews; but, of course, they despised more or less all the subject races. Esther, with her Aryan name, may have passed for a native Persian."
23. 2 Est. 7; Lofts 167.
24. Cf. 5 Singer 235 and 3 Cook 480.
25. 2 Est. 11. Mordecai's accessibility to the harem, coupled with the fact that in those days he had taken a young female cousin into his house, suggests the idea he was a eunuch. 2 Clarke 796, 799; 3 Cook 480. This may account for his abnormal behavior towards Haman. (see infra. pp. 37, 38).
26. 2 Est. 13. "No doubt, the virgins generally took the opportunity—one that would occur but once in their lives—to load themselves with precious ornaments of various kinds." 3 Cook 481.
27. 2 Est. 14. "The Persian monarch seems to have had but one wife, at least but one in chief favor and esteem with him though he must have had many secondary wives or concubines. This was the name of every-

When it came Esther's turn to spend the night with his royal highness, she asked for no trinkets, jewels, or other forms of adornment.[28] Instead, she let Hegai, the eunuch in charge of the virgins, dress her as he thought best.[29] That he did a good job and that Esther was a beautiful woman are attested by the fact that the king fell desperately in love with her. He preferred her to the other virgins, "loved [her] above all the women,"[30] and selected her to be the queen in Vashti's place and stead.[31] This suggests that Esther was either well tutored in the art of love or had had previous experience. Dr. Isidore Singer and his group say that according to some rabbinic accounts Esther had been married before she experienced Ahasuerus.[32] It also supports the idea that she was about forty years old at the time rather than twenty.

In the meantime Mordecai performed a service for Ahasuerus by exposing a plot of two eunuchs, Bigthan and Teresh, to murder the king. Both were hanged.[33]

Haman now enters the scene, and the pot begins to boil. He was a Agagite and presumably a descendant of Agag whom Samuel murdered.[34] Haman was well regarded by the king and was advanced above the other Persian princes to a position comparable to that of prime minister.[35] In that capacity he commanded respect and obeisance from Ahasuerus' subjects.

---

one that was taken from among the virgins (who had a separate house for themselves) and conducted to the king's bed; where, having passed the night, she returned no more to the virgins' apartments but next morning was received into the house of the concubines." 2 Vincent 928.

28. 2 Est. 15.
29. 2 Est. 15; 3 Cook 481.
30. 2 Est. 16, 17, parenthesis added.
31. 2 Est. 17.
32. 5 Singer 234.
33. 2 Est. 21, 23. Why the two eunuchs plotted against the king is unknown. Targum, the Aramaic Version, says Esther intended to have them removed from office, and they planned to kill her as well as the king. 2 Clarke 799.
34. Cf. 1 Scott 861 and The Case Against Samuel, supra.
35. 3 Est. 1.

For some undisclosed reason Mordecai refused to bow to Haman as the latter would enter the king's gate. This was a willful violation of Persian custom and law.[36] Haman did not notice the oversight until it was called to his attention by the king's servants who, at the same time, asked Mordecai, "Why transgressest thou the king's commandment?"[37]

Mordecai did not reply, but many commentators have since undertaken to answer for him. This phase of the matter is important because Mordecai's persistent refusal to acknowledge Haman was the proximate cause of all the bloodshed which followed. Hence it has been discussed at length by biblical scholars. Some say Mordecai had the notion that bowing to Haman was sacrilegious and idolatrous.[38] He may also have considered bowing unmanly.[39] The majority, however, point out that obeisance was not new to the Jews, having been practiced since Joseph's day in Egypt. Critics censure Mordecai for allowing his personal feelings towards Haman, no matter how justified, to jeopardize the lives of his countrymen.[40] It seems to be conclusive that his persistent refusal to acknowledge Haman was a calculated and deliberate insult as well as a breach of Persian law.[41] Whatever the motive, Mordecai's ac-

---

36. 3 Est. 2, 3.
37. 3 Est. 3.
38. Cf. 2 Clarke 799; 3 Cook 483.
39. Ibid.
40. "Mordecai's refusal to prostrate himself before Haman may possibly appear to Europeans as proof of manly self-respect; but among the Hebrews prostration implied no degradation, and had long been customary not only in the presence of sovereigns, but also in the presence of ordinary men.... The behavior of Mordecai is therefore mere wanton insolence, and accordingly Jewish interpreters, as well as some early Christian authorities, have spent much labour in an attempt to devise a justification for it." Cheyne 1403. Cf. 2 Clarke 788 and 1 Scott 860-862.
41. "Mordecai's contumacy increased with time. At first he merely refused to prostrate himself before the minister.... Now he took no notice of his coming, but sate on in the same attitude while Haman passed through the gate. This was ... a serious breach of etiquette, and may well have angered Haman." 3 Cook 488. Cf. also 5 Est. 9.

tions had an adverse effect on Haman. He concluded that all
Jews were as bad as Mordecai and decided "to destroy all (of
them) . . . that were throughout the whole kingdom of Ahasuerus."[42] Such a determination is no more defensible that Mordecai's misdemeanor. It showed Haman's viciousness and vindictiveness. Nothing warranted the destruction of innocent
Jewish men, women, and children because of Mordecai's
churlishness.[43]

Haman took his troubles directly to the king. "There is
a certain people," he told Ahasuerus, "scattered abroad and
dispersed among the people in all the provinces of thy kingdom; and their laws are diverse from all people; neither keep
they the king's laws; therefore it is not for the king's profit to
suffer them.

"If it please the king, let it be written that they may be
destroyed: and I will pay ten thousand talents of silver to the
hands of those that have the charge of the business, to bring it
into the king's treasuries."[44]

Ahasuerus was bored with the whole thing. He brushed
aside the offer of ten thousand talents, told Haman to keep his
money, but "to do with (the Jews) as it seemeth good to thee."[45]
At the same time he gave Haman his signet ring with which to
seal the decree. A law was drafted by the royal scribes and
dispatched throughout Persia calling for the death of "all Jews,
both young and old, little children and women, *in one day,*
even upon the thirteenth day of the twelfth month, which is
the month of Adar, and to take the spoil of them for a prey."[46]

---

42. 3 Est. 6, parenthesis added.
43. Cf. 1 Scott 859-863.
44. 3 Est. 9. Haman's proposal put all the blame on the king instead of
    himself if enacted as a law. 2 Clarke 801. The idea of Haman's offer
    (equivalent to some $10 million) was to compensate the king for the
    loss of tax revenue when the Jews were liquidated. Haman probably
    believed he could be reimbursed from Jewish property seized. Cf.
    Douglas 393.
45. 3 Est. 11, parenthesis added.
46. 3 Est. 13, emphasis added; hereinafter called the Haman Act. 3 Cook
    493. Under this decree "whoever killed a Jew had his property for

The date had been previously selected by Haman and his henchmen by lot.[47]

Now the Israelites were in serious trouble. Throughout the land they heaped all the blame on Mordecai, for, under Persian law, a royal decree could not be vacated, repealed, or set aside by subsequent legislation.[48] Presumably this was based on the theory that there was no need for remedial legislation because the king could do no wrong. The situation was further complicated by the fact that many Persians had intermarried with Jews and would share the same fate; anything could be expected "when a desperate mob had begun to taste of human blood."[49] No wonder the city of Shushan "was perplexed."[50]

Obviously it was up to Mordecai to save his countrymen, and it must be said to his credit that he rose to the occasion. He made a public demonstration by putting on sackcloth and ashes and bewailing the coming fate of his people.[51] More to the point he solicited the aid of Esther because she was a favorite of the King.[52] She dispatched a harem attendant to find out from Mordecai what the trouble was all about.[53] He explained the situation and exhorted her to prevail upon the king to save her people. This was like asking Esther to commit suicide because it was a capital offense for any man or woman to appear before the king unless summoned.[54] Such rashness

---

his trouble." 2 Clarke 802. Septuagint and Vulgate, in defense of the king say it was his "desire to have all his dominions in quiet and prosperity; but that he is informed that this cannot be expected, while a certain detestable people are disseminated through all his provinces, who not only are not subject to the laws, but endeavour to change them; and that nothing less than their utter *extermination* will secure the peace and prosperity of the empire." 2 Clarke 802.

47. 3 Est. 7.
48. Cf. 2 Clarke 810; 8 Est. 8.
49. 2 Clarke 802.
50. 3 Est. 15.
51. 4 Est. 1. Some of the clergy note with astonishment the absence of any supplication to God. 2 Clarke 803.
52. 4 Est. 4.
53. 4 Est. 5.
54. 4 Est. 11.

was excused only if the king touched the culprit with his golden sceptre.[55] Esther's problem was intensified by the fact that she had not been called to spend the night with the king for the past thirty days and there was no telling when she might be called.[56] So she turned down Mordecai's request.

However, he would not take no for an answer. He sent word back to Esther that she would not be excepted from the effect of the so-called Haman Act merely because she was in the king's harem and that she "would be highly culpable"[57] in the eyes of her people if she did not charge into the king's presence at any cost and use her influence with him in their behalf.[58] This convinced Esther. Prior to risking her life, however, she asked Mordecai to "gather together all the Jews that are present in Shushan, and fast ye for me, and neither eat nor drink three days, night or day: I also and my maidens will fast likewise; and so will I go in unto the king, which is not according to the law; and if I perish, I perish."[59]

After the fast Esther put on her best clothes and bravely ventured into the palace, not knowing what fate was in store for her. Luck was with her. She "obtained favour in his (the king's) sight" and he touched her with his golden sceptre, thus sparing her life.[60] He asked,

"What wilt thou, queen Esther? and what is thy request? it shall be even given thee to the half of the kingdom."[61]

The queen's reply demonstrates she was a diplomat of the loftiest order. She did not blurt out that which was uppermost

---

55. Cf. 2 Clarke 803; 4 Est. 11.

56. 4 Est. 11.

57. 2 Clarke 804.

58. 4 Est. 14.

59. 4 Est. 16. This event is celebrated by the Jews as the Fast of Esther followed by a two days' Feast of Purim. The word *purim* is a derivative of *pari*, meaning "lot." It was so named because the date of the intended destruction of the Jews was selected by lot.

60. 5 Est. 2, parenthesis added. Septuagint described Ahasuerus as being enraged at Esther's deportment and she, realizing this, fainted in terror; whereupon the king, suddenly seized with tenderness, took her in his arms and spoke affectionately to her. Cf. 2 Clarke 805.

61. 5 Est. 3.

in her mind. Instead she sparred for time by inviting the king and Haman to dinner.[62] That night "at the banquet of wine"[63] the king asked Esther what she wanted, but again she deferred her request, sensing that she was gaining favor with the king. Women and wine do mix. So she invited the two men to dinner again.[64]

Haman went home in a happy frame of mind. On the advice of his wife and friends he ordered a gallows to be constructed for Mordecai's special benefit.[65] The king, however, was restless after Esther's party and could not go to sleep.[66] He ordered his servants to read from the royal chronicles and, as chance would have it, learned for the first time how Mordecai had frustrated the plans of the two eunuchs to murder him.[67]

The next day the king asked Haman what should be done for a man whom "the king delighteth to honour."[68] Thinking Ahasuerus was referring to him and never dreaming it was Mordecai, Haman suggested the lucky person should be decked out in the king's clothes, placed astride the royal horse, and paraded through the city.[69] Imagine his surprise and chagrin when the king ordered him to bestow that signal honor on Mordecai![70] That marked the beginning of the end for Haman. His downfall was predicted by his wife when he told her what had transpired.[71]

---

62. 5 Est. 4. It was necessary to include Haman to avoid suspicion. 2 Clarke 805. Furthermore, Esther was not sure of her position with the king when it came to opposing Haman, and she decided to let matters develop slowly.

63. 5 Est 6.

64. 5 Est. 8.

65. 5 Est. 9-14.

66. 6 Est. 1. The king probably had indigestion.

67. 6 Est. 2. In all likelihood the king could not read.

68. 6 Est. 6.

69. 6 Est. 8, 9. As it was a capital offense to don the king's clothes without permission, Haman thought this demonstration would confirm his influence at court. Cf. 2 Clarke 807.

70. 6 Est. 10. Dr. Clarke thinks this was a stroke of bad luck. Says he, "O mortifying reverse of human fortune! How could Haman bear this?" 2 Clarke 808.

71. 6 Est. 13.

That evening Haman was worried as he dressed for Esther's second dinner. He must have realized the whole scheme to exterminate the Jews could backfire. During the course of the evening meal Ahasuerus again asked Esther what was on her mind. Now she could tell him without trepidation because Modecai had just been honored and she stated her case most skillfully.

"O king, and if it please the king, let my life be given me at my petition, and my people at my request:

"For we are sold, I and my people, to be destroyed, to be slain, and to perish. But if we had been sold for bondmen and bondwomen, I had held my tongue, although the enemy could not countervail the king's damage."[72]

Well mulled with wine, Ahasuerus seemed to be incensed at the diabolical conspiracy and, either purposely forgetting that difficulty stemmed from him, or not wishing to accept the blame, wanted to know the name of the person who had the temerity to hatch such a plot.[73] When Esther told him it was Haman, Ahasuerus jumped up from the dinner table in a rage and retired to the palace gardens. In the meantime Haman seized the opportunity to entreat Esther to intercede for his life and fell on her couch in a display of humility[74] He was in this position when the king returned, and it caused his highness to wonder if Haman would try to "force the queen also before me in the house?"[75] When told that Haman had built special gallows on which to hang Mordecai, the king ordered his minister's immediate execution on the gibbet.[76]

---

72. 7 Est. 3, 4. "This was very artfully, as well as very honestly, managed; and was highly calculated to work on the feelings of the king." 2 Clarke 808, 809. Even ten thousand silver talents would not compensate the king for the loss of a whole people.

73. 7 Est. 5.

74. 7 Est. 8.

75. 7 Est. 8. The king must have realized that Haman could not violate Esther's person under the circumstances but used it as an additional excuse for ordering his execution. Cf. 2 Clarke 809; 3 Cook 491.

76. 7 Est. 9, 10. As used in the Bible the term hanging means impaling, a most horrible form of punishment that makes you shudder at the mere thought. A stake was planted in the ground with a sharp point

With Haman dead, Esther and Mordecai were in full control of the nation. The latter received the king's ring and became lord chancellor in Haman's place and stead.[77] However, the Jews were still confronted with the Haman Act. Despite Haman's death they still could be killed pursuant to its terms unless it was nullified in some way. Esther pleaded with the king to no avail, for he told her that that "which is written in the king's name, and sealed with the king's ring, may no man reverse."[78] That speech did not stymie Mordecai and the king's lawyers. They were sharp witted. They drew a statute in the king's name similar in form to the Haman Act and sealed it with the king's ring. It permitted the Jews "to gather themselves together, and to stand for their life, *to destroy, to slay*, and to cause to perish, all the power of the people and province *that would assault them*, both little ones and women, and to take the spoil of them for a prey, Upon *one day* in all the provinces of king Ahasuerus, namely, upon the thirteenth day of the twelfth month, which is the month of Adar."[79]

This decree was broadcast throughout the kingdom in the same manner and to the same extent as had been done with the Haman Act. It should be noted here that the two statutes were alike in several respects. Both were effective for one day only, that is, on the thirteenth of Adar. At the end of that day both decrees lapsed and thereafter were ineffective for all purposes. It should be kept in mind also that the so-called Mordecai Act was a shield and not a sword. It was to be used by the Jews only in case anyone attacked them. It did not give them the right to kill except in self-defense. The purpose of

---

at the upper end. The victim was then seated *per anus* on the sharp point and pulled down by the legs until the stake emerged at his neck. "The culprit lives a considerable time in excruciating agonies." 2 Clarke 799.

77. 8 Est. 2; 2 Clarke 810.

78. 8 Est. 8. In framing her plea Esther exercised remarkable discretion and tact, avoiding all intimation that the king himself was responsible for the predicament. Cf. 1 Scott 868-870. Persian laws were unalterable. Concise 462.

79. 8 Est. 10, 11, 12, emphasis added; hereinafter called the Mordecai Act.

the later statute was clearly to nullify the effect of the first under the theory that no Persian in his right mind would attack a Jew.

The Mordecai Act caused great rejoicing in Jewish circles[80] but consternation in Persian camps. Now the Persians knew for sure that Mordecai and Esther were in power at court. They were terror stricken.[81] Thousands professed Judaism as a defense or safeguard,[82] and many went underground.

When the fatal day arrived, the Jews, aided and abetted by the soldiers and officials of Persia[83] and apparently without waiting for anyone to attack them, fell on the populace and killed their enemies, fancied or real. They "smote all their enemies with the stroke of the sword, and slaughter, and destruction, and did what they would unto those that hated them."[84] They killed five hundred people in Shushan including Haman's ten sons. Thousands more were killed in other cities and provinces.[85] Probably the most remarkable part of this nationwide slaughter is that the Book of Esther does not record the death of a single Jew. In the normal course of civil war this would be impossible. It shows that nobody attacked the Jews. They must have been the aggressors throughout.[86]

---

80. 8 Est. 16.

81. 8 Est. 17. A "great terror of the Jews spread over all Persia." 5 Singer 233. "In consequence of these proceedings a dread of the Jews fell upon all people, many proselytes being gained—convinced, apparently, by the logic of events." 1 Hastings (1) , 773.

82. 8 Est. 17. "Probably the chief alarm felt was lest the Jews, when the day came for revenging themselves, should account the large class of indifferent persons among their enemies. Persons of this class avoided the danger by becoming Jews." 3 Cook 493.

83. 9 Est. 3.

84. 9 Est. 5.

85. 9 Est. 6-10.

86. *Per contra*, Dr. Clarke says "it does not appear that the Jews slew any person who did not rise up to destroy them . . .", but he admits it is strange that five hundred persons in Shushan would rise up against those who were in favor with the king. 2 Clarke 812. Reverend Scott also thinks that there was some attack on the Jews. He says: "Neither the fear of God, nor that of the king, could overcome the desparate enmity of numbers against the Jews, whom they had hoped

Not happy with the results of the first day's carnage, Esther, presumably at the instance and request of Mordecai, begged the king to extend the Mordecai Act for another day. Apparently she did not construe the Act as a defensive statute but rather as an unconditional power to kill.[87] She also asked to have the bodies of Haman's ten sons hung in public as a warning, most likely, to anyone who nursed a grudge against the Jews. Both requests were granted.[88]

The next day the Jews again assembled and killed three hundred more people in Shushan.[89] Elsewhere in Persia the slaughter was more pronounced. Seventy-five thousand people were butchered with swords, axes, and irons of different kinds, making a grand total of 75,800 deaths.[90]

The following day (the fifteenth of Adar) the Jews made "a day of feasting and gladness"[91] and inaugurated the Feast of Purim.[92]

The slaughter of the Persians on the thirteenth and fourteenth days of Adar was so appalling that the veracity of the whole story has been challenged by many, including the Jews themselves.[93] Singer and his group question the historical accuracy of the Book of Esther because there is no confirmation of the story in other records and also because the native Per-

---

to extirpate." 1 Scott 872. Reverend Cook says that the Jews "apparently did not remain wholly on the defensive.... Sometimes the one side, sometimes the other, would commence the attack." 3 Cook 494.

87. 9 Est. 13. "Esther had probably been informed by Mordecai, that there were still many enemies of the Jews who sought their destruction, who had escaped the preceding day; and therefore, begs that this *second* day be added to the former permission." 2 Clarke 813.

88. 9 Est. 13, 14.

89. 9 Est. 15.

90. 9 Est. 6, 15, 16; cf. 5 Cath. Encyc. 550.

91. 9 Est. 18.

92. 9 Est. 19-32.

93. 5 Singer 236. Along the same line, Dr. Tuck says that the difficulty with the whole story is that "such a liberty, given to a dependent and captive race, must have put in grave peril the national order and government." Tuck, 293. And Professor Adeney believes that the massacre of the Persians is "highly improbable." 7 Exp. Bible 353; cf. also Lofts 163.

sian nobles would probably have offered "armed resistance to their feeble and capricious sovereign."[94] Possibly it is best to consider the story as a nightmare of the author of the Book of Esther. Here we have a whole nation steeped in its own blood to satisfy the revengeful spirits of Esther and Mordecai. As Professor Adeney says, "we turn with loathing from this gigantic horror, glad to take refuge in the hope that the author has dipped his brush in darker colours than the real events would warrant."[95]

If Esther and Mordecai were not actuated by vindictiveness in seeking a second day on which to kill those who were unfriendly to their people, what was their motive? Some of the expositors insist she was not prompted by a spirit of revenge,[96] but none of them comes up with a substitute. On the other hand, Singer and his collaborators meet the issue squarely and concede that vengeance brought on the second day's carnage.[97]

Maybe some of the blood can be washed from Esther's record if you assume she was dominated by Mordecai. That would be charitable to the lady.[98] But such an assumption does not dovetail with the facts. She displayed remarkable mental dexterity in the way she handled the plight of her countrymen with the king. She was too smart to be relegated to the status of a vine clinging to Mordecai. If anything, the shoe was on the other foot. Knowing Esther's influence with the king was paramount, Mordecai kept his place. For it is possible that

---

94. Ibid.
95. 7 Exp. Bible 359.
96. Cf. 1 Scott 872; 3 McClintock 308.
97. "The queen, not content with a single day's slaughter, then requested the king to grant to her people a second day of vengeance." 5 Singer 233.
98. "But to impute to her the sentiments put in her mouth by the apocryphal author—or to accuse her of cruelty because of the death of Haman and his sons, and the second day's slaughter of the Jews' enemies in Shushan, is utterly to ignore the manners and feelings of her age and nation, and to judge her by the standard of Christian morality in our own age and country instead." 3 McClintock 308.

Esther could have disposed of him as handily as she did of Haman, should her older cousin have incurred her displeasure.

In the first nine chapters of the Book of Esther several crimes appear to have been committed. Initially, Mordecai violated Persian law by refusing to salute the king's chief executive. Haman went too far, of course, in trying to punish all the innocent Jewish men, women, and children for Mordecai's misdemeanor, and no one can condemn Esther and Mordecai for seeking relief from the king. Because Persian law precluded the repeal of a royal edict, the Mordecai Act was a model of sagacity. It nullified the effect of Haman's statute for all practical purposes, leaving everybody concerned in the *status quo ante* (the way they were before). One statute counterbalanced the other and, properly applied, would have caused no fighting at all except for a few minor outbreaks.

Unfortunately the Mordecai Act was miscontrued and misapplied by the very people for whose benefit it was enacted. The decree did not permit the Jews to resort to mass murder but only to kill in self-defense. Such was the purpose of the Act.[99] That Esther and Mordecai and their countrymen violated not only the letter and spirit of their own legislation but the Sixth Commandment as well is conclusively shown by the box score. The figures are 75,800 to zero, with the Persians prevailing in number of deaths.[100]

Criminal responsibility for mass murder must be laid in Mordecai's lap.[101] He was in full charge of the day and could

---

99. Concise 461, 462.
100. "How far the Jews acted according to the strict letter of the edict and 'stood for their lives' only when attacked, is perhaps to be doubted. They had on their side all the executives of the empire (ver. 3), and evidently, to all intents and purposes, the second edict was considered virtually to repeal the first. The Jews, therefore, being in favour at court, and, as was not unnatural after their alarm, ... were probably resolved to use their opportunities while they had the chance. If so, who could object so long as they did nothing against the authorities? and they were on their side. That they did make a bloody use of their opportunity is shown clearly by verse 16." Tuck 293, 294.
101. 7 Ex. Bible 400.

have stopped the massacre any time he saw fit or at least he could have tried to do so. Rather, he preferred to liquidate all Persians suspected of being opposed to the Jews. Probably some of his personal enemies were also killed at the same time. Esther shares criminal complicity as an accessory if not as a principal.[102] She failed to restrain Mordecai. She cheered his efforts. As she was the one who lobbied the defensive statute from the king, it was her duty to see that it was not violated.

The events of the second day clearly show the homicidal intent of both Esther and Mordecai. By the end of the first day the Jews were no longer in jeopardy. There was no need for an extension of the defensive statute.[103] But Esther and Mordecai were not satisfied.[104] Many people who should have been killed on the first day were still alive. More time was needed to dispose of them. It is a huge task to kill 75,800 people in one day with ancient weapons no matter how hard you work. You must stop the sword swinging once in a while to rest, dispose of the bodies, and wash away the blood.

How would you vote if sitting as a juror in Esther's case?

Jezebel

Contrary to popular belief, the name Jezebel signifies chastity and lack of carnal knowledge.[105] But the habits of the lady who first bore that name contrast so sharply with its literal meaning that the passing of more than 2,850 years has imparted a different connotation. Today, a Jezebel is regarded by modern lexicographers as a licentious and treacherous

---

102. Associates share equal criminal responsibility where culpable homicide results from the acts of any one of them. 40 Am. Jur. 2d 318.
103. The right to kill in self-defense begins with the necessity for such defense and ends when the necessity ends. 40 Am. Jur. 2d 412, 413; 40 C. J. S. 986.
104. Professor Adeney finds no excuse for Mordecai or Esther "in begging permission for this awful massacre." 7 Exp. Bible 359.
105. Cf. Fausset 378.

woman.[106] A closer look at the lady herself provokes admiration as well as censure. She lived her life as she saw fit, fervently worshipped her own gods, lived according to her convictions, and met death magnificently. Certainly she did not lack courage. For after Elijah had displayed his miraculous powers and killed four-hundred-and-fifty of her priests, Jezebel sent word to him that in retaliation she would kill him within twenty-four hours.[107] To save his own life Elijah was obliged to flee from the country, all of his supernatural power to the contrary notwithstanding.[108] In one respect Jezebel and Elijah were on an equal footing. When the opportunity arose both of them killed anyone who got in their way.[109]

The daughter of a Phoenician monarch, Jezebel was married to Ahab, king of Israel, as part of a political alliance.[110] The Phoenicians worshipped Baal, and Jezebel lost no time in championing the cause of that god in Israel. In the worship of Baal the ceremonies, or festivities if you prefer, invited lasciviousness in all shape, manner, and form with any person who happened to be handy. Baal, it must be remembered, was the god of fertility of both plant and animal life.[111] This appealed strongly to the Israelites, and a great many of them, including the king, were led into a life of immorality.[112]

On the subject of kingly prerogatives Jezebel was obdurate. She believed that the king was the king and was not to be denied by the whims of a subject. One Naboth had inherited a vineyard which adjoined the palace of Ahab in Jezreel.[113] The king wanted the land and put a proposition to Naboth.

"Give me thy vinyard," he offered, "that I may have it for

---

106. Cf. *Webster's New Standard Dictionary*, 2nd ed. 1162; Fausset 378.
107. 18 I Kgs. 20-40; 19 I Kgs. 1-2.
108. 19 I Kgs. 3. Elijah was discouraged because the miracle at Mt. Carmel did not convert the entire court and the country. 2 Clarke 455.
109. Cf. 18 I Kgs. 4-13.
110. Cf. 8 Cath. Encyc. 404; 7 Singer 186; Douglas 634; Lofts 141.
111. Lofts 155; cf. The Impulsive Prophets (Elijah), supra.
112. 1 Smith 1706; Lofts 151.
113. Ibid.

a garden of herbs, because it is near unto my house; and I
will give thee for it a better vineyard than it; or, if it seem
good to thee, I will give thee the worth of it in money."[114]

Naboth refused. "The Lord forbid it me, that I should give
the inheritance of my fathers unto thee."[115]

Like a spoiled child the king returned to his palace where
he threw himself "down upon his bed, and turned away his
face, and would eat no bread."[116]

When Jezebel heard what had happened she tried to com-
fort her husband: "Dost thou now govern the kingdom of
Israel?" "Arise, and eat bread, and let thine heart by merry:
I will give thee the vinyard of Naboth the Jezreelite."[117]

Here the plot thickens. In the king's name and under his
seal she forged "letters" and sent them to the elders and nobles
of Jezreel commanding them to give a public feast and to invite
Naboth as the guest of honor.[118] She also ordered them to have
two men present to give false testimony against Naboth by
charging him with impious irreverence against God and the
king.[119] After that the elders were to take Naboth outside and
stone him to death."[120]

As he was ignorant of the plot, Naboth didn't even have a
chance to escape. Without a trial and without even being
afforded an opportunity to deny the charges, he and his sons
were dragged from the city and pelted with stones until they

---

114. 21 I Kgs. 2.
115. 21 I Kgs. 3. Hebrew law precluded alienation of a son's inheritance
     from his father. Cf. Miller 475; 25 Lev. 23-28; 36 Num. 7, 8; 2 Cook
     610; 2 Clarke 465.
116. 21 I Kgs. 4. "Poor soul! he was lord over ten-twelfths of the land,
     and became miserable because he could not get a poor man's vine-
     yard added to all that he possessed!" 2 Clarke 466.
117. 21 I Kgs. 7.
118. 21 I Kgs. 8-10.
119. Ibid.
120. 21 Kgs. 10. In "stoning," the victim is stripped and the complaining
     witness tosses the first stone on his chest or head. If that fails to
     produce death the bystanders join in and hurl rocks until death
     ensues. Cf. 9 McClintock 1047, 1048.

died.[121] As soon as Jezebel heard of Naboth's death she broke the news to her husband.

"Arise, she cried, "take possession of the vineyard of Naboth the Jezreelite, which he refused to give thee for money: for Naboth is not alive, but dead."[122]

While the Bible does not inform us if Jezebel told her husband in advance how she intended to get rid of Naboth permanently, there is a strong indication that she did. If so, Ahab was guilty of murder along with his wife. At that time the king did not have absolute power of life and death over his subjects. Apparently they could only be put to death for cause. This may have prompted Jezebel to trump up false charges against Naboth. Otherwise there would have been no occasion for her to resort to such evil measures, unless she wished to neutralize adverse public opinion by finding an excuse for Naboth's sudden and unnatural demise.

Ahab was more concerned, however, with the prospect of possessing the vinyard than with Naboth's fatal misfortune. With Naboth and his sons dead, the vineyard escheated to the crown, thereby giving Ahab the right to take possession.[123] His happiness was soon blunted by Elijah who, on learning of Naboth's passing, denounced the king, predicted his downfall, and prophesied that both he and Jezebel would be eaten by dogs.[124] Ahab had a guilty conscience, and he was so frightened by these prognostications "that he rent his clothes, and put sackcloth upon his flesh, . . . and went softly."[125]

The king must have abandoned the idea of retaining the vineyard because the Lord relented at his humility and announced through Elijah that He would not "bring the evil" upon Ahab but "in his son's days will I bring the evil upon his house."[126] So the sons were destined to pay for the sins of Ahab

---

121. 21 I Kgs. 13; 2 Cook 612; 9 II Kgs. 26.
122. 21 I Kgs. 15; cf. 2 Clarke 467; Lofts 151.
123. 2 Clarke 467; 9 II Kgs. 26; Concise 436.
124. 21 I Kgs. 19-26.
125. 21 I Kgs. 27.
126. 21 I Kgs. 29.

and Jezebel, even though Mosaic law prohibited this transfer of punishment.[127]

Ahab did not live long after Naboth's death. Two years later false prophets talked him into the idea of making war on Syria, and he was killed in the battle of Ramoth-gilead.[128] The blood from his wounds ran over his armor and chariot which were later washed in a pool at Sàmaria where dogs lapped up his blood and the crimson water.[129] Elijah's prophesy was fulfilled.

Jezebel fared better than her husband. She survived another fifteen years and was quite influential at the court of the sons who succeeded Ahab. The last son, Joram,[130] was the victim of a conspiracy hatched by Elisha to seize the thrones of Israel and Judah, and to elevate Jehu. During a truce, Jehu killed Joram and had his remains thrown in Naboth's vineyard as a token of retributive justice[131] Jehu then marched on the city where Jezebel lived.

On learning of her son's death and the conqueror's approach Jezebel, either as an act of regality in contemplation of death or hoping for a new husband in Jehu, adorned herself with jewels and fine robes. After the manner of the East she painted her eyes with antimony to make them more lustrous.[132] Thus arrayed, she hurled a question to Jehu from the seraglio window overlooking the gate of the city,[133] "Had Zimri peace, who slew his master?"[134]

Jehu was afraid to take a chance with Jezebel. He ordered

---

127. 24 Deut. 16; 18 Ezek. 4, 20; 14 II Kgs. 6.
128. 22 I Kgs. 1-40.
129. 22 I Kgs. 38.
130. Also spelled Jehoram.
131. 9 II Kgs. 22-25.
132. Morton 141; 1 Smith 1707.
133. Cf. 1 Smith 1707.
134. 9 II Kgs. 31. This has been regarded either as a defiant welcome or a proposal to Jehu that if he spared her life as Zimri had done to the women of Baasha (16 I Kgs. 11) she would be willing to marry him or become a concubine. 1 Smith 1707. It has also been regarded as a warning to Jehu of the inevitable results of treason. 4 McClintock 915.

two or three eunuchs to throw her out of the window. She landed in front of his chariot and was trampled to death. " (S) ome of her blood was sprinkled on the wall, and on the horses: and he trode her under foot."[135] That evening when Jezebel's servants came to bury her, they found nothing but her skull, her feet, and the palms of her hands, the rest of her body having been devoured by dogs.[136]

Jael

Do you think you could drive a spike through the temple of a sleeping person and fasten his head to the floor or ground? Even the contemplation of such a gory caper is repulsive. It would require plenty of nerve and intestinal fortitude. You might hit the spike a glancing blow, wake up the victim, and have him kill you for your trouble. It would be risky business. That is exactly what happened to Sisera in the year 1285 B.C. at the hand of Jael, the wife of one of his allies.

After his defeat by the Israelites under Barak at Megiddo, an ancient city commanding the Jezreel Valley in Palestine,[137] Sisera, the field general of the Canaanite army, sought refuge in the tent of Jael. She greeted him kindly. "Turn in, my lord, turn in to me, fear not," she said[138]

For a time she was most hospitable and Sisera was reassured. When he asked for water to drink she gave him milk.[139] But when he dropped from exhaustion and fell sound asleep she took a hammer and drove a spike through his temples, fastening his head to the ground.[140]

---

135. 9 II Kgs. 33.
136. 9 II Kgs. 35, 36.
137. Believed to be the site of Armageddon where the final battle between good and evil was to be fought. Cf. 16 Rev. 16 and *Webster's New Collegiate Dictionary*, 7th ed., 48.
138. 4 Judg. 18. "The characteristic duplicity of the Oriental character . . . is very forcibly depicted in this narrative." 2 Cook 148.
139. 4 Judg. 19. "Her friendship increased his confidence and security." 2 Clarke 116.
140. 4 Judg. 21. "The piercing of his temples must have in a moment put him past resistance." 2 Clarke 116; cf. Douglas 596.

Very likely Jael committed this horrible deed to save her own life and the lives of her people, because Barak was in hot pursuit of Sisera.[141] Jael's tribe had been friendly to Sisera. Had Barak found him alive in Jael's tent, there is no telling what might have happened to her, her husband, her tribe, and her family. She must have realized that Barak held the upper hand and would probably kill anyone who befriended Sisera. So when Barak arrived at her camp in search of Sisera, she was able to display the corpse of that gentleman. For this act she was highly praised [142] by Deborah, a prophetess and judge of Israel, in her famous song celebrating the release of the Israelites from the yoke of Canaan.[143]

While the Bible gives no hint that Jael's conduct was divinely inspired, it has been said she might have killed Sisera because he threatened to violate her person.[144] This theory is inconsistent with the physical condition of Sisera at the time. He was completely worn out after the battle and obviously was not seeking intimate relations with any woman, let alone the wife of a friend and ally. Dr. McClintock says, "If . . . we eliminate the . . . monstrous supposition . . . that Sisera was slain by Jael because he attempted to offer her violence . . . the murder will appear in all its hideous atrocity. . . . Surely we require the clearest and most positive statement that Jael was instigated to such a murder by divine suggestion."[145]

Some expositors denounced Jael's act as a violation of the ancient code of hospitality.[146] But circumstances alter cases and hospitality too. It is more reasonable to assume that the unhappy woman pursued the only possible course to extricate

---

141. Cf. 2 Fallows 899.
142. "Blessed above women shall Jael the wife of Heber the Kenite be." 5 Judg. 24.
143. 5 Judg. 1 et seq.
144. 4 McClintock 745.
145. 4 McClintock 745; Douglas 596.
146. "Jael's act, praised in Judges v. 24, is contrary to modern ideas of right and to the obligations of hospitality as recognized in the East to-day." 7 Singer 51. Cf. 4 McClintock 745. Dr. Douglas thinks she was also guilty of "falsehood, treachery, and murder." Douglas 596.

herself from the awkward position in which she had been placed by Sisera's unheralded and unwanted call. She, too, broke the Sixth Commandment, but this homicide can be justified by the law of self-defense.

Other commentators contend that the end justifies the means. Thus it is said that in those rough days such an evil deed cannot be justified but only rationalized on the theory that whatever contributed to Israel's well-being must be condoned.[147] Similarly minded is the Reverend Cook.[148] But the authors of the *Catholic Dictionary* take a different view and contend that the end never justifies the means unless both are free from evil.[149]

The Reverend Tuck joins with Dr. McClintock and Dr. Strong and unhesitatingly denounces Jael's act. "Was not Jael's act in every way dishonourable and disgraceful; and is it not surprising to find that she is so highly praised?"[150]

As noted above, none of the commentators have sought to justify Jael's act on the ground of self-defense, a point worthy of your consideration in passing on her guilt or innocence.

---

147. 2 I.B. 716.
148. "If we can overlook the treachery and violence which belonged to the morals of the age and country, and bear in mind Jael's ardent sympathies with the oppressed people of God, her faith in the right of Israel to possess the land in which they were now slaves, her zeal for the glory of Jehovah as against the gods of Canaan, and the heroic courage and firmness with which she executed her deadly purpose, we shall be ready to yield to her the praise which is her due." 2 Cook 148.
149. Cath. Dict. 334.
150. Tuck 40.

6
Cloak and Dagger

THE ISRAELITES WHO followed in the wake of Judah were not free from evil.[1] To use the words of the author of the Book of Judges, they "went a whoring after other gods."[2]

The Lord in His anger caused them to be subjugated by the king of Mesopotamia. They slaved under him for eight years[3] until rescued by Othniel, a Jewish liberator, who subsequently reigned over them peacefully for forty years.[4]

After Othniel's death the Jews went "whoring" again with the result that they were defeated in 1406 B.C. by Eglon, king of the Moabites, who had allied himself with the Ammonites and Amalekites. These tribes had been "strengthened" by the Lord to punish the Israelites.[5] They served under King Eglon for eighteen years[6] until the advent of a self-appointed liberator

---

1. 2 Judg. 11, 12.
2. 2 Judg. 17.
3. 3 Judg. 8, 9. It should be observed here that the text does not show the women and children of the defeated Israelites were slaughtered wholesale by the victors.
4. 3 Judg. 11.
5. 3 Judg. 12, Cf. supra, p. 17, note 20.
6. 3 Judg. 14.

in the person of Ehud, a left-handed Benjamite,[7] who murdered Eglon.

Whether the assassination of Eglon was justifiable tyrannicide or treacherous murder of the cloak-and-dagger variety is for you to decide for yourself from the evidence and the arguments of the clergy.

Ehud made a two-edged dagger about eighteen inches long. He then wormed his way into the presence of the Moabite king, an exceedingly fat man, with the offer of a present.[8] "I have a secret errand unto thee," he said to the king.[9]

Eglon told him to be quiet. But when the pair had been left alone in the king's summer parlor, Ehud whispered significantly, "I have a message from God unto thee."[10]

With these few words he sidled up to Eglon, pulled out the dagger he had hidden in his cloak, and thrust it so deeply into the king's belly that the fat closed upon the blade and he could not jerk it out.[11] Only the "dirt" came out.[12]

Seeing nobody in sight, Ehud locked the parlor door, took the key, and boldly sauntered from the palace.[13] He then announced the death of Eglon, mustered an army of Israelites, and drove the Moabites to the fords of the River Jordan, where he killed ten thousand "lusty men" who could not escape."[14]

---

7. 3 Judg. 15. Cf. also Jacobus 200, 204
8. 3 Judg. 16, 17.
9. 3 Judg. 19.
10. 3 Judg. 20.
11. 3 Judg. 21, 22. Being left-handed, Ehud was able to reach for the knife without exciting Eglon's suspicions. 2 Cheyne 1250. The Reverend Tuck points to a parallel case occurring in 1589 A.D. when Henry III of France was assassinated by a Dominican monk named Jacques Clement who worked his way into the king's presence and, when alone, plunged a dagger in Henry's intestines and left it there. Tuck 20.
12. 3 Judg. 22. Various meanings have been assigned to the word "dirt." Some say it means Eglon's blood. It has also been interpreted to mean the chamber through which Ehud escaped. 2 Cook 141.
13. 3 Judg. 23-26.
14. 3 Judg. 27-31. Cf. 2 Cook 142.

Tyrannicide has been defined as the killing of a tyrant for the common good.[15] The priests who compiled the *Catholic Encyclopedia Dictionary* maintain that a tyrant may only be put to death by lawfully constituted authority and by due process of law. Thus a usurper who establishes a new government with himself at the head of it may wage war against a tyrant and put him to death. But if one cannot overthrow the regime of a tryrant in that way, he must submit to the jurisdiction of the tyrant. He cannot resort to murder. It should be noted, in passing, that the "Catholic Church condemns tyrannicide as opposed to the natural law."[16]

On this basis it may be said that the killing of Eglon was not justified. Ehud acted without process of law. He had not established a reign or *de facto* government challenging Eglon. He sneaked into the king's presence and treacherously told Eglon he had a message from God. The "message" was a dagger in the stomach.

As in the case of Jael, the clergy and commentators take divergent views of Ehud's conduct.[17] The expositor in *The Interpreter's Bible* consistently reasons that the means are justified by the end. Says he: "By even the most elementary standard of ethics his deception and murder of Eglon stand condemned. Passages like this, when encountered by the *untutored reader* of the Scriptures, cause consternation and questioning. One must see the situation in the light of the times, when the important matter was to help Israel, and the means of doing it were not examined or questioned."[18] The words "untutored reader" are underscored to raise the question, Who is an untutored reader? Apparently the learned expositor means a biblical neophyte. However, it often happens that fresh minds see things more clearly and more accurately than one whose viewpoint has been "tutored" or channeled in any direction.

On the other hand, Dr. Clarke and the Reverend Tuck

---

15. Cath. Dict. 977.
16. Cath. Dict. 978.
17. Wood 174, 175.
18. 2 I.B. 708, 711; cf. also Wood 175.

look on Ehud as a cold-blooded murderer.[19] The latter says that the "assertion that Ehud's act was done in fulfillment of a divine commission strangely confuses our minds concerning the shameful wickedness of all assassinations, but more especially treacherous ones. We see no signs of a special commission to assassinate given by God to Eglon [sic]."[20]

Would you find Ehud guilty?

---

19. 2 Clarke 113; Tuck 18, 19.
20. Tuck 18. The text uses Eglon instead of Ehud; most likely a misprint.

7
War Crimes

THE LAW OF WAR is defined as that phase of international jurisprudence which prescribes rules of conduct to guide belligerents
in their treatment of combatants and of noncombatant civilian
populations. Like the civil common law it is for the most part
unwritten (*lex non scripta*). It developed slowly over the
centuries as human beings attained higher moral levels and
learned the fundamentals of humanity and justice.[1] In the
United States it has always been followed by the courts.[2]

With respect to prisoners, the law of war crystalized at the
Geneva Convention in 1929 A.D. when a compact was made
between civilized nations of the world. This recites in detail
the rights and obligations of war prisoners.[3] The agreement
provides that at all times the prisoners must be "humanely
treated and protected, particularly against acts of violence,
insults and public curiosity."[4] The law of war requires the

---

1. Cf. 2 Winthrop 1203 et seq.; Ex parte Quirin, 317 U.S. 1; Black 1754.
2. Ex parte Quirin, 317 U.S. 1.
3. 47 U.S. Statutes at Large 2021-2073.
4. 47 U.S. Statutes at Large 2031.

same type of humane treatment to be extended to noncombatant civilians.[5]

On the other hand the Deuteronomic law of war was a one-way street.[6] It was a case of "heads I win, tails you lose." A city marked for conquest by the Jews was first requested to make peace, conditioned upon the inhabitants accepting slavery and parting with their worldly goods. War ensued if the offer was refused. The Deuteronomic code spelled out the fate of the vanquished when the city fell into the hands of the Israelites. All of the men were to be killed outright. The code also provided that the women and the "little ones" should be kept alive and parceled out among the victorious Israelites as slaves.[7] It is in the latter respect that the ancients broke their own laws of war. The women and the children were usually butchered instead of being permited to live in slavery.

In many instances the Mosaic law of retaliation, an "eye for eye, tooth for tooth,"[8] was invoked by the Israelites to justify the atrocities which they visited upon their fallen enemies. This was a poor excuse because the shoe was generally on the other foot. The history of the Israelite campaigns shows that the Hebrews were most often the aggressors.

With the foregoing principles in mind let us examine the activities of some of the biblical stalwarts.

Moses

During a successful campaign against the Midianites in 1452 B.C. the Israelites under Moses killed all of the Midianite men including five of their kings and their prophet Balaam.[9] Probably many of these men were prisoners and many more were civilians who had taken no part in the fight. The victors also put a torch to the cities of these people. All of the women

---

5. In re Yamashita, 327 U.S. 1, 13, 14, 15.
6. 20 Deut. 10-14.
7. Ibid.
8. 19 Deut. 21.
9. 31 Num. 7, 8.

and their "little ones"[10] were taken captive together with 675,-000 sheep, 72,000 head of cattle, 61,000 asses, and a large assortment of gold, silver, jewels, and trinkets.[11] The war was exceedingly profitable for the Jews.

Moses sealed the fate of the captive women and children with this order. "Now therefore kill every male among the little ones, and kill every woman that hath known man by lying with him.

"But all the women children, that have not known a man by lying with him, keep alive for yourselves."[12]

This command was duly executed. The boys and the older women were slaughtered, leaving the virgin girls to the pleasure of the victors.[13] Clarke attributes this carnage to an act of God and deems it to be right and proper.[14] Parenthetically it should be observed that while the Hittites, Amorites, Canaanites, Hivites, Perizzites, and Jebusites were marked by the Deuteronomic code for total elimination, the Midianites were not so mentioned.[15] Therefore under the rule that the expression of one or more things excludes all others not mentioned (*expressio unius est exclusio alterius*), there was no mandate from God to kill the Midianites.

While many biblical commentators skip lightly over the Midian atrocity, Dr. McClintock and Dr. Strong try to justify the slaughter and rape of these people because they corrupted the Israelites. They say that *"the leading circumstances of the case"* show that all the Midianite men, women, and children "had deliberately combined and conspired, by wile and stratagem, to wean the Israelites from their allegiance to the God of heaven" and "wantonly to allure them to the commission of the most foul and degrading crimes. Was it inconsistent with

---

10. 31 Num. 9. It is estimated there were some thirty-two thousand Midian women and children. 2 Fallows 1160.
11. 31 Num. 1-54.
12. 31 Num. 17, 18.
13. 31 Num. 17-31.
14. 1 Clarke 729.
15. 20 Deut. 17.

justice for the moral Governor of the universe to punish such guilt?[16]

According to these two commentators their question warrants a negative answer. But a closer look at the "leading circumstances of the case" indicates otherwise. In the first place it is both unreasonable and fatuous to assume that the boys and girls of Midian conspired to do anything. Conspiracy is foreign to children of tender years, and it is doubtful if those infant boys and girls comprehended the machinations and motives of a plot to deflect the Israelites from allegiance to a God unknown to them. Secondly the Israelites had no excuse for allowing themselves to be weaned away from Jehovah in favor of Baal. They provoked the Midianites to fear and hatred. As long as they stayed out of Midian territory harmony and good feeling prevailed. Moses himself enjoyed Midian hospitality after his flight from Egypt. He married into the tribe and profited from the spiritual guidance of his Midian father-in-law.[17] But the Midianites rebelled when the Israelites sought to take over their lands. Too weak numerically or too fearful to stand against the Israelites in battle,[18] they tried other means of preventing Jewish encroachment. With their neighbors the Moabites they sent their prophet Balaam to curse the invaders. This scheme boomeranged when the curse was miraculously changed into a blessing.[19] Worshippers of Baal, the threatened people came to the conclusion that only one way remained to ward off the advance of the Israelites. Balaam prevailed upon the women of Midian to entice the men of Israel into licentious sex orgies, hoping to bring about their downfall in the sight of the Lord.[20] The idea was a huge success from the start as

---

16. 6 McClintock 237, emphasis added.
17. Cf. 2 Ex. 15; 3 Ex. 1; 18 Ex. 1-12.
18. The Midianites and Moabites were painfully aware of the fact that Moses had just destroyed a large segment of the Cannanites, all the men, women, and "little ones" among the Amorites, as well as the men, women, and children of Bashan. Cf. 21 Num. 1-3; 21 Num. 21-25; 2 Deut. 32-34; 21 Num. 33-35; 3 Deut. 1-7.
19. Cf. Num. chaps. 22, 23, 24, 25.
20. 25 Num. 1-18. "The worship of (Baal) ... consisted in such obscene

the Israelites did not need much coaxing. It might have ruined them completely but for the intercession of Moses with his war of conquest.[21] It was during this period of gaiety that Phinehas, a relative of Moses, became so incensed at the immoral conduct of his fellows that he seized a javelin and ran it through the "belly" of Zimri, an Israelite who had bedded down with a Midian princess.[22]

Dr. Robert Watson excuses Moses for ordering the execution of the defenseless Midian women by suggesting there was no other course open to him. They would have died of starvation, says the learned doctor, if they had been sent back to their war-scorched homes. They could not be integrated with the Israelites. So Moses had no other course but to kill them.[23]

Assuming but not conceding that death was the only way of dealing with the women, no apology appears to have been advanced by anybody to justify the killing of the Midian boys, who, with adequate schooling in the ways of the Lord, might have been raised to become respectable citizens.

In summary the evidence shows that the Israelites were not free from fault. The scales of justice, if any there were in those grim days, tilted against them. For it is apparent that they not only sought to take over the territory of other people by force, but they were also willing participants in carnal relationship with the women of Midian.[24] If these women deserved death for offending the Lord by their licentiousness, did not

---

21. Cf. 6 McClintock 237.
22. 25 Num. 8-18.
23. "In apology it has been said, with regard to the slaughter of the women, that when brought as captives by the soldiers they could not be received into the camp, and there was only this way of dealing with them, unless indeed they had been sent back to their ruined encampments, where they would have slowly died." 2 Exp. Bible 367.
24. These women, "it is to be supposed, had been the most instrumental in the crime before mentioned; either by prostituting themselves, or their daughters, to the lust of the Israelites; and thereby drawing them to idolatry; in which sin they were so settled, that there was no hope of reclaiming them; but they might rather (if they had been

the Israelite adult males also deserve death for their part in the affair? Moreover, when the law of retribution is considered in connection with the entire matter, there does not appear to be any act committed against the Israelites calling for payment in kind.

Joshua

Joshua succeeded Moses as leader of the Jewish tribes.[25] He was a contemporary of Moses, having accompanied him part of the way up Mt. Sinai to get the Tables and was the first person to greet him upon his descent.[26] As Moses' lieutenant he must have been familiar with the meaning and purport of the Ten Commandments and with the provisions of Deuteronomic law prohibiting the killing of women and children among war prisoners. Although his character is said to have combined "strength with gentleness,"[27] this description clashes with some of his acts reported in the Bible.

Joshua's mission in life was to establish his people on the choice lands of others. The first city marked for destruction in the wars of conquest was Jericho. Two spies were sent to the city where they were quartered for several days by Rahab, a prostitute.[28] Through her they learned that the city was vulnerable to attack. Joshua then marched on Jericho. In the campaign he was aided by a miraculous division of the waters

---

saved alive) have enticed the Israelites to commit the same again."
1 Patrick 721.

25. 1 Josh. 1 et seq.; 4 McClintock 1025.

26. Cf. 32 Ex. 1 et seq.

27. Joshua was "a devout warrior, blameless and fearless, who has been taught by serving as a youth how to command as a man; who earns by manly vigor a quiet, honored old age; who combines strength with gentleness, ever looking up for and obeying the divine impulse with the simplicity of a child, while he wields great power and directs it calmly, and without swerving, to the accomplishment of a high, unselfish purpose." 4 McClintock 1026.

28. 2 Josh. 1 et seq. "Can secret and deceptive work ever be right in the sight of God?" Tuck 55, 56. No, says the Reverend Tuck, from the standpoint of Christianity; but from practical necessity, yes.

of the River Jordan and the collapse of the city's walls.[29] These phenomena are said to have resulted from a timely earthquake.[30]

After the city fell, Joshua ordered the slaughter of every "man and woman, young and old, and ox, and sheep and ass, with the edge of the sword."[31] No mercy was shown to anybody except Rahab and her family because she had befriended the spies.[32] Everything in Jericho was destroyed except the gold, silver, and vessels of iron and brass.[33] These valuables were placed in the public treasury.

After the battle an Israelite named Achan could not resist the temptation to hold out a Babylonian garment, two hundred shekels in silver, and an ingot of gold valued at fifty shekels, instead of depositing them in Joshua's treasury.[34] This theft was said to have been the cause of Joshua's failure in his first attack on Ai, the second city marked for destruction. Actually his defeat was due to poor generalship. He did not send a force large enough to subdue Ai in the first assault, and his men were repulsed by superior strength. But Achan was blamed for the defeat. At Joshua's command Achan and his sons and daughters were stoned to death and their bodies burned.[35] Attention has been called to the severity of this punishment. But instead of condemning it, Drs. McClintock and Strong say they prefer the supposition that Achan's children "were included in the doom by one of those stern, vehement impulses of semi-martial vengeance to which the Jewish (like all Oriental) people were exceedingly prone, and which, though extreme . . . was permitted" as a warning against mutiny and impiety.[36] This theory, however, overlooks that phase of Deuter-

---

29. 3 Josh. 14 et seq.
30. 6 Jackson 236, 237; 2 Hastings (1) 787; Miller 312.
31, 6 Josh. 21.
32. 6 Josh. 25.
33. 6 Josh. 24.
34. 7 Josh. 1-21. A shekel was worth about sixty-four cents or thirty-two cents depending on its weight.
35. 7 Josh. 2 et seq. Cf. 1 Vincent 548.
36. 1 McClintock 51.

onomic law which precludes the execution of children for the offenses of their fathers.[37] In this connection the Reverend Tuck asks, "On what principles can such sharing of the innocent with the guilty in Divine judgments be explained or justified?"[38] He gives no answer other than to say it was customary in the East for children to suffer for the sins of the parents. Here, again, that portion of the Deuteronomic code denouncing the punishment of children for the overt acts of their parents is ignored. Apparently the idea of justice in those days was to kill all suspects, the guilty and innocent alike, lest one of the guilty should escape. This established presumptions of guilt and guilt by association which are repugnant to the present-day rule that everyone is presumed to be innocent until proven guilty.

Joshua's second assault on Ai was successful. Instead of sending three thousand men, he mustered ten times that number. Ai was outnumbered three to one. When the city fell the king was taken alive and then hanged.[39] All of the inhabitants including the noncombatant women and children were slaughtered. It is estimated that twelve thousand good people were liquidated during this massacre.[40]

Victory over Ai spurred Joshua to more glorious and gory heights. In defense of their people, five kings of nearby cities pooled their forces against him.[41] They beseiged the city of

---

37. 24 Deut. 16.
38. Tuck 50.
39. 8 Josh. 3 et seq.
40. Cf. 8 Josh. 25, 26. The Reverend Tuck asks if such harshness is not "in strange contradiction to the mercy inculcated elsewhere in the Bible, and even to the instincts of nature?" Tuck 26. But he says that careful consideration leads to three conclusions: (1) it was customary to kill everybody on the losing side; (2) there is a distinction between Divine judgment on nations and on individuals; and (3) it was necessary to get rid of such disturbing influence as the people of Ai, including the women and children, because the descendents of Abraham were destined to preserve the "foundations and truths of the Unity, Purity, and Spirituality of God." Tuck 26-28.
41. 9 Josh. 1 et seq.

Gibeon because its inhabitants, preferring slavery to the sword, had surrendered to the Israelites.[42] The Gibeonites called for help, and Joshua responded with such ferocity that the five kings were quickly defeated. The sun stood still and the moon stayed during the fight to accommodate Joshua. These astronomical phenomena are said to be symbolic of his speedy victory.[43] The defeated kings sought personal safety by hiding in a cave.[44] When Joshua ascertained their whereabouts, he trapped them by rolling stones in front of the entrance. He then proceeded as usual to massacre all of the inhabitants of the five cities, including the women and children.[45]

After the massacre Joshua released the five kings from the cave. They were summoned before him. At his command, his captains put their feet on the five regal necks, thus manifesting complete subjugation of the kings. Joshua then killed them with a sword and hung the bodies on trees until nighttime, when they were cut down from the branches and pitched unceremoniously into the cave of refuge.[46]

Joshua continued his wars of conquest until a total of thirty-one kings and thirty-one cities were overthrown and all of the inhabitants put to death.[47] Assuming the cities averaged 10,000 people, Joshua slaughtered about 310,000 people inhabiting that part of Palestine which was reduced to his command.

Gideon

After their deliverance from the Canaanites by Deborah and Barak,[48] the Israelites became once again a corrupt and

---

42. 9 Josh. 3-15, 10 Josh. 5.
43. 10 Josh. 10 et seq. 6 Jackson 237.
44. 10 Josh. 17.
45. 10 Josh. 19-40.
46. 10 Josh. 24-27.
47. 11 Josh. 1 et seq.; 12 Josh. 7-24.
48. Cf. The Female of the Species (Jael), supra.

degenerate people. For this they were punished by the Lord.[49] The chastisement took the form of sporadic raids by the Midianites and Amalekites who swarmed down from the hills, seized all the crops and animals in sight, and virtually impoverished the Israelites.[50] These humiliations were suffered for about seven years until the advent of Gideon.

This prince of Israel mustered an army of thirty-two thousand men to put an end to the marauders who were encamped in the Jezreel Valley southeast of Mt. Carmel. In keeping with the Deuteronomic code of war, about twenty-two thousand chicken-hearted warriors were permitted to withdraw.[51] This reduced Gideon's army to ten thousand. From this force, he selected three hundred men to carry out a tactical plan to defeat the enemy. He divided these men into three groups of one hundred each and stationed them on all sides of the enemy's camp. Every man was given a trumpet, flares, and empty pitchers.[52] After nightfall and at the right psychological moment, Gideon's three hundred cut loose with unearthly din, blowing the trumpets, breaking the pitchers, waving the flares, and yelling, "The sword of the Lord, and of Gideon."[53] In the darkness the Midianites and their allies didn't know friend from foe. Fighting broke out among them and in pandemonic disorder they were frightened headlong into retreat.[54] Under King Zebah and King Zalmunna they fled southeasterly across the River Jordan with Gideon and his main force in hot pursuit. The vanguard of the Israelite army caught up with a segment of the fleeing Midianites, captured two of their princes, Oreb and Zeeb, decapitated the pair forthwith, and

---

49. 6 Judg. 1.
50. 6 Judg. 3-7.
51. "What man is there that is fearful and fainthearted? let him go and return unto his house, lest his brethren's heart faint as well as his heart." 20 Deut. 8. Cf. 7 Judg. 3.
52. 7 Judg. 16.
53. 7 Judg. 19, 20.
54. 7 Judg. 20-23. Oriental armies were superstitious and became disorganized at the slightest provocation. Cf. 3 McClintock 855, 856.

sent the heads back to Gideon, who at that time was still on
the west side of the Jordan.[55]

After he crossed the river, Gideon asked the inhabitants
of the city of Succoth for food and shelter for his weary and
hungry men. He told the city fathers he had defeated the
Midianites and was chasing a disorganized army in hope of
capturing Zebah and Zalmunna. News did not travel fast in
those days and the elders of Succoth were skeptical of Gideon's
report. They refused to aid him because they feared retaliation
from the Midianites. Being on the east side of the River Jordan, Succoth was highly vulnerable to Midianite attack. Hence
the elders decided to proceed with caution. Gideon lost his
temper and all control of himself. "Therefore when the Lord
hath delivered Zebah and Zalmunna into mine hands," he told
the elders, "then I will tear your flesh with the thorns of the
wilderness and with briers."[56]

Gideon then tried to get food and lodging at Penuel, a
city about five miles from Succoth, but was refused for the
same reason. He promised upon his return to tear down the
city's tower.[57]

After he captured Zebah and Zalmunna, he ordered his son
Jether to kill the kingly pair.[58] Young Jether had no stomach
for the gory job so Gideon was obliged to kill them himself.[59]
Gideon then returned to Succoth and carried out his vicious
threat. He flayed seventy-seven of the city's elders with thorns
and briers until they died in excruciating pain.[60] At Penuel he

---

55. 7 Judg. 25.
56. 8 Judg. 7. This meant that Gideon would flay or thresh the elders
    alive, a most cruel form of capital punishment. Cf. 2 Cook 166; 2
    Clarke 133; 2 I.B. 746-747; 1 Amos 3.
57. 8 Judg. 9.
58. 8 Judg. 20. "What a request for a father to make of a son! ... We
    are glad that the lad did not or could not obey his father's brutal
    request," 2 I.B. 747, 748.
59. 8 Judg. 20, 21.
60. 8 Judg. 14-16. The word "taught" in verse 16 means "threshed" or
    flayed. 2 Cook 167; 2 Clarke 134. It means death by torture. 2 I.B. 747.

tore down the city tower and killed all of the men who were present.[61]

Unquestionably Gideon was exasperated by his reception at Succoth and Penuel when he asked for food for his army and was brushed aside by the elders. It must be conceded that these people erred when they refused to aid Gideon or anyone who was not an enemy. But why did Gideon carry his grudge to such extremes? The people of Succoth and Penuel were Jews like himself. Gideon had plenty of time to cool off before he returned to the two cities, and the reader of today must be amazed at the lack of mercy and understanding in his make-up. There are two sides to every argument, and though they were not free from blame Succoth and Penuel had their side. Certainly the citizenry of the two cities did not deserve the cruel and vicious punishment which Gideon handed out. These acts of Gideon have been described as "signal and appropriate vengeance on the coward and apostate towns of Succoth and Penuel."[62] On the other hand, the Reverend Piercy regards the punishment of the cities as "barbarous."[63] How do you regard it?

David

Becoming a national hero overnight has its disadvantages as well as its benefits. David found that out early in life after he killed Goliath, the Philistine champion, with a slingshot. The young man's popularity skyrocketed with everybody in Israel except King Saul, who feared David might attempt to gain the throne.[64] To save his own life David was obliged to

---

61. 8 Judg. 17.
62. 3 McClintock 856.
63. Piercy 308. So does the Reverend Tuck, who asks: "Was not the vengeance of Gideon extravagant, unreasonable, and beyond any justification from the existing conditions?" Tuck 45.
64. 18 I Sam. 7 et seq. Cf. Edman 80; Harrison 184, 186.

leave the country hurriedly.[65] Saul pursued but could not catch
him. So bitter was Saul that he killed eighty-five innocent
priests of the city of Nob because they had unwittingly befriended David in his flight. Along with the priests, all of the
men, women, and children of Nob were also slaughtered by
King Saul's order.[66]

David ultimately succeeded Saul as king of Israel. Before
he attained that regal status, however, he followed the customary pattern of killing everybody among a conquered people, the women and children included. A fugitive from the
jealousy and wrath of Saul, he arrived at Gath, a city in the
Philistine highlands about thirty miles southeasterly of Jerusalem, with an entourage consisting of a couple of wives and
six hundred ardent followers. On learning that he had left
Israel, King Saul abandoned the pursuit of his young rival.[67]

David was welcomed at Gath by King Achish, who extended him the sanctity and hospitality of the realm. The king
was falsely led to believe that David had defected from the
Israelites. At David's suggestion, the king gave him control of
the city of Ziklag.[68] From this vantage point David abused the
hospitality and confidence of his benefactor[69] by conducting a
series of raids on the allies of King Achish and by fattening his
own purse with the lucre taken from them.[70] David lied to
Achish about these activities. He said he had raided Jewish
tribes and their allies.[71] When the king asked David with whom
he had been fighting the latter falsely replied, "Against the
south of Judah, and against the south of the Jerahmeelites, and
against the south of the Kenites."[72]

---

65. 19 I Sam. 1 et seq.
66. 22 I Sam. 9-19; Miller 649.
67. 23 I Sam. 13-29.
68. 27 I Sam. 6.
69. 27 I Sam. 8, 9. Hebrew custom regarded inhospitality as a grave
offense. Cf. Lot and His Daughters, and The Levite's Concubine,
infra.
70. 27 I Sam. 9.
71. 27 I Sam. 10.
72. Ibid.

Dr. Clarke takes his fellow clergymen to task for trying to excuse David's mendacity. He says: "This deception, . . . imposed upon Achish, had the most direct tendency to make him imagine himself secure, while in the utmost danger; and to have a faithful friend and able ally in David, while he was the veriest enemy he could possibly have. Shame on him who becomes the apologist of such conduct!"[73] Along the same line *The Interpreter's Bible* sums up David's deceit in this way: "In modern terms he was a fifth columnist, guilty of sabotage. Instead of responding in loyalty to Achish's kindness, he uses his advantage for despicable treachery."[74]

To guard against the possibility of having these falsehoods brought to Achish's attention by any survivors of the defeated tribes, David exterminated all and sundry, male and female alike.[75] Fear of exposure alone motivated these mass murders and dispels the weird notion of some commentators that they were retaliatory. To use David's own words, he killed these people "lest they should tell on us."[76]

King Achish was a gullible chap. He swallowed David's fantastic stories whole, apparently without a shadow of doubt, on the assumption that David had severed all ties with the Israelites when, in truth and in fact, David had not.[77] In this way David treacherously ingratiated himself with his Philistine host and violated the confidence placed in him. His conduct cannot be justified. As the Reverend Tuck points out, "The sacred historian does not disguise from the reader, that David resorted to unworthy shifts and prevarications and to acts, it may be, of cruelty."[78]

The other Philistine kings were not as naive as Achish. When they gathered for a frontal attack on Saul, they refused to allow David to participate in the fight, believing they might

---

73. 2 Clarke 291.
74. 2 I.B. 1023.
75. 27 I Sam. 9, 11.
76. 27 I Sam. 11.
77. David's sympathies were with the Israelites. Cf. 18 I Sam. 27; 19 I Sam. 1 et seq.; 1 II Sam. 7-16; 4 II Sam. 5-12.
78. Tuck 62.

get the proverbial stab in the back.[79] They overruled Achish's protest, and he was forced to break the news to his guest.[80] "Surely," he said to David, "as the Lord liveth, thou hast been upright, and thy going out and thy coming in with me in the host is good in my sight; for I have not found evil in thee since the day of thy coming unto me unto this day; nevertheless the lords favour thee not."[81]

Was David's face red? Were his eyes downcast because of his friend's unwarranted manifestation of faith and confidence in him? No indeed. The persistent prevaricator squirmed out of it with another lie. He protested his innocence and complained bitterly that the other Philistine kings would distrust him in a battle about to be fought with the people of his own race.[82] This facet of David's character helps to account for his ruthlessness in years to come.[83]

Dr. Clarke admits that David intended to deceive the Philistines but tries to find a way out of the difficulty for the ingrate by arguing that God would not have permitted him to go into a battle in which he was sure to be disgraced irrespective of which side he took.[84] After stating that "leopards do not change their spots, and kindness is often repaid by base ingratitude," one expositor goes on to say that David's realism is a shock to the sentimentalist but adds that "people who are too readily shocked by what their fellows do, and become skeptics because their friends do not do what is expected of them, confuse the revolutionary, cleansing power of religion with a tepid bath."[85] The weakness of this argument lies in the fact that the learned expositor himself has apparently confused realism with deceit. You can be realistic without being a fraud or a traitor.

---

79. 29 I Sam. 1-11.
80. 29 I Sam. 3, 4.
81. 29 I Sam. 6.
82. 29 I Sam. 8.
83. Cf. infra this chapter; also, Lady of the Bath, infra.
84. 2 Clarke 296.
85. 2 I.B. 1031, 1032.

The battle between the Hebrews and Philistines took place at Gilboa. Without David's help, the Philistines won. With his help they might have been defeated through foul play.[86] Saul was fatally wounded.[87] Shortly after Saul's death, David returned to his own people and was chosen king of Judah.[88] Evidently he was glad to get out of Philistine country because the victorious kings might have killed him had he remained. Life was touch and go in those days. Later events proved that the kings were justified in distrusting him.

After ruling over Judah for eight years, David was anointed king of Israel.[89] This consolidated the two kingdoms. From then on he wielded a bloody sword. In 1047 B.C. he turned on his benefactors, the Philistines, and defeated them.[90] Five years later he was again at war with these people and with other old friends, the Moabites. Making war against the Moabites was a willful violation of the Deuteronomic code prohibiting the molestation of that tribe.[91]

After their defeat David forced hundreds of the Moab war prisoners to lie down on the ground in three rows or tiers. Those in the first two rows were cut to pieces with swords. The remaining one-third were kept alive and reduced to slavery.[92] What motivated this vicious treatment of the Moabites is obscure since David had lived with them and had been befriended by them during the time he was nimbly avoiding contact with Saul in order to save his own life.[93] Some do not regard David's severity as being abnormal.[94] However, David's

---

86. Oriental armies were jittery and could be put to flight on the slightest provocation. Cf. Gideon, this chapter, supra. It is conceivable that David, like a fifth columnist, could have caused consternation in the Philistine camp by resorting to some irregularity.
87. 31 I Sam. 1-4.
88. 2 II Sam. 2-4.
89. 5 II Sam. 3.
90. 5 II Sam. 19-25.
91. 2 Deut. 9.
92. 8 II Sam. 2.
93. 22 I Sam. 3, 4.
94. Cf. 2 I.B. 1089, 1090; H. P. Smith 305.

cruelty to the defeated Moabites bothered the Chronicler who omitted reference to it in his work.[95] And the Reverend Tuck asks how such planned cruelty can be reconciled with the characterization of David as a "man after God's own heart."[96] His only excuse for David is that he acted in accordance with the manners of those times.[97]

The next group of people to incur David's displeasure were tortured to death. These people were the Ammonites. Like the Moabites they sprang from the incestuous relationship between Lot and his daughter.[98] Their King Hanun insulted messengers whom David sent to convey sympathetic regards following a death in the Ammonite royal family.[99] Hanun must have been aware of what had happened to David's other friends, such as the Moabites and the Philistines, because he gained the erroneous impression that the messengers were spies. He grossly insulted them by shaving off half of their beards and by cutting off half of their clothes, leaving them indecently exposed with their buttocks bared to the four winds.[100]

The war that followed this caper was disastrous to Hanun and his people. They allied themselves with the Syrians but were thoroughly defeated by Joab (David's field general) at Helam[101] in 1037 B.C. Throughout the ensuing winter David had plenty of time to forget such trivialities as the mistreatment of his messengers and to consider the idea of showing mercy to the defeated Ammonites. He had good reason for doing so because he had just been soundly spanked, figuratively speaking, by the prophet Nathan for his affair with Bathsheba and the murder of her husband Uriah.[102] That winter found David in a repentent mood, crying publicly over his own shortcom-

---

95. 18 I Chron. 2.
96. Tuck 100.
97. Ibid.
98. Cf. Lot and His Daughters, infra.
99. 10 II Sam. 1, 2, 3.
100. 10 II Sam. 4.
101. 10 II Sam. 16-19. Believed to be a town in Syria east of the River Jordan.
102. 12 II Sam. 1-13. Cf. Lady of the Bath, infra.

ings with Bathsheba. Yet, in spite of his ostentations, there was no mercy in his soul. He asked the Lord for mercy but refused to extend it to others. The following spring he sent a task force under Joab to take revenge.[103] Rabbah, the chief city of the Ammonites, was attacked, and after it fell David was hurriedly called from Jerusalem to make a triumphal entry.[104] What happened then is nauseating. It makes the blood run cold, for it was more horrible than the fate of the Moabites.

David assembled all of the men, women, and children of Rabbah and killed these innocent people slowly and painfully. Some were sawed into pieces, others were hacked to death with axes, others were mangled with harrows, and the remainder were forced to walk into a red-hot brick kiln.[105] Even the victorious butchers had no stomach for the wails and piteous cries of the children. In keeping with the age, the children were killed first, leaving the more stoic adults for the last while David, the "man after God's own heart,"[106] wallowed in their blood.

The Reverend Tuck says that unless such cruelties can be explained the reader is left with a very painful impression of David's character. The explanation, says he, is that David was not personally responsible but only "governmentally responsible." This minister then shifts the blame to Joab, concluding that "in all these war movements of David's reign, Joab was the leading, masterful spirit; and such deaths by torture suit his nature better than David's."[107] It is your privilege to accept this explantion. You may also reject it and find David, as a despotic ruler, not only governmentally responsible but also personally responsible.

Commentators disagree on the nature of David's treatment of the Ammonites. Some believe these people were merely reduced to slavery and put to work with saws, axes, and harrows

---

103. 11 II Sam. 1.
104. 12 II Sam. 26-29.
105. 12 II Sam. 31.
106. Cf. Tuck 100; 1 Fallows 502.
107. Tuck 316, 317.

and in brick kilns.[108] This view, however, is not in harmony with that of the Chronicler who says David "brought out the people that were in it (Rabbah), and cut them with saws, and with harrows of iron, and with axes."[109]

The Reverend Cook and his fellow expositors insist that the Ammonites were tortured to death and were not kept alive for slave labor. They argue that the saw is an implement of torture and the harrows of iron are threshing machines designed to strip the living flesh from the bone. They maintain that the last punishment, that of making the people "pass through" the brick kilns, is conclusive of torture and is "indefensible."[110]

It should be added that the cruel executions are also "indefensible" under the Deuteronomic law of war,[111] the Sixth Commandment, and the specific injunction against molestation of the Ammonites.[112]

Is there any proper place in sacred literature for an account of David's atrocities? What purpose do they serve? Should he be condemned as a war criminal? The answers are yours.

---

108. 2 I.B. 1108; 2 Clarke 336; H. P. Smith 326, 327.
109. 20 I Chron. 3, parenthesis added.
110. 2 Cook 410, 411; cf. 12 II Sam. 31.
111. 20 Deut. 10-14.
112. 2 Deut. 19; cf. 10 Judg. 11-13.

8
Kill or Be Killed

IF YOU WERE a king in biblical times, the thing to do was to kill off all collateral heirs and possible aspirants to your throne before any of them killed you. Otherwise your chances of a violent death at the hands of some young hopeful were about even. It was hazardous to trust even your own bodyguards.

The liquidation of all possible contenders to the throne was in one way a matter of self-defense. Either kill or be killed. Assassinations of this kind were common in Eastern kingdoms and are said to have been the result of polygamy. Thus brothers, cousins, and other kin were disposed of promptly by the incoming monarch lest any one of them try to usurp the throne.[1] Evidently royalty regarded the Sixth Commandment as being meant for the masses only.

On the other hand, if you aspired to the throne it was politic to get rid of the incumbent by fair or foul means. Indeed, your supporters expected you to do so. Otherwise the king might kill you and the rest of your group before you could get a knife into his back. So with the claimant, too, it was a case of kill or be killed.

---

1. Cf. 2 Cook 171.

Abimelech appears to have started this vicious cycle among biblical characters in the year 1209 B.C. He was the son of Gideon[2] and a Shechemite concubine.[3] Gideon had seventy other sons by different wives.[4] After he died the situation became acute when Abimelech and his host of half brothers all wanted to step into their father's shoes at the same time. Abimelech appealed to his mother's people and obtained a loan or gift of seventy pieces of silver.[5] With this tidy sum he hired a gang of cutthroats to dispose of his half brothers. These unfortunates were found in the palace at Ophrah[6] where Abimelech's mob descended on them and killed every one except Jotham, who hid from the murderers.[7] After denouncing Abimelech for the slaughter, Jotham fled from the country to save his own life.[8]

Abimelech's reign was short-lived. In a war against the very people who put up the money for the murder of his half brothers, namely the Shechemites, Abimelech killed all of the inhabitants of the city except one thousand men and women who took refuge in a tower. He made short work of this group too. His soldiers stacked some wood around the tower, then set fire to the wood, burning the tower and the people alive.[9]

Abimelech's next campaign was his last one. He attacked the city of Thebez. These people also holed up in a tower for protection, and Abimelech tried the same trick again. But before he could get the fire going, a woman intervened and heaved a millstone from the tower. It hit Abimelech on the head and broke his skull.[10] His death is treated by the author

---

2. Cf. War Crimes, supra.
3. 8 Judg. 31. Shechem was a town in the hills of Ephraim about thirty miles north of Jerusalem.
4. 8 Judg. 30.
5. 9 Judg. 1-4. These coins were worth about $400. Miller 455.
6. A town about fifteen miles northeast of Bethel. Miller 508.
7. 9 Judg. 5. 2 Clarke 138. This is regarded as an atrocious massacre and one of the sad results of polygamy. Miller 509.
8. 9 Judg. 21.
9. 9 Judg. 22-49.
10. 9 Judg. 52-53.

of the Book of Judges as just punishment by the Lord for the murder of his half brothers.[11] This is a rarity since so many biblical murders and massacres went unpunished.

After Saul's death David became king of Judah, while Abner, a capable warrior and Saul's faithful field general, put Ishbosheth on the throne of Israel. Ishbosheth was Saul's weakling son. War ensued between Judah and Israel and the fight was nip and tuck for a while. Then Abner either seduced or married Saul's former concubine, Rizpah. In those days marriage with, or the seduction of, a deceased king's consort was interpreted as a design on the throne.[12] Ishbosheth was infuriated and castigated Abner. The resentful Abner then sought an alliance with David. He was courteously received by David at Hebron and left in peace. But Joab, David's hatchet man, thought it best to dispose of Abner. In the king's name he sent messengers to recall Abner to Hebron. When the unsuspecting Abner reached the gates of the city, Joab "took him aside . . . to speak with him quietly" and then plunged a sword into his ribs.[13]

This murder caused David considerable embarrassment, as Abner had visited him under a truce.[14] He publicly denounced Joab for the treacherous assault on his guest. Whether Joab was too strong politically or whether David was inwardly pleased with Abner's demise is for you to decide. It may reasonably be inferred from David's hypocrisy at Gath[15] that he would stop at nothing to further his own ends—in this instance to gain the throne of Israel since Ishbosheth was putty without the capable Abner. David did not punish Joab, contenting himself with censure and a public display of grief.[16]

Ishbosheth was an easy mark with Abner out of the way. Two of Saul's former captains, hoping to curry favor with

---

11. 9 Judg. 56; 2 Clarke 143.
12. Cf. 3 II Sam. 7-11; Piercy 5, 6; 2 Cook 492.
13. 3 II Sam. 27.
14. 3 II Sam. 28, 29; Maly 55.
15. Cf. War Crimes (David), supra.
16. 3 II Sam. 33, 34; Piercy 5, 6.

David, stealthily entered Ishbosheth's bedroom one dark night and killed him while he was asleep. They cut off his head and took the gory member to David.[17] Ostensibly the king was displeased and rewarded the disappointed captains by first cutting off their hands and feet and then hanging them.[18]

With no aspirant to the throne on the political horizon, David's position as king solidified both in Israel and Judah. But when he was older, his son Absalom challenged him in open revolt. Recalled by David from self-imposed exile after he killed his half brother Amnon in revenge for the rape of Tamar,[19] Absalom became quite popular in Israel.[20] He was the man of the hour, a young, handsome, and personable chap. He quickly sensed that his other half brothers, including Solomon, had regal ambitions similar to his, so he decided the time was ripe to take over the kingdom by force. On the pretext of paying a vow to the Lord, he obtained David's permission to go to Hebron. There he proclaimed himself king and attracted a large following.[21] David was forced to evacuate Jerusalem. He fled across the River Jordan, leaving ten of his concubines at the palace.[22]

This opened the way for Absalom's triumphal entry into Jerusalem. On the advice of counsel, the very first thing he did was to have sexual intercourse in public with all ten of his father's concubines who had been left behind.[23] As previously noted, taking possession of the king's harem was an act of assumed sovereignty.[24] To add insult to injury, these ten indiscretions took place at or near the site of David's carnal

17. 4 II Sam. 5-8.
18. 4 II Sam. 9-12.
19. Cf. The Rape of Tamar, infra.
20. 15 II Sam. 6.
21. 15 II Sam. 7-12.
22. 15 II Sam. 14-17.
23. 16 II Sam. 21, 22. "A shameful public spectacle was arranged for this act so that it happened before the eyes of all men according to (counsel's) advice." Alleman 408, parenthesis added.
24. 2 Cook 426.

advances against Bathsheba. Absalom's promiscuity only wid-
ened the breach between himself and his father.

David, however, was not a man to let temporary reverses
stand in his way. With the aid of the faithful Joab, he recruited
an army, recrossed the River Jordan, and engaged Absalom's
army. Just before the crucial battle, David issued an order that
Absalom was not to be killed.[25]

Absalom was defeated and took flight on muleback. During his mad dash for safety his head caught in the bough or fork
of a tree, jerking him from his mount. There he hung in midair
while the mule raced on.[26] Unless he was knocked unconscious,
it is difficult to ascertain why Absalom did not extricate himself from this ludicrous position, since his hands and feet were
free at the time. Hearing of Absalom's plight, Joab rushed to
the scene and, contrary to David's order, "thrust (three darts)
through the heart of Absalom, while he was yet alive in the
midst of the oak."[27]

Although he mourned his son's death, David did not dare
or desire, as the case may be, to punish Joab.[28] In killing
Absalom, "Joab was dead right; as the king whose throne had
been preserved by the courageous action of his loyal troops,
David could not afford to give the impression that his anger
over the death of his rebellious boy outweighed his gratitude
for the salvation of the kingdom."[29] It is also possible that
David was inwardly pleased that Absalom had been killed and
could never head up another revolt, the first of which was
almost disastrous.

About a year later (1023 B.C.) there was another insurrec-
tion against David. This time the ringleader was Sheba of the
tribe of Benjamin. Apparently piqued at Joab for killing
Absalom, David demoted him as field general and placed Amasa

---

25. 18 II Sam 5.
26. 18 II Sam. 9.
27. 18 II Sam. 14, parenthesis added.
28. Cf. 18 II Sam. 33.
29. 2 I.B. 1144.

in full command of the defending forces. Amasa had been Absalom's field general in the previous conflict. David ordered Amasa to muster the troops and pounce on Sheba.[30] However, Amasa "tarried longer than the time set which he had appointed him."[31] The Bible does not disclose whether the delay was due to circumstances beyond Amasa's control or whether he was treacherous in allowing Sheba's cause to gain momentum. It may have been due to a lack of confidence in Amasa on the part of the troops.[32]

Again David was forced to fall back on the reliable Joab. The latter mustered an army and took after Sheba without delay, hoping to make contact before he became entrenched in some stronghold.[33] Enroute Joab met Amasa returning to Jerusalem and, after a freindly gesture to throw him off guard, ran a sword through his intestines.[34] Joab reasoned that Amasa's delay was tantamount to treason.[35]

Joab caught up with Sheba at the city of Abelbeth-maachad where he made demands on the people to deliver up the insurgent.[36] Rather than be destroyed by Joab's forces, the people of the city, acting on the advice of a woman, not only met the demand but went Joab one better. They cut off Sheba's head and heaved it over the city walls to Joab.[37]

Years passed. David lived a peaceful life. But when he became "old and stricken in years,"[38] his doctors prescribed something which was believed to be a sure cure for old age. A young virgin named Abishag was recruited and forced to sleep with David.[39] This form of medication, or ministration

---

30. 20 II Sam. 4.
31. 20 II Sam. 5.
32. Cf. 2 I.B. 1156.
33. 20 II Sam. 6 et seq.
34. 20 II Sam. 10.
35. 20 II Sam. 11 et seq.
36. 20 II Sam. 15 et seq.
37. 20 II Sam. 17-22.
38. 1 I Kgs. 1. He was about sixty-nine years old. 2 Clarke 378.
39. 1 I Kgs. 2-4. This practice, apparently common in the East, was regarded as an infallible cure for old age. Friar Bacon's *Cure of Old*

if you prefer, was the first link in a chain of events which led to the death of David's son Adonijah, to the death of Joab, and to the banishment of the prophet Abiathar, all at the order of Solomon when he attained the throne.

About this time, Adonijah, being the oldest living son of the king, announced that he would succeed to the throne when David died. He mustered a coterie of supporters, among them Joab and the prophet Abiathar.[40] A public demonstration was made in Adonijah's behalf. All this proved abortive when David, at the instance and request of Bathsheba and the prophet Nathan, proclaimed and annointed Solomon as king.[41]

This put Adonijah and his followers in jeopardy. The latter deserted Adonijah's cause to insure their own personal safety.[42] Joab retired to private life, and Adonijah fled to the sanctity of the church.[43] After turning the matter over in his mind Solomon decided to spare Adonijah's life on condition that Adonijah swear allegiance to him and never again seek the throne.[44] Adonijah agreed to those terms.

Shortly thereafter, David's former bedfellow, Abishag, re-entered the scene. Believing Abishag was still a virgin, Adonijah asked King Solomon through Bathsheba for permission to

---

Age, though somewhat protracted, boils down to this: To regain the vigor of youth old people should sleep constantly with young people. "And it was on this principle that the physicians of David recommended a *young healthy girl to sleep with David in his old age.* They well knew that the aged, infirm body of the king would absorb a considerable portion of healthy energy from the young woman." 2 Clarke, 199.

40. 1 I Kgs. 7. Some think this was a defection from David on Joab's part. It has also been said that Joab had the right to assume that Adonijah rightfully should succeed his father as the oldest living son. 2 Cook 482; 4 McClintock 921.

41. 1 I Kgs. 10-35. A monarch had the right to determine which one of his sons should succeed to the throne. Cf. 4 McClintock 921.

42. 1 I Kgs. 49.

43. That is, the tabernacle. 1 I Kgs. 50, 51. "It was deemed sacrilege to molest a man who had taken refuge there." 2 Clarke 382.

44. 1 I Kgs. 52, 53. Cf. 2 Cook 488; 2 Clarke 382; 1 McClintock 75.

marry her.[45] The king was incensed at his half brother's request
and construed it as being the first step in a plot to usurp the
throne.[46] On the spur of the moment he ordered Adonijah's
execution,[47] and the unfortunate young man died a few hours
later without trial or the opportunity to be heard by way of
defense. This killing has been justified on the ground that
"Adonijah had forfeited his life by his former conduct, as his
pardon had been merely conditional."[48] But. Dr. Clarke sharply
criticizes Solomon, pointing out that Adonijah had cheerfully
given up "all right to kingdom ... to have this young woman,
who, though she had been his father's wife or concubine, was
still in a state of virginity.... He who attempts to varnish over
this conduct of Solomon by either *state necessity* or a *divine
command*, is an enemy, in my mind, to the cause of God and
truth.... That this was an act of cruelty towards Adonijah,
needs no proof. He is suspected, condemned, and slain, without
a hearing."[49]

The next victims on Solomon's list were Joab and Abiathar, the prophet. Presumed to be guilty by association with
Adonijah, they too were disposed of without trial or hearing.
Nothing in the Bible indicates that either of them plotted with
Adonijah against Solomon after the latter's elevation to the
throne. Solomon merely assumed that they did.[50] It is true that
Joab favored Adonijah as David's successor, but after David
made his choice; Joab was willing to let the affairs of state take
the course which the king had laid down.

Abiathar was not executed but was stripped of his worldly
possessions and banished from the priesthood.[51] Joab was
executed at Solomon's command, while clinging for dear life to

---

45. 2 I Kgs. 15-21 Taking a king's consort was regarded as a design on
the throne. Cf. 2 Cook 492; supra note 12.
46. 2 Cook 492.
47. 2 I Kgs. 23-25.
48. 2 Cook 492.
49. 2 Clarke 385-386.
50. 2 I Kgs. 22; 2 Cook 492.
51. 2 I Kgs. 26, 27.

the horns of the church altar.[52] This was unusually harsh because, without the assistance of the able and forceful Joab over the years, Solomon never would have had a throne to inherit. Benaiah, selected by Solomon to execute Joab, came to the tabernacle and yelled to the victim, "Come forth."

"Nay;" Joab replied, "but I will die here."[53]

Benaiah was puzzled. He did not know what to do because it was a sacrilege to kill a man at the altar. So he returned to Solomon for instructions. Solomon told him to kill Joab even if he refused to leave the tabernacle. To justify this order, Solomon delivered a bombastic tirade against his father's benefactor and lifelong friend.

"Do as he (Joab) hath said," the king told Benaiah, "and fall upon him, and bury him; that thou mayest take away the innocent blood, which Joab shed, from me, and from the house of my father.

"And the Lord shall return his blood upon his own head, who fell upon two men more righteous and *better* than he, and slew them with the sword, my father David not knowing thereof, to wit, Abner the son of Ner, captain of the host of Israel, and Amasa the son of Jether, captain of the host of Judah.

"Their blood shall therefore return upon the head of Joab, and upon the head of his seed for ever: but upon David, and upon his seed, and upon his house, and upon his throne, shall there be peace for ever from the Lord."[54]

---

52. "The projecting points on the altar of the holocaust were called horns.... Criminals were free from danger as long as they took hold of these horns." Cath. Dict. 458.

53. 2 I Kgs. 30.

54. 2 I Kgs. 31-33; parenthesis and emphasis added. Some commentators justify the execution of Joab on the theory that he got what was coming to him. Cf. 2 Cook 493; 4 McClintock 921; 2 Clarke 387; 6 Jackson 182; Piercy 839; Miller 336. But the expositor in 2 I.B. 1157 says: "Solomon's statement ... is sheer falsehood.... It became necessary ... to get Joab out of the way. He was an 'Adonijah man'; so Abner and Amasa are canonized and Joab is executed as the arch-villain who has persecuted the saints." Cf. also 2 Cheyne 2462.

The blood of Joab not only colored the altar where he was executed but, figuratively speaking, must have stuck in Solomon's throat. For Amasa was in command of the revolutionary forces against Solomon's father. And if Abner and Amasa were "better" than Joab, it follows that Joab was "better" than Solomon because he owed the preservation of his throne to Joab.

When certain phases of the lives of David, Solomon, and Joab are paralleled, the latter does not suffer by the comparison.

Joab was the personification of loyalty. Like Jonathan, he stood by David through thick and thin. He shared not only the fruits of victory but also the reverses and hazards of defeat. Whenever David was in trouble Joab was always at his side, a willing and able compatriot, ready to smooth over the rough parts. Although he was vicious, he was primarily actuated in all his sword-swinging by a desire to enhance the affairs of state. Personal interest appears to be lacking. Thus, when he assassinated Amasa, Joab realized that Amasa was an unskilled warrior and could not instill confidence in the troops. This was evidenced by Amasa's failure to assemble a force to crush the Sheba rebellion. Nobody wanted to fight under a half-baked general. Consequently, Joab correctly concluded that David's reign would be jeopardized by the inferior leadership of Amasa in the field.

The assassination of Abner served David's cause even more than it may have helped Joab personally. Abner was unreliable. He deserted his own king and came over to David's side after Ishbosheth criticized him for coveting his father's concubine. What price would Abner ask of David for his support? Once a traitor always a traitor reasoned Joab, and he decided the public interest would best be served by Abner's death. This was cruel, but it was also logical.

While he killed Absalom in violation of the king's command, Joab again acted in the national interest. He knew that peace was impossible with Absalom alive, because there was no telling when the young upstart would try again to dislodge his father, and the second attempt might be successful. The safest course was to liquidate the ringleader. In defying the king,

Joab not only risked his life but his fortune as well. He did what he believed was right, despite David's sentimental regard for his wayward son.

Joab was not afraid to assume responsibility at any time. History shows conclusively that he was the strong man of David's regime. Without him David would have been lost in a welter of indecision and might have been overcome by one of his rebellious sons. In that event Solomon never would have ascended to the throne but very likely would have been killed early in life by one of his half brothers, in keeping with the time and the manners.

David has been extolled as the "man after God's own heart."[55] This appraisal appears to stem from a consideration of his virtues without putting his faults in the balance. A habit seems to have developed among many commentators of attributing ideality to some of the biblical characters who were far from being ideal. This is confirmed by Dr. T. K. Cheyne and Dr. Henry Black who say that "the special stress laid upon the innocence of David as well as the reiterated condemnation

---

55. Cf. 1 Fallows 504. See also 2 McClintock 699 where it is said: "The difficulties that attend his character are available proofs of the impartiality of Scripture in recording them.... It has often been asked, both by scoffers and the serious, how the man after God's own heart could have murdered Uriah and seduced Bathsheba, and tortured the Ammonites to death? An extract from one who is not a too-indulgent critic of sacred characters expresses at once the common sense and the religious lesson of the whole matter. "Who is called "the man after God's own heart?" David, the Hebrew king, had fallen into sins enough—blackest crimes—there was no want of sin. And therefore the unbelievers sneer, and ask, "Is this your man according to God's heart?" The sneer, I must say, seems to me but a shallow one. What are faults, what are the outward details of a life, if the inner secret of it, the remorse, temptations, the often baffled, never ending struggle of it be forgotten? ... David's life and history, as written for us in those Psalms of his, I consider to be the truest emblem ever given us of a man's moral progress and warfare here below.' (Carlyle's *Hero and Hero Worship*, page 72)." Note: The difficulty with Carlyle's appraisal is that it assumes David authored some of the Psalms, whereas, in truth and in fact, the authorship is unknown. Cf. Miller 589, 590 and note 65 infra.

of the 'sons of Zeruiah' (Joab and his brother Shemei) reveals the tendency to idealize the character of the great national hero which characterized later ages."[56]

That David had much personal charm and the ability to attract a following cannot be denied. He was an excellent administrator, a shrewd politician, and knew how to capitalize on success. But his nobility is tarnished by too many sour traits.[57] It must be conceded he was self-centered and would lie at any time to further his own ambitions.[58] He had no hesitancy in killing a person whose presence made him uncomfortable.[59] As one group of commentators points out, "It is a curious fact that while David could not murder by trickery in the interests of political intrigue, he could and did murder by proxy to satisfy his personal desire."[60]

History also shows that David was ungrateful and resentful. All his life he leaned heavily on his nephew Joab and owed to him the preservation of the throne. Yet, in his last hours on earth, he rewarded Joab by enjoining Solomon to kill him.[61] That David was petulant is evidenced by his rash and unwarranted elevation of Amasa over Joab.[62] Like a peevish child he whined about his inability to cope with the

---

56. 2 Cheyne 2462, parenthesis added.
57. "Was David, the adulterer, the traitor, the murderer, a man after God's own heart?" 5 Exp. Bible 216; cf. 1 Forlong 514.
58. Cf. War Crimes (David), supra.
59. Cf. Lady of the Bath, infra.
60. 2 I.B. 1155.
61. "David's charge in the light of all Joab did for him seems terribly unfair." 2 I.B. 1157. Cf. 2 I Kgs. 5, 6. The Reverend Tuck asks: "Can any reasonable excuse be made for the revengeful spirit manifested by David in his last hours?" Tuck 43. This minister says that judged by Christian standards the answer is no; but to judge by such standards is unfair because you cannot expect Gospel morality of Old Testament characters. He adds that David was guided by a worldly policy in not punishing or prosecuting Joab. David had as many black marks against his name as did Joab. The kettle ought not call the pot black. Tuck 43-45.
62. Cf. 2 I.B. 1145.

forcefulness of Joab.[63] This may account for the expression of Dr. McClintock and Dr. Strong that "the desire of David's heart is not chiefly for wisdom, but for holiness. He is conscious of an oppressing evil, and seeks to be delivered from it. He regrets and falls, and repents again."[64]

From the biblical account of David's life, it is incredulous that a man of his habits and characteristics could have authored any of the Psalms.[65] One who strips the flesh off of little children with axes and harrows of iron is hardly concerned with the identity of his "shepherd."[66] As some of the Psalms may have been written in David's time or shortly thereafter, it may be safely assumed that his name is attached to those works in the same manner and to the same extent as the name of King James is connected with the King James Version of the Bible.[67] In both instances the association of the king was honorary. James did not write the King James Version and David did not write the Psalms. Oil and water do not mix. David was too much of a realist to be in tune with the infinite.

Solomon, on the other hand, was born with a silver spoon in his mouth. "He grew up as a rich heir in the splendor of a royal court, inheriting certain despotic tendencies and weaknesses, and inclined to prodigality, display, and sensuality."[68] Solomon had the talents and characteristics of a money-maker and a loose spender. He amassed a fortune estimated in excess of $4 billion.[69] But he spent so much money trying to keep up

---

63. 3 II Sam. 39.
64. 9 McClintock 867, supra.
65. Cf. War Crimes (David). "The authors of the Psalms are unknown. ... Psalms attributed to David reveal a noble spiritual insight which seems inconsistent with the more primitive views of David's time as recorded in the historical books." Miller 589, 590. Cf. also 4 I.B. 10; 11 New Cath. Encyc. 935; 12 Cath. Encyc. 539; 22 Encyc. Amer. (Internat'l Ed.) 726.
66. 23 Psa. 1.
67. Cf. 22 Encyc. Brit. (11th ed.) 534; 11 New Cath. Encyc. 935; 12 Cath. Encyc. 537, 539; 22 Encyc. Amer. (Internat'l Ed.) 726.
68. 10 Jackson 497.
69. 9 McClintock 867.

with his wealthy neighbors, the Assyrians and the Egyptians, that towards the end of his reign he was forced to pawn twenty cities.[70] Like other monarchs of the age Solomon disregarded human suffering. He uprooted 153,600 men from their homes together with their wives and children and compelled the men to build his temple, according to some authorities.

While Solomon is noted for his wisdom, even that famous attribute is clouded by the record of his life. Actually he was a fool in many ways.[71] Fallows is similarly minded. He says, "Wise, Solomon doubtless was, but to me he seems to have been only in a very limited sense, for that is surely far from true wisdom which aggrandizes the throne at the cost of the nation, and, after creating an ephemeral and artificial glory, leaves to the next heir only the wreck of a miserable and exploded failure."[72] By national extravagance Solomon set the stage for the invasions which occurred years later when the Babylonians under Nebuchadnezzar swept over Israel, destroyed all semblance of its glory, and took the Jews into captivity.[73]

In contrast with David, Solomon "asks only for wisdom. He has a lofty ideal before him, and seeks to accomplish it; but he is as yet haunted by no deeper yearnings, and speaks as one who has 'no need for repentence.' "[74] This conflicts with the opinion of Clarke who says that Solomon "died in almost the flower of his age, and, it appears, unregretted. His government was no blessing to Israel; and laid, by its exactions and oppressions, the foundation of that schism which was so fatal to the unhappy people of Israel and Judah, and was the most power-

---

70. 10 Jackson 497. Cf. also 4 Hastings (1) 569 where it is said that Solomon "lost the popularity which he had enjoyed in the earlier years of his reign. He had overtaxed and overburdened his subjects, and made a lavish and wasteful use of the national resources, and the selfishness which led him to do so had defeated its own ends." See Maly 169.
71. Edman 92 et seq.
72. 9 Fallows 604.
73. 36 II Chron. 1 et seq. Cf. also Cath. Dict. 911.
74. 9 McClintock 867.

ful procuring cause of the miseries which have fallen upon the Jewish people from that time until now."[75]

After Solomon died, pandemonium broke loose in Palestine. Tired of being overtaxed, overworked, and pushed around for so many years,[76] the Israelites asked Solomon's son Rehoboam for relief. They gained an audience with the new king and a spokesman for the group said, "Thy father made our yoke grievous: now therefore make thou the grievous service of thy father, and his heavy yoke which he put upon us, lighter, and we will serve thee."[77]

Rehoboam told them to come back in three days for his answer.[78] In the meantime he counselled with the elders who advised him to grant the people some relief. He also talked with the young hotheads of the nobility who advised him to be more despotic and abusive than Solomon had been. Rehoboam followed the recommendation of the latter group.

"And now whereas my father," he told the people, "did lade you with a heavy yoke, I will add to your yoke: my father hath chastised you with whips, but I will chastise you with scorpions."[79]

---

75. 2 Clarke 424.
76. So burdensome had Solomon become with oppressive taxation that during the last few years of his reign the people were in open revolt. 11 I Kgs. 1-40. See also 2 Clarke 427, where it is said that in addition to his expensive building program his "inordinate love of women" led him to assume the burden of maintaining "the fearful amount of no less than *seven hundred* (wives). Politicians may endeavour to justify these acts by asserting, that in the Asiatic countries they were matters of sound policy, rather than an argument of the prevalence of an irregular and unbridled passion. Let this stand for its value; but what can such apologists say for the *additional three hundred concubines*, for the taking of whom no such necessity can be pleaded?" (Parenthesis added).
77. 12 I Kgs. 4; see also 10 II Chron. 4. These people were complaining of heavy taxation and forced labor. 2 Clarke 429.
78. 12 I Kgs. 5; 10 II Chron. 5.
79. 12 I Kgs. 11; 10 II Chron. 14. The scorpion is a whip studded with iron points which dug into and ripped the flesh. 2 Clarke 430.

This speech split the kingdom wide open. The Israelites rebelled and set up their own government under Jeroboam, thus separating Judah and Israel into two factions.[80] The full impact of this breach did not dawn on Rehoboam until he sent a tax collector among the Israelites. Instead of paying taxes they stoned the poor man to death.[81] After that "there were wars between Rehoboam (Judah) and Jeroboam (Israel) continually"[82] and, for that matter, for those who followed in their footsteps.

Overindulgence and riotous living typified the reigns of both Rehoboam and Jeroboam.[83] The latter was succeeded by his son Nadab, but in those days of stiff competition for a throne, Nadab didn't last long as king of Israel. About two years later Baasha, the son of a prophet, appeared on the political horizon and hatched a successful coup against the throne. He killed not only Nadab but all of the children, grandchildren, and collateral relatives of the late Jeroboam as well.[84] Thus Baasha became king of Israel.[85]

Baasha was succeded by his son Elah.[86] Shortly thereafter, Elah got the usual treatment, this time from a member of his own bodyguard, Zimri. Elah had made a friendly call on his steward or bartender, and during the evening both of them got dead drunk.[87] In marched Zimri and killed the inebriated Elah. Very likely he killed the steward too. Zimri then announced that he was king of Israel, and to make sure there would be no competition from any source he killed "all the house of Baasha: he left him not one that pisseth against a wall, neither of his kinsfolks, nor of his friends."[88] From this in-

---

80. 12 I Kgs. 16-20.
81. 12 I Kgs. 18; 10 II Chron. 18.
82. 12 II Chron. 15; 14 IKgs. 30, parentheses added.
83. 14 I Kgs. 10-31; 15 I Kgs. 1 et seq.; 12 II Chron. 1-13; 13 II Chron. 1-22.
84. 15 I Kgs. 27 et seq.
85. 15 I Kgs. 16 et seq.
86. 16 I Kgs. 6.
87. 16 I Kgs. 9.
88. 16 I Kgs. 11.

delicate expression it seems clear that Zimri slaughtered all the men, leaving the women for his personal attention.

Zimri's conspiracy boomeranged. When the people learned what he had done, they made Omri "the captain of the host, king over Israel."[89] Omri besieged the city of Tirzah where Zimri had holed up with a small force. When Zimri saw defeat staring him in the face he committed suicide.[90]

In the meantime, Judah was free for several years from internal strife among contenders for the throne. Rehoboam was followed successively by Abijah, Asa, and Jehosaphat. Then Jehoram, the oldest of Jehosaphat's seven sons,[91] ascended the throne upon his father's death. His first regal act was to murder his six brothers and, for good measure, some of the princes of Israel.[92]

About the same time (848 B.C.) the king of Syria became ill and dispatched his servant Hazael to solicit divine help from the prophet Elisha.[93] In payment for such aid or as a manifestation of generosity, the king sent a caravan of forty camels loaded down with valuable gifts.[94] The prophet accepted these presents but failed to help the donor. Instead, he prophesied the old king's death and Hazael's elevation to the Syrian throne. Fortified with this prognosis, Hazael did what he could to accelerate its fulfillment by suffocating the king. He "took a thick cloth, and dipped it in water, and spread it on (the king's) face, so that he died."[95] Hazael then "reigned in his stead."[96]

After Jehoram died from natural causes, his son Ahaziah succeeded to the throne of Judah.[97] At that time, Joram ruled

---

89. 16 I Kgs. 16.
90. 16 I Kgs. 18.
91. Not to be confused with Jehoram, sometimes called Joram, who was the youngest son of Ahab and ruled Israel for a spell.
92. 21 II Chron. 2-4.
93. 8 II Kgs. 7, 8.
94. 8 II Kgs. 8, 9.
95. 8 II Kgs. 15, parenthesis supplied.
96. Ibid.
97. 8 II Kgs. 24, 25. This Ahaziah is not to be confused with a man of

Israel.[98] Ahaziah and Joram followed the teachings and philosophy of the god Baal and other forms of image worship. Joram, being the older of the two and the stronger character, made the inhabitants of both Judah and Jerusalem "commit fornication" and "go a whoring, like the to whoredoms of the house of Ahab."[99] This didn't set well with the disciples of the Lord Jehovah such as the prophet Elisha. During a war with the Syrians, Joram was severely wounded and was obliged to entrust Jehu with the protection of the key city of Ramothgilead.[100] This proved to be a fatal mistake on Joram's part, but one which was difficult to guard against, because Jehu had been a member of Ahab's bodyguard, and Joram had elevated him to the rank of field general for faithful and meritorious service. Joram had every right to rely on the allegiance of Jehu. And Jehu might not have become a traitor but for the intervention of Elisha who fomented trouble by causing him to be annointed king in Joram's place.[101]

The die was cast. It was up to Jehu to kill Joram and Ahaziah, or it was incumbent upon them to kill Jehu. Jehu prevailed; he murdered both Joram and Ahaziah[102] and started a sequence of treachery and butchery which has few parallels in history. Posing as a champion of Jehovah's cause, Jehu ordered the decapitation of seventy of Ahab's sons. On learning of this order, the tutors of the young princes cut off the regal heads and dumped them unceremoniously into fig baskets.[103] That night the grisly objects were toted to the gates of Jezreel where they were thrown into a pile so the people might view

---

the same name who was Ahab's son and ruled Israel after his father's death.

98. 9 II Kgs. 21. Cf. Fausset 317 for an outline of the several accessions in Judah and Israel during those times.

99. 21 II Chron. 11, 13.

100. A stronghold on the Syrian border about thirty miles southeast of the Sea of Galiliee.

101. 9 II Kgs. 1-14.

102. 9 II Kgs. 16-27. Elisha is believed to have approved these killings, but they were later denounced by Hosea. Cf. 1 Hos. 4 and Miller 308.

103. 10 II Kgs. 7.

the ghastly spectacle the following day. Although Jehu had ordered the executions, he falsely disclaimed responsibility by telling the people they took place without his knowledge or consent. He imparted the idea that the assassinations were of divine origin.

"Ye be righteous," he told the assemblage, "behold, I conspired against my master, and slew him: but who slew all these?

"Know now that there shall fall unto the earth nothing of the word of the Lord, which the Lord spake concerning the house of Ahab: for the Lord hath done that which he spake by his servant Elijah."[104]

Two other mass murders can also be laid in Jehu's lap. On their way to visit the young princes who had just been beheaded, forty-two relatives of Ahaziah had the misfortune to meet Jehu. They were killed on the spot.[105] The next massacre was as treacherous and gruesome as any of Jehu's previous affairs. He summoned all the priests of Baal to join him in paying homage to that god. His real intention was to get them together to facilitate their destruction simultaneously. When the priests responded to Jehu's call and assembled in the temple, his armed guards killed everybody in sight, broke the images, and burned the temple.[106]

The most unusual aspect of Jehu's career of carnage and treachery is that it carried the Lord's approval, notwithstanding the Sixth Commandment. The Lord is quoted as saying to Jehu, "Because thou hast done well in executing that which is right in mine eyes, and hast done unto the house of Ahab according to all that was in mine heart, thy children of the fourth generation shall sit on the throne of Israel."[107]

Dr. Farrar says that God did not sanction the subterfuge

---

104. 10 II Kgs. 9, 10. Dr. Farrar says: "With the same cynical ruthlessness, and cold indifference to smearing his robes in the blood of the slain, he carried out to the bitter end his task of policy which he gilded with the name of Divine justice." 6 Exp. Bible 129.
105. 10 II Kgs. 12-14; 2 Cheyne 2355.
106. 10 II Kgs. 19-21.
107. 10 II Kgs. 30.

which Jehu employed but only the extermination of the house of Ahab. This mass murder, he says, "was just; Jehu was ordained to be the executioner. In no other way could the judgment be carried out. The times were not sentimental."[108] But Dr. Farrar also expresses a conflicting view, summing up Jehu's activities in this way: "Thus Jehu murdered two kings, and one hundred and twelve princes, gave Queen Jezebel to dogs to eat; and if priests had but noticed how even Hosea condemns and denounces his savagery, they would have abstained from some of their glorifications of assassins and butchers."[109]

The Reverend Tuck asks if God employs an agent as His executioner, "to what extent must He be regarded as responsible for the way in which the agent's work is done?"[110] Tuck concludes that responsibility rests on the agent (Jehu) alone and not on Jehovah. This conclusion is contrary to the underlying concept of the law of agency that the principal is liable for the acts of his agent done within the actual or apparent scope of his authority.[111] Under this doctrine Jehovah was responsible for Jehu's acts if we can possibly conceive of Jehu being the Lord's agent.

Whether or not you like to concede it, the truth remains that Jehu made a fool of Elisha. The prophet picked Jehu to restore the worship of the Lord Jehovah in Israel. He annointed him king and aided his assault on the throne. Jehu took all this help but in the end he double-crossed his benefactor. In spite of his elevation to the throne through the assistance of Jehovah's followers, Jehu was treacherous to their cause. He "took no heed to walk in the law of the Lord God of Israel with all his heart: for he departed not from the sins of Jeroboam, which made Israel to sin."[112] As a result of this the Lord "cut Israel short: and Hazael smote them."[113]

---

108. 6 Exp. Bible 138.
109. 6 Exp. Bible 133.
110. Tuck 124, 125.
111. 3 Am. Jur. 2d 626 et seq.; 3 C.J.S. 217 et seq.
112. 10 II Kgs. 31.
113. 10 II Kgs. 32.

Ahaziah's death at the hands of Jehu opened the door for more intrigue and slaughter in Judah. When Athaliah[114] learned of her son's death, she killed all her grandchildren and the "seed royal of the house of Judah"[115] and seized the throne for herself.[116] However, Joash, the youngest grandson, escaped when his sister hid him from the villainous grandmother.[117] He was then in swaddling clothes, being about one year old.[118]

Athaliah's reign was short-lived. About six years later, she met her death when the priest Jehoiada gathered a strong force and, aided by her faithless palace guards, put young Joash on the throne. The guards had secretly been enlisted to support Joash. At the opportune time when Athaliah had left the palace, young Joash was rushed to the scene and planted on the throne. A shout went up in his favor. When Athaliah returned to the palace to ascertain the cause of the commotion, Jehoiada's men closed in. "Treason, treason," screamed the aged woman to no avail.[119] Jehoiada's forces cut her to pieces with swords.[120]

Joash prospered under the regency of Jehoiada. After the priest died, the young ruler got too friendly with the wrong people. He also "went a whoring"[121] after other gods, interests, and pleasures, for which he was sternly rebuked by Zechariah, the son of Jehoiada. Joash retaliated by having Zechariah stoned the death.[122] About a year later Joash was defeated in

---

114. She was the daughter of Ahab and Jezebel.
115. 22 II Chron. 10; 11 II Kgs. 1.
116. 22 II Chron. 12.
117. 22 II Chron. 11. Joash is also known as Jehoash.
118. Cf. 22 II Chron 12; 24 II Chron. 1; 11 II Kgs. 3, 21.
119. 23 II Chron. 13.
120. 23 II Chron. 13-15.
121. 2 Judg. 17.
122. 24 II Chron. 21, 22. While Zechariah may have been a busy-body, Joash's act was uncalled for. "What a most wretched and contemptible man was this, who could imbrue his hands in the blood of a prophet of God, and the son of the man who had saved him from being murdered (by his grandmother Athaliah) and raised him to the throne! Alas, alas! Can even *kings* forget benefits?" 2 Clarke 672, parenthesis added.

battle by Hazael, and the people lost their enthusiasm for him. Seeking revenge for the murder of Zechariah, the servants of Joash conspired against him and killed him while he was asleep in bed.[123]

About thirty years later, another Amaziah was on the throne of Judah. Following the usual custom of kings, he also "did turn away from following the Lord" and in consequence thereof was murdered by his servants.[124]

Years later (773 B.C.) Zachariah was king of Israel. He lasted about six months until slain by Shallum.[125] The latter was on the throne for about a month when along came Menahem and killed him.[126] Menahem reigned until his death from natural causes. He was succeeded by Pekahiah who lasted two years until murdered by Pekah.[127] Pekah's reign of some twenty years was terminated when he was murdered by Hoshea.[128]

What is true of Kings in Palestine is also true in other Asiatic countries. For example, Sennacherib, king of Assyria, was knifed to death by his two sons.[129] Still later, Amon, king of Judah, was murdered by his servants. [130] And so on, apparently *ad infinitum,* thus showing a pattern of kill or be killed, which is manifested in the behavior of Herod who, being fearful of the new King of the Jews, ordered all the children of Bethlehem destroyed, thereby causing the flight of the Holy Family into Egypt.[131]

---

123. 24 II Chron. 25; 12 II Kgs. 20.
124. 25 II Chron. 27; 14 II Kgs. 19.
125. 15 II Kgs. 8-10.
126. 15 II Kgs. 13, 14.
127. 15 II Kgs. 25.
128. 15 II Kgs. 27-30.
129. 19 II Kgs. 36, 37.
130. 33 II Chron. 24-25; 21 II Kgs. 23.
131. 2 Matt. 1-17.

Part 2

Sex

9
Lot and His Daughters

LATE ONE NIGHT in the year 1898 B.C., Lot had sexual intercourse with his "firstborn" daughter.[1] The following night he repeated the same performance with his other daughter. Both were young, unmarried women of marriageable age.[2] According to the sacred historian, the idea of the sordid affairs arose in the mind of the older girl.[3]

Lot was well along in years at the time. He was a nephew of Abraham[4] and had been a "judge" in the city of Sodom where he acquired considerable wealth and good standing.[5] Acting on the advice of two angels, Lot, his wife, and their two unmarried daughters quickly got out of Sodom with a few of their belongings just before it was destroyed by fire and

---

1. 19 Gen. 31-34.
2. Cf. 19 Gen. 31, 36.
3. 19 Gen. 31, 32.
4. 11 Gen. 27.
5. 5 McClintock 520-522; 1 Cook 130.
6. 19 Gen. 12-24. Lot had sons and other married daughters who ridiculed his suggestion to vacate Sodom, 19 Gen. 14; 5 McClintock 520, 521.

brimstone from above.[6] For disobeying an angelic injunction not to look back at the city in flames, Lot's wife was turned miraculously into a pillar of salt[7] That reduced the family to three, Lot and his two virgin daughters. They repaired to the city of Zoar but, disliking the place or not being able to afford to stay there, moved out and established residence in a cave on the side of a mountain.[8] Here the oldest daughter became restless and said to her younger sister, "Our father is old, and there is not a man in the earth to come in unto us after the manner of all the earth: Come, let us wake our father drink wine, and we will lie with him, that we may preserve the seed of our father."[9]

Where or how the older girl got the notion that the destruction of Sodom had depopulated the surrounding area of all eligible single men is not explained. In any event, the possibility of finding a husband was of no concern at the moment to the younger daughter, because she readily agreed to her sister's proposal. That night they "made their father drink wine" and, after he had become well saturated with the juice, the older girl crept into his bed and the pair indulged in sexual intercourse.[10] It is reported that Lot was so drunk he "perceived not when she lay down, nor when she arose."[11]

The following night the same incestuous act was repeated under similiar circumstances. However, this time the younger daughter was the recipient of her father's "seed."[12] Lot got drunk as before and, we are told, did not know what transpired while the younger girl was in his bed.[13]

Both young women became pregnant. In due time the

---

7. 19 Gen. 17, 26.
8. 19 Gen. 22, 23, 30. Zoar, Sodom, and Gomorrah are said to have been located on the southeasterly side of the Dead Sea. The site of each city is probably now covered with water due to the rise of the sea level.
9. 19 Gen. 31, 32.
10. 19 Gen. 33.
11. 19 Gen. 33.
12. 19 Gen. 32, 34, 35.
13. 19 Gen. 35.

older daughter gave birth to a son, Moab, who became the progenitor of the Moabites.[14] The younger girl aso produced a son whom she named Benammi. Years later he sired the Ammonites.[15]

Some interesting questions arise from these facts. Were any crimes committed, and, if so, who was guilty of what?

In the commission of every crime, it is settled law that there must be a union of criminal act and criminal intent. *Actus non facit reum, nisi mens sit rea.* When intent is not admitted by the suspected person, it may be established by circumstances incidental to the offense, because a person who is possessed of his normal mental faculties intends the ordinary consequences of his own acts.[16]

The irregularities committed by Lot and his daughters are commonly known as incest and fornication. Incest is defined as intermarriage or sexual intercourse between a man and a woman related to each other in any degree of affinity which precludes marriage.[17] Fornication is defined as carnal copulation between two unmarried persons.[18] While the incestuous acts of Lot and his daughters had not been denounced specifically in the Bible as crimes prior to the time they were committed, it may be safely assumed from the Seven Commandments of Noah and the history of the Deluge that such acts were prohibited.[19] All the clerical commentators so indicate and agree. Despite extenuating circumstances, the two maidens were obviously guilty of both incest and fornication. They admitted they arranged the preliminaries for each session with their father; they knew what they were doing.

Biblical scholars do not agree, however, on the issue as to whether the daughters acted from a craving to satisfy a sexual impulse or whether they were motivated solely by a desire to insure the continuation of the human race and the survival of

14. 19 Gen. 36-38.
15. Ibid.
16. 29 Am. Jur. 2d 257 et seq.; 31A C.J.S. 193 et seq.
17. Cf. 42 C.J.S. 503; Black 904; 4 McClintock 540; 18 Lev. 1-30.
18. Black 781; 3 McClintock 625; cf. 23 Deut. 18.
19. 8 Jackson 184.

the family. Maybe the two girls were actuated by both factors. Dr. William Jenks leans to the side of sensuality. He says in part: "His daughters laid a very wicked plot to bring him to sin, and theirs was doubtless the graver guilt.... Whatever their pretense, their project was very wicked and vile and an impudent afront to the very light and law of nature.... No sufficient excuse can be made for either of them or for Lot."[20] This view is shared by the Reverend Cook, who says: "It is too apparent that the licentiousness of Sodom had had a degrading influence upon their (the daughters') hearts and lives."[21]

The Reverends McClintock and Strong do not discount the possibility that the two young women had a strong sexual urge, stating that the whole "contrivance...has in it the taint of Sodom."[22] They rebut the argument that the affairs in the cave may be condoned because the girls believed their father was the only man alive who could, through them, preserve the human race. These learned gentlemen say that "it is incredible that they (the girls) could have entertained any such belief. The city of Zoar had been spared, and they had been there. The wine also with which they made their father drunk must have been procured from some men, as we cannot suppose that they had brought it with them from Sodom."[23] That statement makes sense.

At the same time these two clergymen present the other side, pointing out that "Whiston and others"[24] are unable to see any wicked intent on the part of the daughters because (1) they did not think it proper to marry outside their own family or tribe and (2) they felt an urgent need, born of womankind, to resort to any measures to preserve the family

---

20. 1 Jenks 100.
21. 1 Cook 130, parenthesis added.
22. 5 McClintock 522. The word *sodomy* has become synonymous with carnal sensuality.
23. 5 McClintock 522, parenthesis added.
24. Ibid. William Whiston was an English theologian and mathematician (1667-1752).

and the race.[25] Quoting from H. Gunkel's *Schopfung und Chaos in Urzeit und Endzeit* (1895), Dr. Skinner says: " 'When the existence of the race is at stake, the woman is more eager and unscrupulous than the man.' "[26] He argues that the possibility of barrenness and race suicide left the girls with no other course. They had to reproduce through their father. And so he concludes: "The truth seems to be that while incest was held in abhorrence in Israel . . . it was at one time regarded as justified by extreme necessity, so that deeds like those here related could be told without shame."[27]

Dr. Jenks, however, cannot accept the possibility of race suicide as an excuse for the conduct of the daughters. He says that "Lot lived to repent; yet there is no proof that his daughters did."[28] And all apologies for the girls are brushed aside by the Reverend Cook with these words: "Iren . . ., Chrysostom . . ., Ambros . . . (and) Theodoret . . . excuse this incestuous conduct of the daughters of Lot on the ground that they supposed the whole human race to have been destroyed excepting their father and themselves. Even if it were so, the words of St. Augustine would be true, that 'they should have preferred to be childless rather than to treat their father so.' "[29]

Lot himself presents a more difficult problem. Was he guilty also? At first it may look as if Lot were the innocent victim of his daughters' culpability. Yet an analysis of the facts indicates otherwise. The authors of Genesis tell us that Lot did not know when either of his daughters "lay down, nor when she arose"[30] because he was drunk. It follows as day

---

25. Cf. 5 McClintock 520; 1 Clarke 133; 1 I.B. 631.
26. Skinner 313.
27. Skinner 314.
28. 1 Jenks 100.
29. 1 Cook 130, parenthesis added. Iren. is an abbreviation for Irenaeus, a renowned clergyman of the first or second century A.D. Ambros. stands for Ambrose, a bishop of Milan of the fourth century. Chrysostum was an orator of the Greek Church and Theodoret was an ecclesiastic of the fifth century.
30. 19 Gen. 33, 35.

follows night that if he was unconscious of their behavior, he was at the time physically incapable of having sexual intercourse with either one of them. In that case, neither the younger daughter nor the older daughter could have become pregnant. A prerequisite of pregnancy would normally be sexual penetration, and that would not be possible unless Lot was physically potent at the time. However, it has been indicated that a man who is *unconscious* from alcoholic overindulgence is physically unable to have sexual intercourse or to ejaculate.[31] Consequently the pregnancy of the daughters shows that Lot was *not* so drunk that he did not know what was transpiring when his daughters got into bed with him on successive nights.[32] He was either playing possum or overplaying the role of an unconscious participant. Probably he did so to save face and to avoid embarrassment when the family met the following mornings at breakfast.

The idea that Lot knew he was having sexual intercourse with his daughters finds support among some commentators and expositors. Although Dr. Clarke excuses Lot's conduct on two other grounds,[33] he concedes that Lot "must have been sensible that some person had been in his bed, it would be ridiculous to deny."[34] Similarly minded is Dr. Lange, who says that in any event "a certain measure of voluntariness must be assumed . . . and therefore his intoxication can only be urged

---

31. Cf. Masters 266, 267; McCary 301-309; Kaufman 67; Lamb 161; Wharton 125; 18 Ala. 521. The late D. E. F. Easton, M.D. of San Francisco expressed the opinion that even manipulation would not produce an erection when a man is unconscious from an excessive intake of liquor.

32. The narrative "lacks probability" assuming "Lot was so intoxicated both times that he should know nothing of what took place, and still, as an old man should, with all this, be capable of begetting seed." 1 Lange 440.

33. (1) Lack of "accurate knowledge of what took place either on the first or second night" and (2) lack of knowledge of the power of wine and the inability to cope with a strong intoxicant. 1 Clarke 133.

34. 1 Clarke 133.

as an excuse, since the intoxication was, like the deed itself, immediately repeated."[35]

To mollify Lot's part in the affair Dr. Clarke comes up with the suggestion that he might have thought he was having sexual intercourse with "some of his female domestics, which it is reasonable to suppose he might have brought from Zoar."[36] This supposition is not supported by the facts. The Bible makes no mention of anyone in the cave besides Lot and his daughters. Secondly, when Lot arrived in Zoar, he was destitute. He rushed out of Sodom leaving most of his worldly goods behind.[37] When he arrived at Zoar he was without funds to rent or buy a house. That is why he was forced to seek shelter in a cave. Dr. Hastings describes Lot as "the man who once was rich in 'flocks and herds and tents'—was, as a result of his own actions, stripped of his possessions, and reduced to living penuriously in a cave."[38] In short Lot didn't have the where-withal to hire or purchase any female domestics.

Generally speaking, voluntary intoxication is no defense to the commission of a crime.[39] Thus, in sex crimes such as rape or incest, drunkenness affords no legal excuse. On the other hand, proof of incapacity is a defense to a charge of committing such crimes.[40] Thus, a male who has not attained the age of puberty or who is impotent may prove such a fact in defense of an accusation of committing rape, because sexual penetration is an essential element of that crime.[41] While intoxication is no defense, it has been recognized that a man may be so drunk as to be physically incapable of committing some of the sex offenses. In that case the defense is not intoxication but physical incapacity brought on by intoxication. In *Nugent*

---

35. 1 Lange 440.
36. 1 Clarke 133.
37. Cf. 19 Gen. 15-22.
38. 3 Hastings (1) 152.
39. 22 C.J.S. 213.
40. Cf. 75 C.J.S. 466, 485; 65 Am. Jur. 2d ed. 779 et seq.
41. 75 C.J.S. 485; 65 Am. Jur. 2d ed. 779 et seq.

v. State[42] the evidence showed that for several days prior to the time Nugent was accused of seducing a ten-year-old girl, he had been in a state of intoxication. He was convicted. On appeal, the Supreme Court of Alabama reversed the judgment of conviction and sent the case back to the lower court for a new trial. In discussing the question of intoxication as affecting a man's physical ability to commit a crime in which sexual penetration is a necessary element, the court said:

"The testimony tended to show that about the time the offense is alleged to have been committed, the physical system of the accused was greatly weakened and debilitated from drink. . . . It is true that the drunken condition of the accused would, neither in a moral, nor legal point of view, excuse or palliate the crime, if in fact committed, but drunkenness may not only render one entirely incapable of committing the crime, with which the prisoner is charged, but it may, by the prostration of his system, render him less capable of committing it. The effects, therefore, of the drunken condition of the accused upon his physical capacity to commit the crime, was a matter to be considered by the jury, in coming to their conclusion whether the prisoner did the act with which he is charged. A certain degree of excitement from drink may increase the passions, the cravings of which lead to the commission of such unnatural and monstrous crime, *but drunkenness may be so excessive as to render the party partially or totally incapable of committing it.*"[43]

This language of the Alabama court bears on the question of whether Lot knowingly committed incest.

One other phase of the matter should also be considered before you pass on the guilt or innocence of Lot and his daughters. Two strangers (angels) enjoyed the hospitality of his home the night before he vacated Sodom.[44] When some of the citizens of Sodom heard of this visit, they demanded the

---

42. 18 Ala. 521.
43. 18 Ala. 521, 526, 527, emphasis added.
44. 19 Gen. 1-3.

persons of Lot's guests in order to commit sodomy with them.[45] Lot refused. To stave off the insistent demands of the rabble, he offered to give them his two virgin daughters instead.

"Behold now," he told the mob, "I have two daughters which have not known man; let me, I pray you, bring them out unto you, and do ye to them as is good in your eyes: only unto these men do nothing; for therefore came they under the shadow of my roof."[46]

The Sodomites refused Lot's offer and tried to break into the house to get at his male guests. Some of them were blinded by the angels.[47] This incident shows that Lot had little, if any, respect or love for his daughters and, hence, he might well have had no compunction whatever in having sexual relations with them. St. Chrysostom thought it virtuous of Lot not to protect his daughters at the risk of failing to perform his duty as a host.[48] But St. Ambrose believes the lesser sin (omission to show hospitality) is preferred to a greater one (offering your daughters to a bunch of Sodomites) [49] And Dr. Hastings places Lot in error for thinking that his duty as a host was paramount to his obligation to his daughters.[50]

Applying the language of the Alabama court to the events which took place in Lot's cave and keeping in mind all the lurid details of the story, what is your verdict? The Reverend Cook tells us that "the sacred writer relates the history simply and without comment, not holding up Lot as an example for imitation, but telling us his faults as well as his virtues, and leaving us to draw the inferences."[51] That being so, you may conclude in your own mind whether Lot was conscious or unconscious of his daughters' nocturnal visitations and whether you would hold all participants equally guilty.

---

45. 19 Gen. 4, 5.
46. 19 Gen. 8.
47. 19 Gen. 9-11.
48. Cf. 3 Hastings (1) 151; Jerome 21.
49. Ibid.
50. Ibid.
51. 1 Cook 127.

10
The Maltreatment of Sarah

IN BIBLICAL TIMES if a king were a sensualist at heart and saw a beautiful young girl, she was his for the taking.[1] He didn't even have to ask her or her family. He merely put a squad of palace guards on her trail, and they would quickly take her into protective custody and deposit her in the harem. Although the king was not obliged to consult the girl's family, it was courteous to do so if the opportunity arose. Such was the regal life of royalty.

An unmarried daughter was a chattel and, as such, was the property of her father. Therefore it was customary for the king to give him something of value in return for the person of the girl.[2] This was called a mohar, or purchase price of a wife or concubine.[3] Jewelry, livestock, and slaves were often a medium of payment. That apparently satisfied the girl's family, and everybody was happy with the transaction except possibly the girl herself. The same rule of thumb applied when the father was dead and a sister was taken from her brother.[4]

---

1. Cf. Fausset 6; Skinner 248, 249, 346.
2. Cf. Fosdick (2) 102, 103; 22 Ex. 17.
3. Skinner 319, 346; cf. The Levite's Concubine, infra.
4. Cf. Tuck 25.

However, it was not quite so easy for the king to latch on to somebody's wife. Marriage complicated the situation because the existence of the husband was a stumbling block. The law of the East frowned on one who snatched a wife from her husband. Even despots came under the ban.[5] It was just not the thing to do. But as there was nothing to bar the taking of a widow, the problem was more academic than real. All the king had to do was to kill the woman's husband.[6] The woman of his choice then became a single woman and could be hustled into the harem forthwith. It was that easy to circumvent the law.

Once in the harem the king's prospective bedfellow was put through a series of treatments known as "purification."[7] This lasted for several months.[8] As previously pointed out, the purpose of "purification" was to assure the chief eunuch or keeper of the women that the lady was not pregnant and did not have venereal or some other loathsome disease before she was ushered to the king's bed for a night of revelry with his royal highness.[9]

With this background of early law and custom in mind, let us consider Abraham and his wife Sarah.[10] At the Lord's suggestion the happy couple moved out of Haran, the land of their nativity.[11] They wandered into Canaan and from there to Sichem and Moreh.[12] Famine forced them to move on, and they journeyed south to Egypt.[13] This trip jeopardized Abraham's personal safety, because he foresaw that the Egyptian king might want to lay hands on his beautiful wife. Pharaoh

---

5. Ibid.; Lofts 115.
6. Alleman 185; Lofts 7.
7. 2 Esther 3, 9, 12; 1 Cook 104.
8. Cf. 2 Esther 12.
9. Cf. The Female of the Species (Esther), supra.
10. Abram and Sarai changed their names to Abraham and Sarah. 17 Gen. 5, 15.
11. Cf. 11 Gen. 28; 12 Gen. 4. Haran is near the source of the Euphrates River.
12. 12 Gen. 5, 6, 7.
13. 12 Gen. 9, 12. "Nothing is said of his having asked counsel from

could not do so if Abraham were alive. So Abraham said to Sarah, "Behold now, I know that thou art a fair woman to look upon:

"Therefore it shall come to pass, when the Egyptians shall see thee, that they shall say, This is his wife: and they will kill me, but they will save thee alive.

"Say, I pray thee, thou art my sister: that it may be well with me for thy sake; and my soul shall live because of thee."[14]

Sarah did not demur to her husband's request. When they reached Egypt, she was spotted by Pharaoh's henchmen. To keep Abraham out of danger, the couple told the king's men they were brother and sister. Neither one of them revealed their marital status.[15] So Sarah was taken to the seraglio at once.[16]

This suppression of the truth by Sarah and Abraham was tantamount to a deliberate falsehood.[17] The Reverend Cook says that Abraham "has been defended as having 'said she was his sister, without denying that she was his wife, concealing the truth but not speaking what was false.' . . . But though concealment may not necessarily be deception, we can scarsely acquit Abraham either of some disingenuousness or of endangering his wife's honour and chastity, in order to save his own life."[18]

In keeping with the times and the manners, Pharaoh paid

---

heaven before taking this important step; and succeeding events lead rather to the inference that he trusted to his own judgment in this matter, and consequently fell into error." Deane 48.

14. 12 Gen. 11-13. The Reverend Tuck poses this question: "Can such an incident be recorded in Scripture for our imitation?" Tuck 24. And Dr. Skinner says: "There is no suggestion that either the untruthfulness or the selfish cowardice of the request was severely reprobated by the ethical code to which the narrative appealed." Skinner 249.

15. 12 Gen. 15, 16. Though married, Abraham was the half brother of Sarah.

16. 12 Gen. 14, 15.

17. Cf. 37 C.J.S. 242-249 and 37 Am. Jur. 2d 20 et seq., defining fraud as including the supression of the truth as well as the utterance of a deliberate lie.

18. 1 Cook 133.

for Sarah's person. He presented Abraham with "sheep, and oxen, and he asses, and menservants, and maidservants, and she asses, and camels."[19] The patriarch accepted payment for his wife apparently without qualms of conscience because, as is hereinafter noted, he did not return the slaves and the livestock to Pharaoh when he got his wife back again.

The Lord was displeased with the whole affair. With Sarah bought and paid for and safely ensconced in the harem for purification, He intervened by bringing down "great plagues" on Pharaoh and his house.[20] Just why the Lord did not punish Abraham, the real offender, instead of the innocent victim of the deception is one of the unsolved riddles of the Scriptures. None of the commentators whose works have been examined attempt to answer the question. In some way, though most likely from the frightened Sarah,[21] Pharaoh learned the truth. He then gave Abraham a scathing denunciation. "What is this," he asked Abraham, "that thou hast done unto me? why didst thou not tell me that she was thy wife?

'Why sayest thou, She is my sister? so I might have taken her to me to wife: now therefore behold thy wife, take her, and go thy way."[22]

With these few words Pharaoh banished Abraham and Sarah from Egypt. While Pharaoh did not demand the return of the chattels he gave for Sarah's person,[23] there is no mention in poverty but left with wealth acquired by deceit and dis- been the fair and equitable thing to do. But Abraham preferred to keep the ill-gotten gains. He and Sarah entered Egypt in poverty but left with wealth acquired by deceit and dis-

---

19. 12 Gen. 16. "These presents could not have been refused by him without an insult which . . . the king did not deserve." 1 McClintock 29. These gifts were the foundation of Abraham's wealth. Skinner 249.

20. 12 Gen. 17. It was during the period of purification "that God *plagued Pharaoh and his house with plagues,* so that Sarai was restored before she would have been taken to the bed of the Egyptian king." 1 Clarke 100.

21. 1 Cook 103, 104.

22. 12 Gen. 18, 19.

23. 12 Gen. 20; Lofts 7.

simulation. Commenting on this phase of Abraham's life, the
Reverend Tuck offers the following poignant remarks:

"Craft is the weak side of the strong Abrahamic race; the
evil into which their characteristic quality runs. Their caution
and skill in retaining what they possess, which makes the Jews
good bankers and money-lenders, made them suitable for the
Divine purpose as depositaries of the primary religious truths,
and their conservators until the fulness of times should come.
But caution easily degenerates into craft and guile. In Abraham we find traces of the evil which comes out prominently in
Jacob."[24]

Abraham was the founder of the Hebrew nation. He and
his family have been regarded as "a type of the Church of God
in after ages. They, indeed, constituted God's ancient Church."[25]
Nevertheless, Abraham has been subjected to severe criticism
for his part in the sordid transaction with Pharaoh, and he
has been compared unfavorably with the Egyptian king.[26]
"The man of God was rebuked by the man of the world: a
thing singularly humiliating. It is common to find men of the
world whose honor and integrity is a shame to every Christian;
and common enough to find men of religious feeling and
aspiration, of whom that same world is compelled to say that
whenever they are tried in business there is always something
found wanting. . . . Morality is not religion; but unless religion is grafted on morality, religion is worth nothing."[27]

The Reverend Cook excuses and accuses Abraham in the
same breath. "We see in the conduct of Abram an instance
of one under the influence of deep religious feeling and true
faith in God, but with a conscience imperfectly enlightened

---

24. Tuck 26. Abraham and Sarah could now "gloat together . . . over the
    wealth which their brief separation had brought them." Lofts 8.
25. 1 McClintock 27, 32. Cf. 12 Gen. 1 et seq.
26. Cf. 1 I.B. 581.
27. Robertson 53. Dr. Skinner adds, "Yahwe's (God's) providence puts
    in the wrong the man who is justified at the bar of human con-
    science; He is not here the absolutely righteous Being proclaimed
    by the prophets." Skinner 250.

as to many moral duties, and when leaning to his own understanding suffered to fall into great error and sin. The candour of the historian is shown by his exhibiting in such strong relief the dissimulation of Abram as contrasted with the straightforward integrity of Pharaoh."[28]

The Reverend J. R. Dummelow holds that the conduct of Abraham in Egypt is inexcusable. "The patriarch on this occasion appears in a very unfavourable light. Admitting the great dangers which threatened him at the hands of a licentious despot, admitting also that among Easterns duplicity is admired rather than scorned, the readiness he showed to risk his wife's honour in order to secure his own safety, and his lack of trust in God's protection, are inexcusable."[29]

It would seem that after Abraham's humiliating experience in Egypt he would have learned the lesson that honesty is the best policy. Evidently he didn't. Several years later we find him up to the same trick again. Having become rich by pawning his wife on one occasion, he decided to press his luck. As before, his deception was capped with success, thanks again to the intervention of the Lord on the wrong side of the case.

Arriving at the city of Gerar,[30] Abraham passed his wife off as his sister.[31] On this occasion she was taken to the harem of King Abimelech. Jehovah came to Sarah's rescue a second time he got "sheep, an oxen, and menservants, and women- which her true status was revealed.[32]

The next day the king confronted Abraham with the false-

---

28. 1 Cook 103. Abram is a different spelling of Abraham.
29. Dummelow 21.
30. A Philistine city southwest of Jerusalem.
31. 20 Gen. 2. "It is not to be wondered at that the same danger should twice have occured to Sarah, if we remember that the customs of the heathen nations, among which she was sojourning, were such as to induce Abraham to use the artifice of calling his wife his sister." 1 Cook 133. It might be observed here that the idea works well for Abraham; but how about Sarah? It leaves her continually in somebody's harem.
32. 20 Gen. 3-7.

hood. To justify himself Abraham said apologetically, "Because I thought, Surely the fear of God is not in this place; and they will slay me for my wife's sake.

"And yet indeed she is my sister; for she is the daughter of my father, but not the daughter of my mother; and she became my wife.

"And it came to pass, when God caused me to wander from my father's house, that I said unto her, This is thy kindness which thou shalt shew unto me; at every place whither we shall come, say of me, He is my brother."[33]

This excuse is very lame and is so regarded by many commentators.[34] As Dr. Clarke says: "I have not told a lie; I have suppressed only a part of the truth. In this place it may proper to ask, *What is a lie?* It is any action done or word spoken, whether true or false in itself, which the doer or speaker wishes the observer or hearer to take in a *contrary* sense to that which he knows to be true. It is, in a word, any action done or speech delivered with *the intention to deceive,* though both may be absolutely true and right in themselves."[35] This is in keeping with the current rule that fraud may arise from the suppression of truth or a failure to disclose information which should be disclosed.[36]

To make a long story short, the affair climaxed the same way as before. Abimelech returned Sarah to Abraham after first loading the patriarch down with more merchandise. This time he got "sheep, and oxen, and menservants, and womenservants" coupled with "a thousand pieces of silver."[37] He was also permitted to remain in Gerar with all the profits of his deception. Abraham did all right for himself. But on this occasion Sarah was "reproved"[38] as well as her husband.

---

33. 20 Gen. 11-13.
34. Cf. 1 McClintock 29 where it is said: "This mends the matter very little, since by calling her his sister, he designed to be understood as saying she was *not* his wife." See also Tuck 26.
35. 1 Clarke 136.
36. 37 Am. Jur. 2d ed. 19 et seq.
37. 20 Gen. 14, 16.
38. 20 Gen. 16.

"Behold," the king said to her, "I have given thy brother a thousand pieces of silver: behold, he is to thee a covering of the eyes, unto all that are with thee, and with all other."[39]

In discussing these two chapters in the lives of Abraham and Sarah, the Interpreters offer this interesting comment: "Only at two points does the second story have any important difference from the first: the scene is changed; and there is an evident concern to palliate Abraham's actions by suggesting that he did not completely lie, since Sarah, although she was his wife, was also his half sister. Notwithstanding these differences in details, the purpose of the two narratives remains identical. It was to express the faith ... that God's *protection* of his people of the covenant would never fail."[40] It is difficult to understand why the Lord, as the protector of Abraham and Sarah, would permit the patriarch to profit by deception and why Abraham was not punished for the maltreatment of his wife. Sparing the rod spoiled Abraham. Both he and Sarah could have been protected without being permitted to benefit from wrongful acts. If God would never fail, as the Interpreters say, in the protection of the chosen race, then why did He not take a simpler course of protecting Sarah before she got into anybody's harem? Had He done so, Abraham would not have had to resort to chicanery. Instead of protecting Abraham, it looks as if Jehovah put a dent in his moral armor.

Abraham's deceptive trait became deeply imbedded in his sons. Years later we find Isaac telling the same falsehood about his wife Rebekah in order to insure his personal safety.[41] This time Isaac related the "sister" story to the people of Gerar where he and Rebekah went to live. Either Abimelech was still the king or his son (also named Abimelech) was on the

---

39. 20 Gen. 16. A "covering of the eyes" implies that Abraham should protect his wife and screen her from the view of all men. 1 Cook 135. But the Reverend Dummelow thinks that the gift was intended to cause Sarah to overlook the wrong to which she had been exposed. Dummelow 29.

40. 1 I.B. 633, 635, emphasis added.

41. 26 Gen. 7.

throne.[42] After Isaac and Rebekah had resided in the city for a considerable period, the king looked out of the palace window one day and saw him "sporting"[43] with her. He realized at once they were husband and wife and not brother and sister. The king took Isaac to task. "Behold, of a surety she is thy wife," he said accusingly, "and how saidst thou, She is my sister?"[44]

Isaac's excuse was as lame as his father's.

"Because I said, Lest I die for her."[45]

That answer did not satify Abimelech. He rebuked Isaac for denying his wife, fearing that some of his subjects unwittingly might have taken the fair lady for a concubine.

"What is this," he asked Isaac, "thou hast done unto us? one of the people might lightly have lien with thy wife, and thou shouldest have bought guiltiness upon us."[46]

After this verbal castigation the king let Isaac and Rebekah off without punishment. The couple remained in Abimelech's territory and prospered. They became so weathly as to menace the position of the king, and for that reason he subsequently asked them to leave the country.[47]

In considering Isaac's duplicity, the question again arises why he was favored by the Lord instead of being punished. These stories of Abraham and Isaac put a premium on false-

---

42. The same man dealt with both Abraham and Isaac. Miller 3. But according to others there were two Abimelechs, father and son. Cf. Piercy 4; 1 McClintock 19.

43. 26 Gen. 8. In the Revised Standard Version of the Bible the word *fondling* is substituted for *sporting*. Rheims-Douay uses the word *playing*. Whether Isaac and Rebekah were in a marital embrace at the time is not disclosed in the Bible but Clarke says that "whatever may be the precise meaning of the word, it evidently implies that there were liberties taken and freedoms used on the occasion, which were not lawful but between man and wife." 1 Clarke 169.

44. 26 Gen. 9. In referring to Rebekah as his sister, Isaac's falsehood was not even a half truth. Abraham and Sarah were half brother and sister. Rebekah had no such relationship to Isaac.

45. Ibid.

46. 26 Gen. 10. Cf. also 1 Cook 158.

47. 26 Gen. 12-16.

hood. They deride truth and integrity. Indeed, they discount the fact that the Supreme Being has supreme intelligence and give rise to the suposition that Abraham, Sarah, Isaac, and Rebekah were not aided by Divine intervention but were just lucky. Supreme intelligence could have protected Sarah and Rebekah without obliging their respective husbands to stoop to trickery and device. One expositor says that the purpose of the tales is to affirm the theory of God's watchfulness over His chosen people.[48] Elsewhere in the same work it is suggested that Isaac represented Rebekah as his sister to show the stupidity and gullibility of his Philistine hosts.[49] The latter theory is hard to follow since Isaac himself conceded he lied to assure the prolongation of his own life even though Rebekah might have been despoiled.[50]

Arguments pro and con on Isaac's case, which are applicable to Abraham as well, are presented by the Reverends McClintock and Strong in this summation: "No passage of his life has produced more reproach to Isaac's character than this. . . . On the one hand, this has been regarded by avowed adversaries of Christianity as involving the guilt of 'lying and endeavoring to betray the wife's chastity,' and even by Christians, undoubtedly zealous for truth and right, as the conduct of 'a very poor, paltry earthworm, displaying cowardice, selfishness, readiness to put his wife in a terrible hazard for his own sake.' But, on the other hand, with more reverence, more kindness, and quite as much probability, Waterland[51] . . . concludes that the patriarch 'did right to evade the *difficulty* as long as it could lawfully be evaded, and *to await and see whether Divine providence might not, in some way or other, interpose before the last extremity.* The event answered. God did interpose' (*Scriptures Vindicated*, in *Works*, iv, 188, 190) ."[52] Dr. Waterland's idea of watchful waiting affords no excuse or little help

---

48. 1 I.B. 673.
49. 1 I.B. 671, 673.
50. 26 Gen. 9.
51. Daniel Waterland, D.D., an English theologian (1683-1740) .
52. 4 McClintock 668, emphasis added.

for Isaac because it is inconceivable that falsehood and deceit will ever constitute a lawful evasion of any "difficulty." Time alone does not extenuate duplicity.

On the basis of this summary, what is your verdict? Would you hold for Abraham and Isaac or against them? Do such capers have a rightful place in sacred literature?

11
Lady of the Bath

IT WAS HOT and muggy in Jerusalem that spring day of the year 1037 B.C. David's forces under Joab were engaged in a war of revenge against the Ammonites and had besieged the principal city of Rabbah.[1] David remained at home. In keeping with the custom of the country, he took the usual siesta at noon to ward off the heat of the day. He arose from his bed about three o'clock in the afternoon,[2] yawned, stretched, and then strolled leisurely to the palace roof garden to get a breath of fresh air. Right before his eyes on a nearby roof or patio was the voluptuous Bathsheba, stark naked. She was taking a bath[3] and was clearly visible to the unaided eye from many directions.

While it cannot be said conclusively that all the troubles which subsequently beset the house of David were proximately caused by Bathsheba's ablutions, the events of that torrid afternoon marked a pivotal point in David's career. He committed

---

1. Cf. War Crimes (David), supra.
2. 11 II Sam. 2. "Eveningtide" began about 3:00 P.M. 2 Cook 405.
3. 11 II Sam. 2. Some believe that this particular bath followed Bathsheba's menstrual period (15 Lev. 19-33), but it is not to be inferred therefrom that Jewish women bathed only once a month. Cf. 2 I.B. 1099; 2 Clarke 330.

adultery[4] with Bathsheba and she with him. To hush up the
affair he was obliged to murder her husband, Uriah. Then
things went from bad to worse for the whole royal family.
Within a short time David's son Amnon raped his sister. Absalom, another son, murdered Amnon, then rebelled against his
father, chased him out of Jerusalem for a time, and had sexual
intercourse in public with ten of his concubines. Later on
Solomon killed his half brother Adonijah and during his reign
squandered the wealth of the nation, leaving the country impoverished and setting in motion a chain of events which produced never-ending wars, assassinations, internal strife, degeneracy, the Babylonian invasion, and the Captivity of the Jews.[5]

Bathsheba's timing was perfect unless you wish to assume
that her nakedness on the terrace and David's concurrent appearance on his own veranda were purely coincidental. To the
contrary, it is plausible that she studied the daily routine of
the king. If he could see her from the palace terrace, she could
see him. Bathsheba probably expected David to capitulate to
her charms for she "was very beautiful to look upon."[6] Dr.
Clarke criticizes her performance as an act of indelicacy,[7] and
asks if she knew she could be seen from the king's terrace.[8]
This question warrants an affirmative reply. What Bathsheba
wanted was a man, not a warrior; and he might as well be the
king as anybody else. Her husband, Uriah, had gone to war,
swinging a sword in David's behalf. That did not help Bathsheba. Even when he was at home on leave Uriah was such a
stickler for form that he would not have marital relations with
her. Protocol demanded that warriors abstain from sexual

---

4. Adultery is defined as "carnal intercourse of a married person and
   another who is not the wife or husband." Cath. Dict. 14.
5. Cf. War Crimes (David), supra. and Kill or Be Killed, supra. Of
   David it has been said: "Sorely he sinned, and sorely did he suffer
   for it; he sowed one *grain* of sweet and reaped a long *harvest* of
   calamity and woe. 2 Clarke 332.
6. 11 II Sam. 2.
7. "How could any woman of delicacy expose herself where she could
   be so fully and openly viewed?" 2 Clarke 330.

intercourse, presumably to give them greater strength for battle.[9]

All the evidence points to Bathsheba's complicity in the adulterous act which she and David committed later that afternoon. If Bathsheba was not seeking male companionship, why did she cavort naked on the roof garden? It would have been much easier to take a bath inside of her house. Certainly it would have been more decorous. But she preferred to go outside and expose herself to the leering glances of David or any other interesting male. As people often intend the consequences of their own acts,[10] it is likely that Bathsheba's exposure of her body to the elements was for no good purpose.

Unlike Uriah, David was a man of action when it came to women. He dispatched a palace guard to ascertain her identity and was informed she was none other than "the daughter of Eliam, the wife of Uriah the Hittite."[11] Nevertheless, her marriage to one of the ranking officers[12] of his army did not deter David at that exciting moment. Established principles never bothered him. To hell with Uriah! And damn the consequences! He must have that woman now. Once more he sent a messenger to her home, and she was hustled over to the palace where without further ado both of them satisfied their sexual impetuosity.[13] There is no evidence that Bathsheba showed any reluctance in joining David.[14] Reluctant or not, she went home pregnant.[15]

"I am with child," she bluntly announced to David in due time and thus put it up to him to find a way out of the mess.[16]

Now the fat was in the fire. Under Mosaic law, the punish-

---

8. 2 Clarke 330.
9. 21 I Sam. 4; 2 I.B. 1100.
10. 31A C.J.S. 193 et seq.; 29 Am. Jur. 2d ed. 257 et seq.
11. 11 II Sam. 3.
12. Cf. 2 I.B 1099
13. 11 II Sam. 4; Lofts 112, 113.
14. 2 Clarke 330.
15. 11 II Sam. 5.
16. Ibid.

ment for adultery was death for both participants.[17] Although this law made no exception of kings, it has been said that the monarch could not be punished for such a crime as his death meant the death of the soul.[18] But Dr. Clarke takes a contrary view and thinks David could have been made to suffer the extreme penalty.[19] Abortion was not praticed in those days, and it would soon become apparent that Uriah was not the prospective papa. David would be exposed to public censure and ridicule because Bathsheba showed no inclination to cover up for her paramour. Something had to be done and done quickly. It would be a good idea, David reasoned to himself, to get Uriah home so he could "lay" with his wife.[20] Then the child just conceived could be palmed off as Uriah's. It was a very clever idea especially for "the Lord's annointed."[21] One expositor thinks David was as much concerned with protecting Uriah's home as he was with having his own adultery become public knowledge.[22] This is illogical because David could have protected Uriah's home in the first place by refraining from sexual intercourse with his wife.

However, David's plan did not work. He ordered the gallant captain to return to Jerusalem on the pretext of ascertaining "how the war prospered."[23] When Uriah arrived at the palace he was ushered into the king's presence. David went through the preliminaries by asking for war news and then got to the point.

---

17. 20 Lev. 10; 22 Deut. 22; Lofts 3, 115.
18. Cf. 2 Cook 409.
19. "He thought therefore that either Uriah must die, or he and Bathsheba perish for their iniquity; for that law (Mosaic) had made no provision to save the life of even a king who transgressed its precepts." 2 Clarke 332, parenthesis added.
20. 11 II Sam. 4.
21. 1 II Sam. 14.
22. 2 I.B. 1098.
23. 11 II Sam. 7. "The degrading falsehood and dissimulation to which David was forced to stoop in the vain hope of hiding his sin is most instructive. Truly they are deeds of darkness which require to be enveloped in lies and hypocrisy." 2 Cook 405; cf. Lofts 113.

"Go down to thy house, and wash thy feet," he told Uriah.[24] Expecting the captain to follow the suggestion to go home to his wife, David set a "mess of meat" after him as a gift.[25] But Uriah did not go home. He slept all night "at the door of the king's house,"[26] and had nothing to do with Bathsheba.

This was maddening. Uriah would not follow David's well-hatched plan. It left the king with no alternative but to try again.[27] The next day he asked Uriah, "Camest thou not from thy journey? why then didst thou not go down unto thine house?"[28]

"The ark, and Israel, and Judah abide in tents," Uriah replied, "and my lord Joab, and the servants of my lord, are encamped in the open fields; shall I then go into mine house, to eat and to drink, and to lie with my wife? As thou livest, and as thy soul liveth, I will not do this thing."[29]

David was stumped by this speech, but not for long. This time a better idea flashed through his mind. He would arouse Uriah's passion with a reasonable amount of alcohol. So he invited Uriah to dinner and to spend the night at the palace, telling him that "tomorow I will let thee depart."[30] If David could arouse Uriah's masculinity with liquor, he might forget the sexual restrictions on soldiers and rush home to Bath-

---

24. 11 II Sam. 8. "David's design was that he (Uriah) should go and lie with his wife, that the child now conceived should pass for his, the honour of Bath-sheba screened, and his own crime concealed." 2 Clarke 330.

25. 11 II Sam. 8. The "mess of meat" probably means dinner for two.

26. 11 II Sam. 9. Probably in a spare room at the palace.

27. The Reverend Cook suggests that Uriah may have been informed of the affair between David and Bathsheba. 2 Cook 405; cf. also Lofts 114.

28. 11 II Sam. 10.

29. 11 II Sam. 11. Some doubt has been expressed whether Uriah's declaration was sincere or ironic. 2 I.B. 1100. Dr. Clarke says it was "the answer of a brave, generous and disinterested man ... Had Uriah no suspicion of what had been done in his absence?" 2 Clarke 331.

30. 11 II Sam. 12.

sheba.[31] This scheme failed too. Uriah got well stimulated but spent the night at the palace and would not go home.[32] That marked the beginning of the end for poor Uriah who, parenthetically, may be regarded by many people as a fool.

The next day David sent Uriah back to the battlefront with a letter to Joab, the field general, who was ordered to "set . . . Uriah in the forefront of the hottest battle, and retire ye from him, that he may be smitten, and die."[33] This treacherous act on David's part could well mark the nadir of his career. To make sure that Uriah would be killed David ordered Uriah's comrades to desert him in the thick of battle. A review of the comments of the clergy on this facet of David's character will serve no useful purpose here. Most of them agree with the Reverend Thomas Scott who brands David's action as "deliberate murder" with "malice prepense."[34] Suffice it to say that nobody yet has come up with any plausible excuse for the one reputed to be the "man after God's own heart"[35] and, except in one instance hereinafter noted, none of them try.

This time David's evil plan could not help but succeed. With a handful of men Uriah was assigned to that part of the

---

31. David "tries every wile he can think of to conceal what has happened. . . . When the first attempt fails David tries to overcome Uriah's resistance by making him drunk. But all his plans are foiled by Uriah's reverence for the taboo which forbade sexual intercourse to warriors who had been consecrated for battle." 2 I.B. 1099, 1100; cf. also Lofts 115.

32. 11 II Sam. 13. "The Providence of God is here manifest, defeating David's base contrivances, and bringing his sin to the open light. It is no less clear how mercy was at the bottom of this severity which issued in David's deep repentance, and has also given to the Church one of the most solemn and searching warnings as to the evil of sin which is contained in the whole Bible." 2 Cook 405, 406.

33. 11 II Sam. 15. "This was the sum of treachery and villainy. He made this most noble man the carrier of letters which prescribed the mode in which he was to be murdered." 2 Clarke 331.

34. "Whatever casuistry David might use with his conscience this was *deliberate murder of many persons with malice prepense,* aggravated exceedingly by the circumstance, that these men were slain in the very act of fighting for him and his kingdom." 1 Scott 552.

35. Cf. 1 Fallows 504.

besieged city of Rabbah most strongly defended.[36] In the melee Uriah and his squad were deserted by Joab's main force, leaving the unfortunate group surrounded. All of them were cut to pieces by hostile swords.[37]

Joab then dispatched the glad tidings to his majesty, who by that time was irritated to the point of distraction. To be sure, David could rely on Joab to carry out the order to murder Uriah without asking embarrassing questions. This was one of the things David liked about Joab. At the same time the king did not relish the position in which he had been placed with his field general. He felt mean and cheap. Joab sensed, if he didn't actually know, that David was squirming, so he, running true to form, did not pass up the opportunity to needle his royal highness by instructing the messenger to hold back the news of Uriah's death until the end of the report.[38]

At last David could breathe easily. But now that the dirty work had been done, what did Joab think about it? This worried David. In keeping with his role as perennial hypocrite, he said to Joab's mesenger, "Thus shalt thou say unto Joab, Let not this thing displease thee, for the sword devoureth one as well as another: make thy battle more strong against the city, and overthrow it: and encourage thou him."[39]

When Bathsheba learned of her husband's death, she "mourned."[40] About ten days later she married David, and seven or eight months after that she gave birth to a son.[41]

The king's marriage to Bathsheba did not end the affair.

---

36. 11 II Sam. 16.

37. 11 II Sam. 16, 17.

38. 11 II Sam. 18-24.

39. 11 II Sam. 25. "What abominable hypocrisy was here! He well knew that Uriah's death was no *chance-medley;* he was by his own order thrust on the edge of the sword." 2 Clarke 332.

40. 11 II Sam. 26. Dr. Clarke thinks Bathsheba's mourning was insincere. "She lost a *captain* and got a *king* for her spouse; this must have been deep affliction indeed: and therefore ... 'She shed reluctant tears, and forced out groans from a joyful heart.'" 2 Clarke 332. Mourning lasted for about a week after which custom permitted the surviving spouse to remary. Cf. 2 Cook 407.

The Lord was displeased with David's antics and dispatched the prophet Nathan to censure the culprit king. Nathan gave David a severe tongue-lashing. It took the form of a parable in which the prophet described a rich man with many "flocks and herds"[42] who took the poor man's "one little ewe lamb"[43] which the latter had cherished and nourished.[44] David became incensed at the villainy of the rich man and proclaimed that whoever had done such a dastardly thing "shall surely die."[45] He further decreed that the rich man should restore four lambs to the poor man because "he had no pity."[46]

Unless David was feigning righteous indignation for the benefit of Nathan, imagine, if you will, the king's suprise when the prophet hit him squarely between the eyes with these words, "Thou art the (rich) man."[47]

Nathan then reviewed all the good fortune which the Lord had bestowed on David[48] and prophesied the ill wind which blew through the house of David for years,[49] including the death of the unlawfully conceived child.[50]

It must be said for the king that he took Nathan's verbal chastisement in good grace. What criminal doesn't do likewise when he gets a lecture along with probation from a judge? David's life would be spared, said Nathan.[51] He would not be

---

41. 11 II Sam. 27.
42. 12 II Sam. 2.
43. 12 II Sam. 3.
44. 12 II Sam. 1-5.
45. 12 II Sam. 5. Some doubt has been expressed that David was so dense as not to see through Nathan's parable. Cf. 2 I.B. 1102.
46. 12 II Sam. 6.
47. 12 II Sam. 7, parenthesis added.
48. 12 II Sam. 7, 8.
49. 12 II Sam. 10-12. Cf. supra. note 5. "The sword of calamity did not depart from his house, from the murder of wretched *Amnon* ... to the slaughter of the sons of *Zedekiah*, before their father's eyes, by the king of Babylon. His *daughter* was dishonoured by her own brother, and his *wives* contaminated publicly by his own son." 2 Clarke 333.
50. 12 II Sam. 14-19.
51. 12 II Sam. 13.

punished with death according to the Mosaic code. He was suppliant before the prophet since the elite, as well as the uneducated masses, were extremely superstitious in those days and feared anyone alleged to be an emissary of Jehovah.[52] "I have sinned against the Lord," David said humbly to Nathan.[53]

He must have meant what he said because, according to some commentators, his acts in the immediate future showed deep repentence.[54] From this some of the clergy find fuel to light up his character. For example, it has been said: "Heinous as was his double crime, he but exercised dictatorial powers in behalf of self-advantage—a common enough procedure upon the part of Eastern monarchs devoid of ethical sensibilities. The point of the biblical narrative is not the gravity of the sin but David's humble acnowledgment of its gravity."[55] This language typifies the tendency to excuse the criminal acts of some biblical characters on the grounds that such was the custom of the age and that all the culprit had to do was to repent and bewail his misdeeds. He could then escape the punishment prescribed by Mosaic law. There was nothing unusual or outstanding about David's acknowledgment of his overt acts or his acceptance of responsibility for the existence of a child illegitimately conceived. A great many men have done the same thing since his time and a great many men will probably do the same thing in years to come.

---

52. Cf. The Case Against Samuel, supra.
53. 12 II Sam. 13. "The silence with which David listened to the long and terrible harangue of Nathan sufficiently shows the prostration of his spirit under the sense of guilt." 2 Cook 408. Cf. also the thirty-second and fifty-first Psalms.
54. 12 II Sam. 16-20. "The death of the infant child of one of the numerous harems of an Oriental monarch would in general be a matter of little moment to the father. The deep feeling shown by David on this occasion is both an indication of his *affectionate and tender nature,* and also proof of the strength of his passion for Bath-sheba." 2 Cook 409, emphasis added. It is hard to accept this appraisal of David as having an "affectionate and tender nature" in view of his torture of the Ammonites and the Moabites and his other vicious deeds. Cf. War Crimes (David), supra.
55. 2 I.B. 1098.

After the ill-gotten infant died, Bathsheba conceived again and Solomon was born.[56] While she is regarded by one expositor as a woman of "low status to begin with,"[57] the Reverends McClintock and Strong say that the "rabbins describe her as a woman of vast information and a highly-cultivated mind, to whose education Solomon owed much of his wisdom and reputation, and even a great part of the practical philosophy embodied in his Proverbs."[58]

Whether true love developed between David and Bathsheba in later years is for you to resolve in your own mind. It can hardly be said to have existed at the start of their relationship. Some think it never did exist. "The story nowhere indicates that David was especially devoted to Bathsheba."[59] But the Reverend Cook thinks otherwise,[60] and his theory is bolstered by the fact that David put Bathsheba's son on the throne in preference to his other sons who were older than Solomon. The Reverend Tuck seems to agree: "The favour shown to Solomon, and the consequent setting aside of the other children of David, tends to lighten our estimate of the moral fault of Bathsheba and David."[61]

Dr. Clarke sums up the case this way: "Drs. Delaney, Chandler, and others have taken great pains to excuse and varnish this conduct of David; and while I admire their ingenuity, I abhor the tendency of their doctrine, being fully convinced that he who writes on this subject should write like the inspired penman who tells the TRUTH, the WHOLE TRUTH, and NOTHING BUT THE TRUTH. . . . The criminal king and his criminal paramour are for the moment concealed; and one of the bravest of men falls an affectionate victim for the safety and support of him by whom his spotless blood is shed! . . . let this *David*, I say, be considered an awful example of *apostasy* from religion, justice, and virtue; *Bath-sheba*, of lightness and conjugal in-

---

56. 12 II Sam. 24.
57. 2 I.B. 1099.
58. 1 McClintock 695.
59. 2 I.B. 1098.
60. 2 Cook 408, 409.
61. Tuck 141.

fidelity; *Joab,* of base, unmanly, and cold-blooded cruelty; *Uriah,* of untarnished heroism, inflexible fidelity, and unspotted virtue; and then justice will done to each character."[62]

The authors of *The Jewish Encyclopedia* come to David's defense. They advance the idea that he was not guilty of either adultery or murder.[63] Based on certain Talmudic authorities, they argue that David did not commit adultery with Bathsheba because in those days "all women obtained letters of divorce from their husbands who went to war, to use in case the latter should die on the field."[64] This is illogical. If a warrior husband was killed in battle, his wife would be widowed by death rather than divorce. The divorce papers would be redundant if they were not to be used until the husband died in battle. It hardly could be said that such papers legalized promiscuity on the part of the wives at home. Another weakness of this theory is that neither David nor Bathsheba was free from a sense of guilt arising out of their intimate relations. If Bathsheba had a divorce decree, neither of them relied upon it. In that case there would have been no occasion for David to try to cover up the affair. Moreover, there would have been no point in recalling Uriah from battle to prevail upon him to "lay"[65] with his wife so that the child already conceived could be said to be his. David's actions in this respect rebut the contention that Bathsheba was divorced.

Next it is said that David was blameless of Uriah's death because "the latter had committed a capital offense in refusing to obey the king's command—to return to his wife."[66] This point is weak also because it places Uriah "betwixt the devil

---

62. 2 Clarke 332. Dr. Delaney is probably Patrick Delaney, an Irish clergyman (1686-1768) although the reference may be to William H. Delancey, Bishop of the Protestant Episcopal Church of New York (1797-1865). Dr. Chandler is either Edward Chandler, Bishop of Dublin (1670-1750) or Samuel Chandler, an eminent English minister (1693-1766).

63. 4 Singer 455, 456.

64. 4 Singer 455.

65. 11 II Sam. 4.

66. 4 Singer 456, citing II Sam. xl, 8, 9; Shab. 56a; Kid., 43a. (Talmudic versions).

and the deep sea."[67] Assuming the king had enjoined him to go to Bathsheba, Uriah was also under order to refrain from having sexual intercourse during a war. It should be noted, however, that David's words to Uriah ("Go down to thy house, and wash thy feet") [68] were precatory rather than mandatory. They were merely a friendly suggestion, and Uriah so construed them. The king was not angry with Uriah the next day when he learned the latter had not visited Bathsheba. He was only dumbfounded. Lack of anger is manifested by the cordial invitation David extended to Uriah to be wined and dined at the palace. If David thought Uriah had disobeyed a royal command, it is reasonable to assume he would have punished Uriah with death at once, since Uriah was *persona non grata* and a fly in the regal ointment. The king's invitation dispels the idea that Uriah had committed a capital offense by refusing to return to his wife.

As far as David is concerned, one final observation may bear repetition. It pertains to his insincerity and inconsistency. Maybe he had a Jekyll and Hyde complex. He was quite willing to penalize the rich man of Nathan's parable "because (the rich man) had no pity."[69] Yet a short while later we find him subjecting the men, women, and children of the city of Rabbah to pitiless torture.[70] Thus David's lamentations after his denunciation by Nathan have all the appearance of an insincere and ostentatious display of grief to assuage public resentment against him for the Bathsheba affair. How do you look at it?

---

67. Erasmus, *Adagia*, Chap. III, Cent. IV, 94.
68. 11 II Sam. 8.
69. 12 II Sam. 6, parenthesis added.
70. Cf. War Crimes (David), supra.

12
The Rape of Tamar

BENEATH THE SURFACE of this tragic story is a solemn word of warning to womankind. The sad tale shows that illicit sexual intimacy often leaves the male participant cold.[1] After Amnon ravished Tamar, he rudely dismissed her from his presence and wanted nothing further to do with her. But in the end he paid with his life for the rape of his unwilling victim.

All this happened in the year 1033 B.C., approximately four years after David's notorious carnality with Bathsheba.[2] Amnon, the oldest son of David and heir apparent to the throne, took one look at the lovely Tamar[3] and immediately felt the cosmic urge. He could not conceive of any way to have intimate relations with her unless they were illegal.[4] She was his half sister, and at that time marriage between a half brother and sister was taboo. Moreover, she was a virgin, and the sexual molestation of a virgin was also prohibited by Levitical law.

---

1. Cf. 13 II Sam. 15; 2 I.B. 1113; H. P. Smith 329.
2. Cf. Lady of the Bath, supra.
3. Tamar was the full sister of Absalom and a half sister of Amnon. All of them were sired by David. Cf. 2 I.B. 1111; 10 McClintock 192, 193.
4. 13 II Sam. 2.

This only aggravated Amon's frantic passion.[5] He became so aroused that he "fell sick for his sister Tamar."[6]

While thus afflicted, he received a call from his cousin and confidant, one Jonadab, who asked, "Why art thou, being the king's son, lean from day to day? Wilt thou not tell me?"[7]

"I love Tamar," Amnon said simply, though he also may have explained the impossibility of obtaining lawful access to the girl.[8]

The wily Jonadab had a brilliant idea. Sensing that David would not deny his son anything within reason, he advised Amnon to pretend illness and, when his father called, to request the presence of Tamar at his bedside to prepare palatable food for him.[9] Amnon decided to try his luck. When the king visited him at his bachelor quarters, Amnon said, "I pray thee, let Tamar my sister come, and make me a couple of cakes in my sight, that I may eat at her hand."[10]

Complying with this apparently innocent request, David ordered Tamar to wait upon her half brother. The girl called at his apartments and "took flour, and kneaded it, and made cakes in his sight, and did bake the cakes."[11] When the cakes came out of the oven she offered them to Amnon, but he refused to eat.[12] The bounder was obviously more interested in Tamar's curves than in her culinary accomplishments.

---

5. 13 II Sam. 2. "It has been well remarked that 'the passion of love is nowhere so wasting and vexatious, as where it is unlawful.' " 2 Clarke 337.

6. 13 II Sam. 2. Cf. also 10 McClintock 192, 193.

7. 13 II Sam. 4.

8. Ibid.

9. 13 II Sam. 5. Jonadab was "an evil genius (who) ... was smart enough to tell Amnon how to get what he wanted, but he was not smart enough to tell him how to avoid the ... consequences of his rash act." 2 I.B. 1112, 1113; parenthesis added.

10. 13 II Sam. 6.

11. 13 II Sam. 8. The baking of the cakes by Tamar showed the simplicity of court life. 10 McClintock 193.

12. 13 II Sam. 9.

He summarily dismissed all of his servants and then roughly seized the unlucky girl and drew her down to him on the bed. Without any romantic preliminaries whatever he bluntly put his proposition: "Come lie with me, my sister."[13]

"Nay, my brother, do not force me;" she replied beseechingly, "for no such thing ought to be done in Israel: do not thou this folly. And I, whither shall I cause my shame to go? and as for thee, thou shalt be as one of the fools in Israel Now therefore, I pray thee, speak unto the king, for he will not withhold me from thee."[14] This speech implies that David would overlook incest and sanction her marriage to Amnon.[15]

The young prince would not listen to reason. Maybe he did not believe his father would allow him to marry Tamar. But even if his father should approve the match, it is more likely that he did not want to marry her anyway, because it might make him a lawbreaker in the public eye and subject him to ridicule and ill will.[16] So by superior physical strength he held her down on the bed and raped her. From the biblical account of the affair Amnon did not have an easy time accomplishing his purpose. It is said that Amnon "being stronger than she, forced her, and lay with her."[17] The use of the words

---

13. 13 II Sam. 11.

14. 13 II Sam. 12, 13.

15. "In her touching remonstrance two points are remarkable. First the expression of the infamy of such a crime 'in *Israel*' implying the loftier standard of morals that prevailed as compared with other countries at that time; and, secondly, the belief that even this standard might be overborne lawfully by royal authority.... It is enough to suppose, what evidently her whole speech implies, that the king had a dispensing power which was conceived to cover even extreme cases." 10 McClintock 193. Dr. Fausset sums up Tamar's plea this way: "She remonstrated at his force, dwelling twice on such baseness being wrought 'in Israel' where a higher law existed than in heathendom." Fausset 674. Cf. also 18 Lev. 9; 20 Lev. 17; 27 Deut. 22.

16. Cf. 2 I.B. 1113. Marriage with a half sister was permitted at that time, some believe. Cf. Concise 424.

17. 13 II Sam. 14.

"stronger" and "forced" indicates that Tamar put up a fight for her honor and struggled with her assailant, yelling, screaming, biting, and clawing to no avail.

After Amnon expended himself in Tamar he "hated her exceedingly; so that the hatred wherewith he hated her was greater than the love wherewith he had loved her."[18] Without so much as giving her a chance to catch her breath, get off the bed, and arrange herself, he ordered her out of the house. "Arise, be gone," he said with ill grace.[19] Tamar didn't move. "There is no cause;" she retorted indignantly, "this evil in sending me away is greater than the other that thou didst unto me."[20]

But Amnon wanted no more of Tamar. Her presence annoyed him. He summoned his servants and said contemptuously, "Put now this woman out from me, and bolt the door after her."[21]

The servants seized Tamar, jerked her to her feet, and ushered her hurriedly to the street. She must have known by this time that Amnon had no intention of marrying her. Her unhappy predicament is vividly described by Doctors McClintock and Strong who say that "when the guard at Amnon's door had thrust her out and closed the door after her to prevent her return, she, in her agony, snatched handfuls of ashes from the ground and threw them on her hair, then tore off her royal sleeves, and clasped her bare hands upon her head, and rushed to and fro through the streets screaming aloud. In this state she encountered her brother Absalom, who took her to his house, where she remained as if in a state of widowhood."[22]

---

18. 13 II Sam. 15.
19. Ibid.
20. 13 II Sam. 16. Apparently Tamar meant that Amnon should rectify the   wrong he had done to her by marrying her.
21. 13 II Sam. 16-17. Amnon's reference to Tamar as "this woman" shows his brutality towards his victim. Cf. 2 I.B. 1113, 1115.
22. 10 McClintock 193. Long sleeves were worn by women of the royal court as a mark of distinction. Cf. also 13 II Sam. 18-20.

When David heard the news he became "very wroth."[23] However, to get angry was about all he did, although it has been suggested he may have sternly lectured his wayward son.[24] If so, Amnon probably regarded his father with a sardonic grin. David was in no position to reprimand Amnon. He was vulnerable himself. His affair with Bathsheba and the murder of her husband made it awkward for him to punish or criticize his son.[25] Amnon was merely a chip off the old block. Why shouldn't he take Tamar? If his father could commit adultery and then murder the lady's husband without punishment,[26] what was wrong with raping a half sister? He was an heir apparent to the throne, and the difference between his father and himself was a trifling one of time and degree. His attitude reflects the baseness of David's court. "Even the king of Israel must wink at the offenses of his son."[27]

Realizing that his father's shortcomings virtually precluded punishment of the rapist, Absalom advised Tamar to do nothing impulsive. "Hath Amnon thy brother been with thee? but hold now thy peace, my sister: he is thy brother; regard not this thing."[28]

---

23. 13 II Sam. 21. "To this verse the *Septuagint* add the following words: 'But he would not grieve the soul of Amnon his son, for he loved him, because he was his first-born.' The same addition is found in the *Vulgate* and in *Josephus*, and it is possible that this was once made a part of the Hebrew text." 2 Clarke 338.

24. "David probably said a good deal to Amnon; tragically for all concerned, he did nothing. Absalom said nothing, and tragically . . . did the *wrong* thing." 2 I.B. 1115, emphasis added. It may be of interest to observe here that since the Old Testament preaches the doctrine of retributive justice, what was "wrong" about Absalom's invocation of *lex talionis* of Levitical law and killing Amnon? In H. P. Smith, page 329, it is suggested that family ties prevented summary venegeance. Others say that David was "afraid or unwilling" to punish Amnon. 10 McClintock 193.

25. 2 I.B. 1109.

26. Cf. Lady of the Bath, supra.

27. 5 Exp. Bible 199; cf. also Harrison 195.

28. 13 II Sam. 20.

That ended the matter as far as Tamar was concerned but not for Absalom. He was made of sterner stuff than his father and was determined not to take Amnon's insult lying down. His resentment smouldered for a long time before the opportunity arose for revenge.[29] Two years later he prevailed upon David to let Amnon join him in a sheep-shearing venture.[30] One night during the encampment while Amnon was "merry with wine" Absalom ordered his servants to kill him.[31] And they did.[32] It broke up the party then and there. The other sons of the king who were present, thinking Absalom may have had designs on the throne by their elimination also, fled to the sanctity of the palace.[33] Absalom did not return to David's court. He took refuge with his mother's people, the Geshurites.[34] Three years later he was recalled to Jerusalem by his father who had ceased to grieve for Amnon and yearned to see his younger son.[35]

The vicious rape of Tamar was a crime denounced by Levitical law.[36] There is no possible excuse for Amnon unless it be said, in the light of his father's misdeeds, that it was a case of "monkey see, monkey do." In any event David's criminal activities furnished no legal or ethical excuse for Amnon's crime.

As it was then, so is it today. The woman pays. Tamar was the real sufferer. She was confined to Absalom's house for the rest of her life and was denied the benefits of her sex, namely, a husband, a home, and children.[37]

While Absalom broke with his father for a long time, he

---

29. 13 II Sam. 23.
30. 13 II Sam. 23-27.
31. 13 II Sam. 28.
32. 13 II Sam. 29.
33. 13 II Sam. 29. At that time it is evident that Absalom did not aspire to the throne. He killed Amnon as a punishment for the rape of Tamar. Cf. 2 I.B. 1116, 1117.
34. 13 II Sam. 37.
35. 13 II Sam. 37-39; cf. also 2 Clarke 339.
36. 18 Lev. 11; cf. also note 15, supra.
37. 13 II Sam. 20.

became a court favorite upon his return; only to fall out again with David when he tried to overthrow his father's reign by force and violence. In this Absalom may have been actuated in part by David's shabby treatment of Tamar. One thing is certain—David had no control over his children.[38] He brushed aside his duties as a king and acted as a lenient father towards Amnon. This must have been discouraging to David's other sons and also to his supporters when they realized that fundamentally he was a weakling. To commit a crime is bad enough, but intentionally to let the culprit go unpunished is worse. As the Reverend Dummelow says, (David's) sin was finding him out, and he was tasting the first bitter fruits of it in the death of one son and the alienation of another."[39]

---

38. Cf. 2 I.B. 1109; Jerome 176.
39. Dummelow 201, parenthesis added.

13
The Levite's Concubine

Woman's lot in life was a sorry one during Old Testament times. She was a chattel, the property of her father before marriage and that of her husband afterwards. A drudge all of her life, she was subordinated to the male members of the family.[1] Her primary function was to perpetuate the race, and she was afforded every opportunity to do so. The Hebrew woman, however, was better off than those of other Oriental kingdoms.[2] She was protected by the Ten Commandments and many provisions of the Mosaic code.[3] When she attained marriageable age she was sold by her father for a mohar[4] to the most eligible man who, presumably, was the fellow with the most money. Her feelings were of no concern to anyone but herself.[5]

There were, of course, exceptions to the general rule. Some

---

1. Cf. 11 I Cor. 8, 9; 2 I Tim, 13; Fosdick (2) 102, 103; Miller 821.
2. Cf. 3 Smith 1785; Lofts 2.
3. Cf. 22 Deut. 1-30; 24 Deut. 1-5.
4. A mohar was the purchase money for a wife. Cf. Skinner 319. "Ruth the Moabitess . . . have I purchased to be my wife." 4 Ruth 10; Chase 163.
5. "The consent of the maiden was sometimes asked . . . but this appears to have been subordinate to the previous consent of the father and the adult brothers." 2 Smith 249.

women rose to positions of prominence and power. Take
Esther, for example, who virtually ruled a huge Persian kingdom in the early part of the sixth century, B.C. as the wife of
King Ahasuerus.[6] Others like Deborah, Rebekah, Rachel,
Sarah, and Jezebel made their mark in history also. But for
the run-of-the-mill, a woman was lucky if she attained and kept
the status of a full-fledged wife. She might be a secondary wife
or concubine. Worse yet she might be a slave.

Despite woman's inferior position, a violation of her person was not tolerated in biblical times. This stemmed from the
fact that she was a chattel and would become damaged merchandise if anyone had unlawful sexual relations with her.
To illustrate, the sexual mistreatment and murder of the unknown concubine of an unknown Levite led to civil war,
pillage, carnage, mass murder, and the rape of six hundred
other women. On a wave of mass hysteria the punishment soon
engulfed the original crimes, and the situation got completely
out of hand. All this occurred in the days of the judges (about
1406 B.C.) and at a time when there was no king over Israel.[7]
It came about in this way.

Some Levite residing in Ephraim took a concubine. She
later "played the whore against him"[8] and returned to her
father's house in Bethlehem. She was there for several months
before her husband, the Levite, "went after her, to speak
friendly unto her, and to bring her (home) again."[9] The
young woman's father was overjoyed at the prospect of patch-
ing up the differences between the couple and entertained his
son-in-law lavishly for several days.[10]

---

6. Cf. The Female of the Species (Esther), supra.
7. Emphasis at the beginning and end of the story (19 Judg. 1 and 21
   Judg. 25) upon the fact that there was no king indicates the sordid
   affairs never would have occurred had there been a king.
8. 19 Judg. 1, 2. It has been said these words do not connote infidelity
   but only the existence of a domestic quarrel of some minor nature.
   2 Clarke 176. But Bishop Vincent and his associates think she did
   commit adultery. 2 Vincent 618.
9. 19 Judg. 3, parenthesis added.
10. 19 Judg. 3, 4.

Late in the afternoon of the fifth day the Levite determined to start home with his concubine and with the servant
and two donkeys he had brought with him. Their departure
was protested by the concubine's father, who begged the Levite
to remain overnight and get an early start in the morning.[11]
It was dangerous to be out after dark. However, the Levite
insisted upon making a start. The travelers pressed on until
nighttime when they found themselves at Gibeah, a tribal city
of the Benjamites.[12] They were unable to obtain lodgings, and
nobody offered any hospitality to the wayfarers until an old
man happened to pass by on his way home from work in the
fields.[13] After introducing themselves to each other, he invited
the Levite and his concubine and servant to spend the night
at his home, warning him not to "lodge . . . in the street."[14]

In the meantime the presence of the Levite in the city had
not gone unobserved. Later that evening while the Levite and
his host "were making their hearts merry"[15] with the latter's
supply of wine, certain "sons of Belial"[16] gathered outside the
house and hammered at the door.

"Bring forth the man that came into thine house, that
we may know him," they yelled to the old man.[17] The host
refused to do so but countered with an offer of his virgin
daughter and the Levite's concubine.

"Nay, my brethren, nay, I pray you," he replied, "do not
so wickedly; seeing that this man is come into mine house, do
not this folly.

"Behold, here is my daughter, a maiden, and his concubine; them I will bring out now, and humble ye them, and do

---

11. 19 Judg. 9.
12. 19 Judg. 13-15. Gibeah is about four miles north of Jerusalem. 2
Cook 211.
13. 19 Judg. 16.
14. 19 Judg. 17-21.
15. 19 Judg. 22.
16. They were profligate fellows and "were genuine sodomites as to their
practices." 2 Clarke 178. Cf. also 19 Judg. 22 and 2 I.B. 812.
17. 19 Judg. 22. There is little doubt that the demand meant the Levite
was to be used for sexual purposes. Cf. 2 I.B. 812.

with them what seemeth good unto you; but unto this man do not so vile a thing."[18]

The old man's proposal to submit his own virgin daughter as well as the Levite's concubine to the lust of the vicious townsmen has been deplored by biblical scholars.[19]

The sodomites wanted neither one of the women. They wanted the Levite and threatened to break into the house to get him. This frightened him into action. Without wasting further time he ordered his concubine to leave the house and submit to the demands of the gang on the outside. The poor woman pleaded piteously with her husband to no avail. When she shrank into a corner for whatever protection it might afford, the Levite seized her and dragged her to the door. With a shriek of terror she was pushed out of the house by her cowardly husband[20] and, like a pack of wolves, the sodomites closed in. They grabbed her, tore the clothes from her body, and "knew her, and abused her all the night."[21] The Bible leaves to your imagination the precise nature of the abuse to which she was subjected.

In the morning the men let her go.[22] The unfortunate

---

18. 19 Judg. 23, 24.
19. "There is nothing resembling chivalry in the (Levite's) willingness to deliver his concubine to the rioters in place of himself, and one is aghast at the Ephraimite father's offer to give his virgin daughter . . . instead of his guest." 2 I.B. 814, parenthesis added. Clarke says: "Such a proposal was made by *Lot* to the men of Sodom, Gen. xix, but nothing can excuse either. That the rights of *hospitality* were sacred in the East, and most highly regarded, we know: and that a man would defend, at the expense of his own life, the stranger whom he had admitted under his roof, is true; but how a *father* could make such a proposal relative to his *virgin daughter,* must remain among those things which are incomprehensible."   Clarke 178.
20. 19 Judg. 25. This shows the low status of women. "The woman would not go out to them; but her graceless husband *forced* her to go, in order that he might save his own body. He could have but little love for her, and this was the cause of their separation before." 2 Clarke 178.
21. 19 Judg. 25.
22. 19 Judg. 25. "Their turpitude could not bear the full light of day." 2 Clarke 178.

woman staggered to the door of the old man's house where she dropped dead, "her hands were upon the threshold."[23] In this position the Levite found her. Not realizing she was dead, he greeted her unceremoniously, "Up, and let us be going."[24]

When she did not answer, he rolled her over and discovered he had lost his concubine forever. He then cut her body into twelve pieces[25] and sent one of the gory members to every tribe of Israel, indicating that if she was not avenged "may ye be hewn in pieces like the abused and murdered woman."[26] In response to this grim message hundreds of Isrealites assembled at Mizpeh[27] and listened to the Levite relate the horrible details. "I came into Gibeah that belongeth to Benjamin," he told the assemblage, "I and my concubine, to lodge.

"And the men of Gibeah rose against me, and beset the house round about upon me by night, and thought to have slain me: and my concubine have they forced, that she is dead.

"And I took my concubine, and cut her in pieces, and sent her throughout all the country of the inheritance of Israel: for they have committed lewdness and folly in Israel."[28]

The Israelites were infuriated, quite naturally, by the Levite's story. It is very evident he did not make a full disclosure of all that had occurred. Oddly enough, nobody asked him how he happened to be alive, or how the sodomites obtained access to the lady's person. "As one man" the tribesmen arose against Benjamin.[29] Demand was made on them to deliver up the culprits that they might be put to death.[30] The

---

23. 19 Judg. 26, 27. This language points to the culpability of the Levite and the old man. Cf. 2 Clarke 178.
24. 19 Judg. 28.
25. Symbolic of the twelve tribes of Israel. 19 Judg. 29.
26. 2 Clarke 178, 179.
27. 20 Judg. 1.
28. 20 Judg. 4-7.
29. 20 Judg. 8.
30. Cf. 2 I.B. 816.

haughty and powerful tribe refused,[31] and a bloody civil war ensued.

The first two frontal assaults on Gibeah were beaten off by the Benjamites.[32] In these two battles the Israelites lost approximately forty thousand men.[33] How many defending tribesmen were killed or wounded is not told. The third assault was implemented by strategy and proved successful. In this fight the Israelites adopted the same plan Joshua had used many years before at Ai. A small force launched an attack on the city and then feigned retreat hoping to draw the Benjamites out and leave the city undefended. Their hopes were not in vain. The Benjamites swarmed out of the city in hot pursuit of the retreating Israelites. In the meantime a large section of the Israelite army was lying in ambush. When the Benjamites moved out the city the main body of the Israelites moved in. They set fire to the place and killed all of the inhabitants, including, of course, the women and children.[34] The outwitted tribesmen were flabbergasted when they looked back and saw their city in flames. Panic-stricken, they fled in all directions while the Israelites mopped up by burning all other cities of Benjamin and killing every man, woman, and child that could be found.[35] Only six hundred men of the tribe escaped the carnage by making a dash for Rock Rimmon, a natural fortress inaccessible to an attacking force.[36]

Before the war started the Israelites vowed never to give

---

31. 20 Judg. 13, 14. The Israelites "were all struck by the enormity of the crime, and considered it a sovereign disgrace to all the tribes of Israel." 2 Clarke 179.

32. 20 Judg. 20-26.

33. 20 Judg. 21, 25.

34. 20 Judg. 30-48.

35. 20 Judg. 48. "These terrible transactions seem to have made a deep impression upon the mind of Israel, since we find them referred to by the prophet Hosea several centuries after (Hos. ix, 9; x, 9) where, however, it is the conduct of the Benjamites that is held up to reprobation." 2 Cook 220.

36. 20 Judg. 47.

their daughters in marriage to the Benjamites.[37] Now that the tribe was almost destroyed the impulsiveness of the Israelites underwent a change. Anger turned to alarm lest the tribe be exterminated forever.[38] That would never do. Benjamin must be preserved. But how? All the women and children of the tribe had been killed. Only six hundred men perched on Rock Rimmon remained alive, and the Israelites had vowed not to permit their daughters to marry them. The problem now was not how to destroy but how to revive Benjamin. The war had gone too far. Women for the six hundred surviving males had to be provided if the tribe was to be rehabilitated.

To remedy the situation an army was dispatched forthwith to Jabesh-gilead,[39] a city which had remained neutral in the war against Benjamin, with instructions to kill "every male, and every woman that hath lain by man."[40] In the melee that followed only four hundred virgins were found. They were summarily carted off and married to four hundred Benjamites after peace had been made with the men on the Rock.[41] However, the Israelites were still shy of women. They needed two hundred more virgins for the remaining tribesmen. The latter were instructed to attend the annual festival at Shiloh[42] and, when the girls of that city came out to dance, each man was to catch a girl and carry her away to the land of Benjamin as his wife.[43] The kidnapping of these women is generally deplored,[44] though Bishop Vincent and his group of expositors advance the idea that the ill fate of the girls was attributable

---

37. 21 Judg. 1.
38. 21 Judg. 17.
39. Jabesh is a city in Gilead on the east side of the River Jordan about twenty miles south of the Sea of Galilee.
40. 21 Judg. 10, 11; cf. 4 McClintock 722.
41. 21 Judg. 11-14.
42. A city about fifteen miles north of Jerusalem.
43. 21 Judg. 19-23.
44. Cf. 2 Cook 223; 2 Clarke 185.

to their frivolity.[45] This seems to be rather a lame excuse for the conduct of the Israelites and the Benjamites.

Thus, all in all, six hundred virgins were kidnapped from the cities of Jabesh and Shiloh in order to preserve the Benjamin tribe. The problem of providing these men with wives had been solved. The only remaining difficulty was to pacify the fathers of the Shiloh girls. These men were asked to overlook the kidnapping and rape of their daughters because, by doing so, they would be discharging an obligation to Israel.[46] In this way the Israelites circumvented their vow not to permit their daughters to intermarry with Benjamin, thereby adding perjury to rape, fraud, and murder.[47]

It cannot be denied that the lewd men of Gibeah were guilty beyond all reasonable doubt and to a moral certainty when they raped, otherwise abused, and murdered the Levite's concubine. Today the Levite himself could also be held criminally responsible for the fate of his concubine, either as a principal or as an accessory. An accessory is a person who stands by, aids, assists, or encourages another to commit a crime.[48] The Levite aided the rioters by forcing his concubine into their arms. He knew she was going to be sexually abused when he shoved her out of the house. Consequently the sexual

---

45. "Dancing, even without mixture of sexes, often renders persons an easy prey. And who knows how often the ambuscades of evil spirits transport souls from the dancing-floor into everlasting destruction." 2 Vincent 622.

46. Cf. 21 Judg. 22. "Our translation seems to give as a reason to the men of Shiloh why they should pardon this rape, that as they had not permitted the women to live in their war with Benjamin, therefore these men were now destitute; and the concession which they wish them to make may be considered as more of an obligation to the Israelites than to the Benjamites." 2 Clarke 185. Cf. also 2 I.B. 825.

47. "When the thirst of revenge, however, had abated, they (the Israelites) found means to evade the letter of the oath, and to revive the tribe again by an alliance with them." 1 McClintock 753, parenthesis added.

48. Cf. 21 Am. Jur. 2d ed. 197; Black 29; United States v. Burr, 8 U.S. 470, 492.

mistreatment of the unfortunate woman, coupled with her murder, is as much attributable to him as it is to the sodomites. A person who forces another into a lion's cage is responsible if the victim is clawed or chewed to death.

It has been suggested that the Levite should be pardoned for the surrender of his concubine to the sodomites because he acted in self-defense.[49] Self-defense does not include the appeasement of an assailant by subjecting another person to sexual assault, battery, and felonious homicide. *Per contra* it includes the use of an amount of force *against the assailant* which is reasonably necessary to prevent bodily harm or injury to property.[50] The Levite would have been justified in using force against the sodomites to protect himself and his concubine, even if he had to kill the mobsters. But he didn't use any force *against them*. Instead, he heaved his woman out of the house. The doctrine of self-defense is dignified and has never stooped to the level of the Levite's conduct.

The Israelites, of course, went too far in one direction and not far enough in the other to avenge the concubine's death. They should have punished only the Gibeah sodomites. Instead they resorted to murder and rape on a national scale which could also be classified as war crimes.[51] It is true that Israel hoped to avert war by making demands on Gibeah to surrender the culprits. But hysteria soon prevailed over reason. Once Gibeah had been captured, the culprits could have been apprehended and punished. That would have closed the case. There was no justifiable reason to have pursued the matter further by burning the city and killing all of its innocent men, women, and children, a great many of whom probably never heard of the sodomites. Nor was there any justification for punishing the people of the other cities of Benjamin. They had not aided or abetted the affair at Gibeah in any way. Worse yet, the innocent citizenry of Jabesh did not deserve extermination. They merely elected to refrain from engaging

---

49. 2 Hastings (1) 168.
50. Cf. 6 Am. Jur. 2d ed. 133, 134.
51. Cf. War Crimes, supra.

in a civil war. They were the peacemakers who were blessed with death.

Dr. John H. Vincent and his associates do not share these views. They believe that all the people of Jabesh and Gibeah were as guilty as the few sodomites who violated the person of the Levite's concubine. They say: "It ought not to be forgotten in reflection on the whole of this painful narrative, that the people of Gibeah had been guilty of a crime so heinous and abominable that it was calculated to bring disgrace upon the whole land. The tribe of Benjamin condoned the crime by refusing to give up the perpetrators; and the people of Jabesh-gilead practically became *partakers of the guilt* by refusing to unite with their brethren in bringing the guilty to punishment."[52] This theory that guilt attaches through failure to join a vigilance committee could lead not only an individual but also a tribe or nation into serious trouble. It is odd that the good bishop and his group did not urge punishment for the Levite himself as a "partaker of the guilt." He was directly connected with the crime while the citizens of Jabesh were not even remotely connected with it. Moreover, only a few in Gibeah had a voice in the refusal to deliver the culprits. The bulk of the townspeople were an inarticulate mass. Yet they were slaughtered for the offense of others.

Neither Vincent and his group nor other commentators find justification for the kidnapping and rape of the daughters of Shiloh. They pass over the incident with the observation that the misfortune of the girls stemmed from dancing.[53] But the Reverend Scott calls a spade a spade and refers to the Shiloh affair as the "mere *evasion* of the vow (that) ... gave a direct license to fraud, violence, and the marriage of children without the consent of their parents."[54]

It has also been said that the surviving Benjamites acted honorably towards the captured virgins by marrying them.[55]

---

52. 2 Vincent 622, emphasis added.
53. Cf. 2 Vincent 622.
54. 1 Scott 467, parenthesis added.
55. 2 Clarke 185, 186.

These men did not have any choice in the matter; they had to marry the girls. That was stipulated when they came off the Rock Rimmon. Had they reneged, it is almost certain the Israelites would have killed them to the last man.

The Reverend Tuck sums up the whole sorry affair with this pertinent question: "Does not such a dreadful story of atrocity and bloodshed dishonour the pages of God's Holy Word?"[56] What is your answer?

---

56. Tuck 93.

14
Dinah and Shechem

AT FIFTEEN (or seventeen) years of age Dinah was an attractive and sprightly girl.[1] She was the daughter of Jacob and Leah, and Simeon and Levi were her brothers of the full blood.[2] Her beauty and charm are attested by the reference in rabbinical literature to the fact that her father hid her in a box during his historic meeting with his twin brother Esau for fear the latter might want her for a concubine.[3] Having swindled his brother and fearing retaliation against his person, Jacob was in no position to refuse any request Esau might have made.[4]

After his reconciliation with Esau, Jacob bought a tract of land near the city of Shechem[5] and set up a camp for his family and entourage.[6] Dinah, however, was no homebody.

---

1. 1 Cook 184.
2. Cf. 29 Gen. 33, 34; 34 Gen. 1.
3. 4 Singer 605.
4. Cf. 27 Gen. 1-46.
5. Shalem and Shechem are about forty miles north of Jerusalem. 33 Gen. 18; Miller 667, 670. Some say the word *Shalem* signifies "in peace," and that Jacob pitched camp peacefully outside the city of Shechem. 1 Clarke 213.
6. 33 Gen. 19.

She yearned for the company of girls of her own age and liked
to keep in touch with the times. One day she wandered into
the city "to see the daughters of the land."[7] Whether she first
secured permission from her mother or father or whether she
went surreptitiously is not revealed by the biblical historian.
In any event she was not chaperoned.[8]

While roaming about the city she was observed by Shechem, the son of Hamor, who in turn was a prince of the
country.[9] Either through a whirlwind courtship or by sheer
force he deflowered Dinah. We are told in the Bible that he
"saw her, he took her, and lay with her, and defiled her."[10]

Whether the girl fell in love with Shechem is an open
question. At least we know he fell violently in love with her.[11]
It is even possible Dinah consented to the intimacy with
Shechem.[12] The Reverend Scott is of this opinion, believing
she may have been a willing partner in her own defilement.[13]
On the other hand Dr. Clarke sees nothing in verses 2 and 4

---

7. 34 Gen. 1. Apparently she went to a festival in town. 1 Clarke 214.
8. She was merely seeking the comapionship of girls of her own age.
   Cf. 1 I.B. 733. Dr. Fausset thinks that a desire "to see novelties,
   worldly fashions and worldly company ruins many." Fausset 172. And
   Dr. Clarke suggests that the safest couse is to keep young girls at
   home. 1 Clarke 217.
9. 34 Gen. 2.
10. Ibid.
11. 34 Gen. 3-19; 1 Clarke 215; 1 I.B. 733.
12. Cf. 1 I.B. 734 and 4 Singer 605. In the latter text it is said: "Dinah is
    blamed for the affair with Shechem because she 'went out' (Gen.
    xxxiv, 1) and her brothers had to drag her away from Shechem by
    force."
13. "There is nothing in the narrative, which implies that Shechem
    commited a rape on Dinah; nay, the contrary is denoted in these
    words, 'Should he deal with our sister as with an harlot?' (31) for
    force is not used with harlots. The Jewish expositors, however, assert
    that he ravished her. Perhaps they devised this, in order to palliate
    the cruelty and injustice of Jacob's sons, by the greatness of the
    provocation. But Shechem rather seems to have used the common
    arts of seduction; and to have detained Dinah with the promise of
    marrying her, till she was afterwards taken away by her brethren."
    1 Scott 77.

(34 Gen.) so indicating.[14] This aspect of the matter is immaterial because Dinah was probably too young to give legal consent.[15]

When Jacob heard the news he did nothing until his sons returned that evening from work in the fields.[16] He told his sons what had happened, and they became highly and justifiably incensed.[17] Whether Jacob was also perturbed is not disclosed in the Bible. His lack of concern, if such were the case, may be traceable to Oriental theory that a brother is more dishonored by the defilement of a sister than is the father or husband, since the woman may leave the family of the father or husband by marriage or divorce but she never ceases to be the brother's sister.[18]

Shechem lost no time in trying to make amends and to do the right thing by Dinah. He asked his father Hamor to " (g)et me this damsel to wife."[19] That evening both the father and son called on Jacob's family. Hamor addressed the group after the formalities of introduction, "The soul of my son Shechem longeth for your daughter: I pray you give her him to wife.

"And make ye marriages with us, and give your daughters unto us, and take our daughters unto you.

"And ye shall dwell with us: and the land shall be before you; dwell and trade ye therein, and get you possessions therein."[20]

Before either Jacob or his sons could answer Shechem intervened with his own plea, "Let me find grace in your eyes, and what ye shall say unto me I will give.

"Ask me never so much dowry and gift, and I will give

14. "It appears sufficiently evident from this (vs. 3) and the preceding verse that there had been no *consent* on the part of Dinah, that the whole was an act of *violence* and that she was now detained *by force* in the house of Shechem." 1 Clarke 215.

15. Cf. infra. p. 252.

16. 34 Gen. 5.

17. 34 Gen. 7.

18. Cf. 1 Cook 186.

19. 34 Gen. 4.

20. 34 Gen. 8-10.

according as ye shall say unto me: but give me the damsel to wife."[21]

When Jacob did not reply his sons spoke up, "We cannot do this thing," they said, "to give our sister to one that is uncircumcised; for that were a reproach unto us:

"But in this will we consent unto you: if ye will be as we be, that every male of you be circumcised:

"Then we will give our daughters unto you, and we will take your daughters to us, and we will dwell with you, and we will become one people.

"But in this will we consent unto you: If ye will be as we we will take our daughter, and we will be gone."[22]

While Shechem's plea did not rectify the defilement of Dinah, you must concede that his protestations of love coupled with his request to marry the girl were sincere. He held out the olive branch to Jacob's family. He had every right to assume from the tenor of their reply that his offer had been accepted in good faith, that peace and harmony would prevail, and that Dinah would be given to him as a wife provided he and his men were circumcised according to the Hebrew rite.[23]

Shechem's confidence proved to be misplaced. The sons of Jacob had no intention whatever of abiding by their commitment. Their suggestion of circumcision was a means to two nefarious ends. One was to handicap the men of Shechem

---

21. 34 Gen. 11, 12. "This was the utmost he could do in such a case. And in this he is a saint of the first order when compared with the noble and ignoble profligates who, while blaspheming the *Christian* name by continuing to assume it, commit all kinds of breaches on the virtue of simple females, and the peace of respectable families, and not only make no reparation, but glory in their shame." 1 Clarke 217.

22. 34 Gen. 14-17. Rheims-Douay classifies these remarks as being made "deceitfully." 34 Gen. 13.

23. "Because the uncircumcised were not in the covenant of God; and to have given an heiress of the promise to one who had no kind of right to its spiritual blessings, from whom might spring children who would naturally walk in the way of their father, would have been *absurd, reproachful* and *wicked*. Thus far they (Jacob's sons) were perfectly right." 1 Clarke 215, parenthesis added.

physically so as to make them easy victims of mass murder.[24] The other was to rob the Shechemites of all their possessions and wealth. The latter purpose could not be accomplished unless the men of the tribe were dead. Here was calculated deceit at its worst. Unquestionably Jacob's sons were also actuated by a spirit of revenge. Subsequent events, however, show conclusively that Simeon, Levi, and the others sought mainly to enrich themselves at the expense of the Shechemites by stooping to the tactics of a thief.

Not doubting the *bona fides* of the Jacobs, Hamor and his son appealed to their people and won the consent of the men to submit to circumcision.[25] This must have been a painful ordeal without the benefit of anesthetics, sterile knives, antiseptics, or narcotics. The Bible tells us that on the third postoperative day "they were sore."[26] Inflammation set in and the men were racked with fever and pain. They were entirely incapacitated.[27]

It was then that Simeon and Levi, aided by a coterie of servants and probably some of their brothers, took swords and without challenge entered the city.[28] There was no reason for the Shechemites to suspect treachery or to become alarmed. A

---

24. To make the holy principle or circumcision "a cloak for their deceitful and murderous purposes, was the full sum of wickedness.... This was a bait held out for the poor unsuspecting people of Hamor by their prince and his son, who were not much less deceived than the people themselves." 1 Clarke 215, 216.

25. 34 Gen. 24. Either the people of Hamor had "great affection for their chief and his son" to submit to this rite, or were under "the influence of the most passive obedience." 1 Clarke 216.

26. 34 Gen. 25.

27. On the third day, "the inflammation was at its height, and a fever ensued which rendered the person utterly helpless, and his state critical." 1 Clarke 216.

28. "We are not to suppose that Simeon and Levi without help from others attacked and slew all the males: they had no doubt a retinue from their father's household with them, and perhaps were accompanied by some of their brothers." 1 Cook 186. Cf. also 1 Clarke 216, 217.

bargain had been struck, a deal had been made, and peace had been declared. Why should they suspect foul play? Unfortunately, the Shechemites did not know of Jacob's previous capers and the deceitful characteristics of the family.[29] The townspeople soon discovered their fatal error. At a sign from Simeon or Levi, the gang of murderers cut loose with swords and fell on the sick men of Shechem. Hamor and his son and every man in the city were killed outright. With blood spattered all over them, Simeon and Levi dragged Dinah, probably shrieking and hysterical, from the house of her lover.[30]

Not satisfied with carving the innocent and helpless men of Shechem into fine pieces, the Jacobs proceeded to mop up. They sacked the city and stole all of the livestock, jewels, gold, and "wealth" in the place. The women and children were captured and reduced to slavery.[31] When they returned to their tents, Jacob used a very pungent word to describe the actions of his sons. He said they made the whole family "stink."[32]

"Ye have troubled me to make me stink among the inhabitants of the land, among the Cananites and the Perizzites;" he complained, "and I being few in number, they shall gather themselves together against me, and slay me; and I shall be destroyed, I and my house."[33]

"Should he deal with our sister as with an harlot?" Simeon and Levi replied laconically.[34]

This reply did not dispel their father's misgivings. The incident throws a strong light on Jacob's character. Breach of the contract with Hamor and Shechem did not disturb him. Nor was he concerned about the murder of innocent men, the burning of a city, the capture and enslavement of women

29. Cf. 27 Gen. 1-46. It is said that the sacred writer is impartial in "bringing out into prominence whatever traits of excellence there were in the characters of Shechem and Hamor, while he does not conceal the cunning and falsehood of the sons of Jacob." 1 Lange 564.
30. 34 Gen. 25, 26.
31. 34 Gen. 27, 28, 29.
32. 34 Gen. 30.
33. Ibid.
34. 34 Gen. 31.

and children, or the theft of their goods. He really feared for his own life—that some of the neighboring tribes, on learning of the treachery, might band together and kill him.[35] The Reverend Cook is of a similar mind and points out that "it seems strange that Jacob should have reproached his sons as having brought him into danger, not as having been guilty of treachery and murder. This is only another instance of Jacob's weak character."[36] Drs. McClintock and Strong share the same opinion.[37] Dr. Clarke, however, does not regard Jacob in this way, contending that he honorably discharged his duties as a father by reprimanding his sons.[38] It is difficult to find anything in Jacob's remarks to support Dr. Clarke's view. Jacob berated his sons because they furnished cause for retaliation, not because they committed any crime.

Nobody can deny that Shechem raped Dinah. Her consent to the intimacy with the young prince or her lack of consent, as the case may be, is immaterial. She was too young to comprehend the full significance of her act. In most states and countries today a girl of fifteen or seventeen cannot legally consent to sexual intercourse outside of wedlock. In other words, a violation of her person constitutes the crime of rape whether she consents or not. If this rule is good for young sophisticates of this day and age, it is equally applicable to Dinah. Therefore, Shechem cannot be excused even if she did acquiesce.

But the punishment for rape does not warrant the wholesale commission of other crimes by the family of the aggrieved female. If somebody rapes a member of your family, you do not have the right, legally or morally, to shoot everybody in the city where the offender resides. The punishment for the rape of Dinah should have been limited to Shechem. There was no justification for killing the innocent townsmen, for

---

35. Jerome 35.
36. 1 Cook 186.
37. 2 McClintock 802.
38. "Jacob, to his great honour, remonstrated against this barbarous and bloody act." 1 Clarke 217.

sacking the city, for stealing all the "wealth" and livestock, and for making slaves of the women and children. The punishment, if it may be dignified by that name, did not fit Shechem's crime.

In order to eliminate the threat of reprisal, it is possible Simeon and Levi believed it was necessary to liquidate all of the men in the city if they killed the young prince. Assuming this is true, their fears did not justify robbery of the surviving women and children or making them captive slaves.[39] Rape is not punishable by murder, theft, and kidnapping under any code in existence then or now.

Clarke suggests it was wrong to let Dinah go out alone and unchaperoned[40] This point is well taken unless Dinah wandered away from camp without her parents' knowledge or consent. Right or wrong, her sightseeing is an insignificant part of the whole affair. The worst aspect of the case is the fraud and deceit practiced by Jacob's sons.[41] Most people recoil from treachery as they do when suddenly confronted by a snake. Did Jacob know or suspect what his sons had planned? It is almost certain that he did not because he was too fearful of repercussions and would have restrained his sons had he known their intentions. He was too much of a physical coward to have reacted otherwise.

In the light of all the evidence, Jacob compares unfavorably with Shechem. The latter sought to make amends for his mistreatment of Dinah, and he does not deserve to be con-

---

39. "Great as the provocation was ... this was an act of unparalled treachery and cruelty.... It was *diabolical* in *Jacob's sons* to slay a whole tribe for the offense of one man, especially as (Shechem) offered ... restitution." 1 Clarke 216, 217, parenthesis added.

40. 1 Clarke 217.

41. "Nothing can excuse the deceit." 1 Clarke 215. Cf. also 2 McClintock 802. Resentment is voiced by the expositor in 1 I.B. 736 where it is said: "But what they did was worse than the original offense.... Its ugly details are written in the story, and they include the smooth advances and calculated deceit, then treachery, then pitiless slaughter." This expositor might have added robbery and kidnapping to round out the list. However, Dr. Fausset, while denouncing the way in which Simeon and Levi vindicated "Israel's sacred calling" thinks that the "vindication ... was right." Fausset 173.

demned to everlasting perdition. Like many men in every age, he lost control of himself through hot impulse.[42] On the other hand, Jacob did not even try to rectify the wrongs done by his sons or to make them atone for their crimes. He could have released the captured women and children and restored their property to them. Instead, he and his sons kept all of the loot, including the captives, and dashed out of the country before any one of the neighboring tribes could act against them.[43] Like the leopard, Jacob did not change his spots. On his deathbed he must have been pricked by his conscience because he practically disinherited Simeon and Levi and gave them a scathing denunciation for their acts of cruelty and treachery.[44]

Dr. Singer and his group think that the entire story is allegorical. Dinah, they say, "represents a clan; Shechem is the well-known city. The tribe Dinah has been made captive by Shechem, and the closely consanguineous tribes of Levi and Simeon, in an attempt to capture the city and release the sister clan, came to ignominious grief."[45] That is a nice way at looking at a painful episode.

---

42. Cf. 1 I.B. 735.
43. 35 Gen. 1-6.
44. 49 Gen. 5-7. There is little doubt that Jacob's dying words refer to the affair at Shechem. 1 Clarke 217; 1 Cook 186.
45. 4 Singer 606; Concise 353.

Part 3

Miscellaneous Offenses

15
Daniel Out of the Lions' Den

DANIEL WAS A pathetic figure while in the lions' den. He is to be admired for his faith and for his confidence in the timely arrival of help from Heaven. Assuming for the moment that he actually came in personal contact with the lions, he warrants the world's sympathy during those trying hours. For it was fatal to share the same quarters overnight with an aggregation of hungry wild beasts.

But the whole picture changes when Daniel leaves the den. No longer does he inspire pity or admiration. Instead, he appears in the role of a revengeful man, unwilling to help people more innocent that he out of the same perilous predicament. He allowed the innocent wives and children of his accusers to be cast into the lions' den and torn to shreds without raising his voice in protest or lifting a helping hand. At the time he was so popular with the Babylonian king that a word from him might have saved not only his accusers but also their innocent wives and children. At least it was worth a try. Previously, he had saved the lives of others by speaking to the king.[1] But this time he remained mute, and the death of these unfortunates can be attributed indirectly to Daniel, all of which ill becomes a prophet.

Two aspects of the story of Daniel and the lions should be kept constantly in mind. Daniel *did* break the law. The prescribed penalty was to be "cast into the den of lions."[2] His accusers *did not* bring a false indictment. Daniel was guilty as charged, and the king to save face was obliged to put him into the lions' den. Secondly, if Daniel was entitled to divine protection because of his "innocency,"[3] so were the innocent women and children who suffered because of his deliverance. The pertinent facts of the story are summarized here to refresh your memory and to aid the discussion.

About 607 B.C. the forces of Nebuchadnezzar swept over Palestine, reduced the Jews to political subjection, and wreaked havoc in Jerusalem.[4] The walls of the city were torn down, the palaces burned, and the city sacked. In the campaign, the Babylonians "slew (the) young men with the sword in the house of their sanctuary, and had no compassion upon young man or maiden, old man, or him that stooped for age."[5]

The king and the princes of Israel together with all of the treasure were carted off to Babylon. Among the captives was Daniel. He was a young man of noble descent, a good physical specimen, and one of the intelligensia selected for further education in the palace of Nebuchadnezzar.[6] Like Joseph centuries before him, Daniel rose to power and prominence by interpreting the king's dream. The king had forgotten his own dream, but nevertheless called upon his magicians not only to relate the facts of the dream but to interpret it as well. Failing to do this, they were condemned to death but were saved by the intervention of Daniel[7].

---

1. 2 Dan. 24-30.
2. 6 Dan. 7-9.
3. 6 Dan. 22.
4. 36 II Chron. 12-20.
5. 36 II Chron. 17, parenthesis added.
6. 1 Dan. 1-6.
7. 2 Dan. 1-49. Nebuchadnezzar is said to have been afflicted with lycanthropy. The victim of this disease believes in werewolves, hobgoblins, etc. Cf. Montgomery 220.

After Nebuchadnezzar died, Daniel retired from public life but again came into favor at the court of Belshazzar when he interpreted some handwriting which miraculously appeared on the palace wall during a royal orgy.[8]

Belshazzar died shortly thereafter and Darius succeeded to the Babylonian throne. He appointed one-hundred-and-twenty satraps to govern the various regions of the empire. Over this group he named Daniel and two other nobles to act as "presidents."[9] Daniel was "preferred" over the other two. This provoked envy and discord among the courtiers.

The other two presidents and some of the lesser lights decided it was time to get rid of Daniel. He was too popular with the king. The nobles saw an opportunity to dispose of Daniel through his steadfast devotion to his own God. As it was Daniel's custom to pray several times each day, they cunningly suggested to Darius that he enact a statute prohibiting everybody from praying to "God or man" for thirty days on pain of being cast into a den of lions.[10] Darius liked the idea and signed a royal decree to such effect.[11] Daniel was advised of this law but decided to violate it.[12] The Lord did not require Daniel or anybody to say his prayers three times a day or even once a day. Daniel could have waited out the thirty-day period, had he been a law-abiding citizen. Instead he broke the law. The violation was reported to Darius who reluctantly imposed the prescribed penalty on Daniel.[13] He was placed in a cave or den. A huge stone was rolled across the opening which was then sealed with the king's ring.[14]

"Thy God whom thou servest continually, he will deliver

---

8. 5 Dan. 13-31. *Mene, mene, tekel, upharsin.* These words are generally construed to mean that Belshazzar's days had been numbered, that he had been weighed, and was found wanting. Cf. 3 Cheyne 3020.

9. 6 Dan. 1-3.

10. 6 Dan. 4-7.

11. 6 Dan. 9.

12. 6 Dan. 10.

13. 6 Dan. 12-16.

14. 6 Dan. 17.

thee," the king said to Daniel as he closed the mouth of the cave.[15]

Darius spent the night worrying about Daniel. Early on the following morning he rushed to the entrance of the den and called to Daniel. From the inside the prophet proclaimed his innocence.

"My God hath sent his angel, and hath shut the lions' mouths, that they have not hurt me: forasmuch as before him innocency was found in me; and also before thee, O king, have I done no hurt."[16]

The stone was then rolled away from the adit and Daniel emerged, *but not the lions*. Why they didn't dash out at the same time is anybody's guess. The fact that Daniel was unscathed sealed the fate of the other two presidents and their collaborators. There was no plea for mercy forthcoming from Daniel or any manifestation of forgiveness in appreciation of his own deliverance.[17] Without further ado the king ordered "those men which had accused Daniel" to be cast into the lions' den together with "their children, and their wives." The lions then "brake all of their bones in pieces" before they reached "the bottom of the den."[18]

The historical accuracy of the Book of Daniel has been challenged on several occasions.[19] If it is questionable in one respect, it is questionable in others. Hence the report that Daniel was saved by divine intervention provokes serious doubt and raises what is perhaps the most interesting question of the entire story. Did the hungry lions have access to Daniel? This question must be answered negatively.

---

15. 6 Dan. 16.
16. 6 Dan. 22.
17. It must be kept in mind that Daniel saved the lives of Neubuchadnezzar's magicians, who could not comply with the king's request to relate the facts of a dream which he himself had forgotten.
18. 6 Dan. 24.
19. "Some of the historical references in Daniel are correct; others erroneous." Miller 126; cf. also 3 Jackson 350, 358 and 2 McClintock 668.

From the account of the Bible we know for sure that Daniel was placed in the entrance to a cave or den. The entrance was then closed by rolling a stone in place. Obviously the lions did not have access to the den at the time of Daniel's incarceration.[20] Otherwise they would have escaped or made an attempt to do so. They must have been restrained in some manner farther inside. We also know that after the stone was rolled in front of the entrance the closure was sealed with the king's ring. "All this *precaution* served the purposes of the Divine Providence. There could be no trick or collusion here; if Daniel be preserved, it must be by the power of the Supreme God."[21] However, the fact that the entrance was closed does not preclude the possibility of subsequent intervention by some mortal, collusive or otherwise. There is nothing in the Bible to indicate that the lions were released so they could get within striking distance of Daniel after he had been placed in the cave. The evidence points just the other way. If the lions had been released on the inside after the opening had been closed, they would have been able to regain their freedom along with Daniel when the den was opened the following morning. But there is no evidence that the lions were present when Daniel emerged from the cave. It is not the nature of the king of beasts to retreat when the opportunity presents itself for food and freedom. Therefore the conclusion is inescapable that the lions did not have access to Daniel's person during the night. Either Darius or some friend of his gave secret orders not to release them from confinement on the inside of the cave, or the keeper of the zoo restrained the animals himself either because he liked Daniel or hated his accusers.

This theory of feline inaccessibility is bolstered by a comparison with the manner in which Daniel's accusers and their families were tossed to the beasts. The biblical historian conveys the idea that these people were thrown into a hole or

---

20. The "lions were kept in captivity to be released for a royal hunting party." Jerome 455.
21. 4 Clarke 602.

pit. They were torn to pieces by the lions *before they "came at the bottom of the den."*[22] There was no need to close or seal the opening because the lions could not jump out. Dr. Farrar gathered the same impression. He says that these unfortunate people "did not reach the bottom of the pit before 'the lions got hold of them and crushed all their bones.' They are devoured, or caught, by the hungry lions in mid-air."[23] The same thought is shared by Dr. Montgomery who says that the "king thereupon commanded that his accusers with their families should be cast into the den. These became the prey of the ravenous beasts before their bodies reached the bottom; the story depicts them falling into the open mouths of the lions."[24] Daniel, however, was not tossed to the lions in that way. If he had been, it is not unlikely that he would have met the same fate as his accusers and their families.

The idea that Daniel was saved by divine intervention is also discounted by the fact that the prophet claimed he was spared because of his innocence.[25] Of what was he innocent? Instead of being innocent he was guilty. He broke the law intentionally and was sentenced to the prescribed penalty.[26] He was placed in the lions' den but there were no lions present. True, the accusers hatched an unsuccessful plot to do away with Daniel. But such a plot was not a crime denounced by Babylonian statutes. The accusers merely suggested the ordinance to Darius.[27] The king was a one-man legislature. "Silly"[28] as

---

22. 6 Dan. 24, emphasis added.
23. 13 Exp. Bible 229.
24. Montgomery 278.
25. 6 Dan. 22.
26. Cf. 2 McClintock 662.
27. While "lobbying" by improper methods to influence the official conduct of legislators is decried, present law does not forbid all efforts to secure the adoption of desired legislative measures. 54 C.J.S. 659, 660; 17 Am. Jur. 2d ed. 579 et seq.
28. "What pretense could they urge for so silly an ordinance? Probably to *flatter* the ambition of the king, they pretended to make him *a god* for *thirty* days; so that the whole empire should make prayer and supplication to him, and pay him divine honours! This was the bait, but their real object was to destroy Daniel." 4 Clarke 600, 601.

his statute may have been, he could not disregard it when acting in his judicial capacity and passing judgment on Daniel. As a magistrate he had to follow the law.[29]

Certainly the wives and children of Daniel's accusers were guiltless, blameless, and innocent. If divine providence saved Daniel because of his "innocency," why did it overlook these women and children when they were cast into the den? Discrimination of this kind doesn't make sense, and surely nobody can say that divine providence is senseless. If the Lord intervened to save Daniel, He would again have intervened to save the innocent women and children who broke no law whatever and did not even participate in the scheme to do away with the prophet.[30] It follows *a fortiori* that Daniel was not exposed to the claws and fangs of the lions.

---

29. The wisdom of the legislative act is no concern of the courts, and laws should be enforced as written even though they may bring unwise results. Cf. Packard Motor Car Co. v. National Labor Relations Board, 330 U.S. 485; cf. also 73 Am. Jur. 2d ed. 435.

30. "It was perfectly just that they (the plotters) should have suffered that death to which they had endeavored to subject the innocent; but it was savage cruelty to destroy the *women* and *children* who had no part in the transgression." 4 Clarke 602, parenthesis added. See also 13 Exp. Bible 228, 229.

16
Noah's Nudity

In exactly one-hundred-and-forty-nine words the Book of Genesis tells of a degrading interlude in the lives of Noah and his sons.[1] The story leaves so much to the imagination that it has engendered pages and pages of comment from the clergy and biblical scholars. Their minds are far apart on many aspects of the case. But at least we are sure of two things. Noah got dead drunk on wine of his own vintage and indecently exposed himself.

While in that sorry condition one of three things happened. He was either (1) derided, (2) subjected to a sodomitical attack or (3) castrated by his son Ham or by his grandson Canaan. For the sake of propriety, most of the clergy prefer the first of the three alternatives. A few of them, however, find it difficult to reconcile derision with the severity of the punishment imposed on Canaan. Hence they suggest that in keeping with the morals of the age Noah may have been subjected to some form of sexual mistreatment. In rabbinical literature the idea is advanced that he was emasculated, and this theory is not inconsistent with the facts given us in Genesis.

---

1. 9 Gen. 20-27.

Noah is regarded as the "Second Father of Mankind"[2] because of all Adam's progeny he and his family alone survived the Deluge. Consequently humanity had to spring from them. But whether Noah of the Ark and Noah of the vineyard were one and the same man is question upon which all biblical expositors are not agreed. The majority, however, are of the opinion there was only one Noah,[3] and their opinion is supported in part by the dates assigned to the events of his life. According to various editions of the Bible, the Deluge occurred in 2348 B.C. The following year (2347 B.C.) the Lord made His covenant with Noah. Later in the same year Noah got drunk and the events of this discussion occurred.

After the waters of the Deluge receded Noah "began to be a husbandman, and he planted a vineyard."[4] The vineyard flourished. Noah harvested the crop and fermented the grape juice. He then "drank of the wine, and was drunken; and he was uncovered within his tent."[5] His son Ham "saw the nakedness of his father, and told his two brethren without."[6] The other two sons, Shem and Japheth, "took a garment, and laid it upon both their shoulders, and went backward, and covered the nakedness of their father; and their faces were backward, and they saw not their father's nakedness."[7] Shortly thereafter "Noah awoke from his wine, and *knew* what his younger son had done unto him."[8] Here the biblical account of the story ends abruptly, leaving you in midair. For the precise nature of what the "younger son" did to Noah is not disclosed. Nor are you told by which of the five senses Noah "knew" what had happened to him. Did he see, hear, feel, smell, or taste it? The

---

2. 10 New Cath. Encyc. 480; cf. also 7 McClintock 144 and 3 Cheyne 3425.

3. Cf. 1 Scott 34, 35; 9 Singer 322; 1 Jamieson 23; 1 Cook 80; 1 Exp. Bible 75; 1 I.B. 553.

4. 9 Gen. 20.

5. 9 Gen. 21.

6. 9 Gen. 22.

7. 9 Gen. 23.

8. 9 Gen. 24, emphasis added.

answer to this question would help to determine the precise nature of Noah's mistreatment.

Some commentators fill the gap with the observation that Ham or Canaan, as the case may be, derisively mocked Noah or made some caustic comment about his awkward and embarrassing position.[9] This is pure speculation and is entitled to no more weight than any idea you may have. The Catholics suggest that Cham (Ham) "found his father lying naked in his tent, and made a jest of his condition."[10] Along the same line Dr. Patrick believes that Ham told his brothers publicly of their father's plight and that such public irreverence justified the punishment meted out by Noah.[11] The difficulty with this notion is that the affair occurred too soon after the Deluge for there to have been any public. A populace does not spring up in one year like a crop of weeds.

The Reverend Cook thinks that the extreme brevity of the story makes it impossible to explain it fully. According to Cook, "Something therefore there plainly is, which requires to be *supplied* in order fully to clear up the obscurity."[12]

In keeping with this concession that some aspects of the story must be "supplied," a number of clergymen come forward with the idea that Noah was subjected to an indecent sexual attack. This theory is supported by the fact that sodomy was a common custom both before and after the Deluge.[13] The Bible indicates that Noah lived in a period of moral degeneracy which prompted the Lord's decision to destroy the human race.[14] Of a similar mind is James Gray who says: "Noah's drunkenness leads to sensuality on the part of his son."[15] Others share this view. "In the primary, popular form of the story there probably occurred here . . . an account of an indecent

---

9. 1 Scott 34; 7 McClintock 145; 2 Cheyne 1944; 1 Clarke 87; 1 Lange 336.
10. 11 Cath. Encyc. 88.
11. 1 Patrick 34.
12. 1 Cook 81; cf. also note 9, supra.
13. Cf. Lot and His Daughters and The Levite's Concubine, supra.
14. 8 Jackson 183; 11 Cath. Encyc. 88.
15. 1 Gray 45.

attack by Canaan on his father. This J¹ omitted for motives of delicacy."[16]

The belief that Noah was subjected to an indecent sexual attack or to castration is bolstered by the severity of the punishment which was visited upon Canaan. After Noah "knew" what had happened to him, he cursed Canaan and relegated him to the status of a "servant of servants . . . unto his brethren."[17] It was intended that this servile condition should attach to Canaan's posterity indefinitely. Parenthetically it should be noted here that Canaan was punished for what seems to be the overt act of his father, Ham. This is unreasonable and unfair unless Canaan was the real offender, or unless he collaborated in some way in the assault on Noah.

Possibly the most logical explanation of what happened to Noah is advanced by the Talmudists. They think Ham castrated Noah because he did not want his father to have a fourth son. Ham thought Noah had enough sons already without adding to the trio and causing a further split in the inheritance. Consequently Noah let his curse fall upon Ham's fourth son Canaan who was conceived on the Ark. At least this theory supplies a clear-cut answer to the question of why Canaan was punished instead of Ham. It also shows how Noah "knew" what had happened to him when he awoke from his drunken stupor, thus obviating the need to supplement the biblical text by showing the manner in which that intelligence was imparted. Dr. Singer and his group succinctly state the proposition in these words:

"Ham is represented by the Talmudists as one of the three who had intercourse with their wives in the Ark, being punished therefore in that his descendents, the Ethiopians, are black. . . . Some explained the obscure passage in Gen. ix. 22-24 as follows: Ham emasculated his father, saying, 'My father has three sons already; and now he wishes a fourth son.' Therefore

---

16. 1 I.B. 556. J¹ refers to one of the early documents or narratives of Hexateuch, the first six books of the Bible.

17. 9 Gen. 25-27.

Noah cursed Canaan, Ham's fourth son, saying, 'Thou hast hindered me from having a fourth son; I will curse thy own fourth son.' ... Another opinion declares that the mutilation of Noah was committed by Canaan, but was really caused by Ham mentioning his father's nakedness in the presence of Ham's youngest son. ... Possibly Ham saw Canaan's deed and did not condemn him for it. ... Ham was punished by having his descendents led into captivity with· the buttocks uncovered."[18]

Unless this Talmudic version of the affair is accepted, the average person will find it hard to reconcile that portion of the story where Ham appears in the role of a sinner with that part where he goes free and the supposedly innocent Canaan is punished. Patently this would be unjust. The Reverend Cook says that some scholars believe this inequity may be explained by the custom of visiting punishment on children for the sins of their father.[19] But this explanation is weak, because the punishment was limited to Canaan alone. Ham had other sons besides Canaan, and none of them were punished. An attempt is made to jump this hurdle by suggesting that the curse was laid on Canaan as the youngest son of Ham "just as Ham was the youngest son of Noah."[20] This idea falls flat, too, because Ham was not the youngest son of Noah. He was the "middlemost" son.[21]

Another explanation of what appears to be an unjust and unwarranted punishment of Canaan is that Canaan, instead of Ham, was the youngest son of Noah and not his grandson.[22] Many biblical scholars reach this conclusion. They say the ref-

18. 6 Singer 186. Castration may constitute the crime of mayhem under common law and most statutes. 53 Am. Jur. 2d ed. 490. Mayhem at common law is the violent deprivation of such members of the body as renders a person helpless. 57 C.J.S. 461 et seq.

19. 1 Cook 81.

20. Ibid.

21. 1 Patrick 43; 6 Gen. 10; 7 Gen. 13; 10 Gen. 1.

22. "The conclusion is not to be evaded that the writer follows a peculiar genealogical scheme in which Canaan is the youngest son of Noah." Skinner 184.

erence to "Ham, the father of"[23] is a redactional insertion and clearly arbitrary exegesis.[24] From this it follows that Canaan was the youngest son of Noah and the real culprit of the story.

Noah has been both condemned and condoned for getting drunk. It is suggested he was unacquainted with the potent effects of wine[25] and that he drank in order to cure an infirmity.[26] Kitto says that Noah "innocently and without suspicion ... drank of the alluring beverage, as if it had been water from the spring."[27] The number of men since Noah's time who also have drunk an "alluring beverage" as if it were "water from the spring" must run into the millions. Some say Noah got drunk for two reasons: one was to escape temporarily from the problems and vexations of life and the other was to relieve his nerves which had been shattered by the ordeal of living on the Ark with a collection of wild and domestic animals. This had overtaxed Noah's nerves.[28]

Some of the rabbis, however, hold no brief for Noah. "He lost much if not all of his former merit. He was one of the three worthless men that were eager for agricultural pursuits; ... he was the first to plant, to become drunken, to curse, and to introduce slavery; ... God blamed Noah for his intemperance, saying that he ought to have been warned by Adam, upon whom so much evil came through wine ..."[29]

In this rabbinical dissertation is a story which many people might consider the best sermon ever to be delivered on the subject of temperance in the use of alcoholic beverages. Ac-

---

23. 9 Gen. 22.
24. 1 I.B. 555; Skinner 184; 2 Cheyne 1944; 2 Cheyne 2330. "Wellhausen has made it plain that in ix. 22 (9 Gen. 22) the words 'Ham, the father of' are an intrusion by the editor to bring the section into harmony with its context (that is, the punishment of Canaan)." 2 Jackson 376, parenthesis added. Wellhausen is Julius Wellhausen, a German Protestant theologian (1844-1917).
25. 11 Cath. Encyc. 88; 7 McClintock 145; 1 Clarke 87.
26. 1 Cook 80, 81.
27. 2 Kitto 426.
28. Cf. 1 I.B. 553.
29. 9 Singer 321.

cording to Pirke Rabbi Eliezar, "Noah took into the ark a vine-branch which had been cast out with Adam from paradise. He had previously eaten its grapes, and their savor induced him to plant their seed, the results of which proved lamentable. When Noah was about to plant the vineyard, Satan offered him his help, for which he was to have a share in the produce. Noah consented. Satan then successively slaughtered a sheep, a lion, an ape, and a hog, fertilizing the ground with their blood. Satan thereby indicated to Noah that after drinking the first cup of wine, one is mild like a sheep; after the second, courageous like a lion; after the third, like an ape; and after the fourth, like a hog who wallows in mud."[30]

---

30. 9 Singer 321. Pirke Rabbi Eliezar refers to haggadic-midrash, a term applied to the oldest Jewish exposition of the Scriptures.

17
Pottage and Pothunting

THE REMARKABLE AND fascinating story of the twin brothers Esau and Jacob begins in their mother's womb. It ends on the fields near Peniel years later when the cowardly and suppliant Jacob, grown to manhood, groveled in the dirt before his older brother, while Esau earned the distinction of being one of the world's first Christians by displaying a degree of magnanimity and benignity scarcely heard of until the Sermon on the Mount.[1]

Jacob and Esau were the sons of Isaac and Rebekah. Esau was born first. Being a few minutes older than Jacob, he was Isaac's natural heir. As such, he held primogenitive rights and seniority over his twin brother Jacob.[2]

The Bible tells us that during Rebekah's pregnancy "the children struggled together within her."[3] This may relate to a reported embryonic dispute between the two foeti. "Yakub (Jacob) was actually older than his twin brother Esau. When he was going to be born in front of the latter, Esau was angry,

---

1. Cf. Matt. chaps. 5, 6, 7 and 33 Gen. 1, 2, 3.
2. 1 Hastings (2) 205; Douglas 594.
3. 25 Gen. 22.

and the two brothers quarrelled even in the mother's womb. Esau then said: Wallah, if thou wishest to be born first, I shall close up my mother's womb and kill her. Yakub then yielded and Esau was the first born."[4] This fantastic story is the first of a number of hypotheses conjured up to excuse Jacob for his shabby treatment of Esau in later years.

As the boys grew Esau became a daring and "cunning hunter," a man's man, and the apple of his father's eye.[5] Jacob developed into a typical mama's boy, a timid but crafty "stay-at-home"[6] tied to Rebekah's apron strings.[7] He preferred to till the soil and tend the sheep and was favored by his mother.[8] "As between her twin sons, she wanted Jacob to have the best of everything, no matter how he got it; and to that end she would not scruple at trickery and unfairness both toward her husband and her son Esau."[9]

One evening Esau returned from the hunt empty-handed. He was weary and worn out, even to the point of fainting.[10] Jacob had a "pottage of lentils"[11] cooking when the famished Esau entered the family home. "Feed me, I pray thee, with that same red pottage; for I am faint," he said to Jacob.[12]

Realizing Esau's physical weakness Jacob seized the opportunity to make exorbitant demands. "Sell me this day thy birthright."[13]

"Behold," Esau replied despairingly, "I am at the point to die; and what profit shall this birthright do to me?"[14]

Thus a bargain was struck. Esau "sold his birthright unto

---

4. 2 Islam 555, parenthesis added.
5. 25 Gen. 27, 28.
6. 1 Gray 105.
7. 25 Gen. 27, 28.
8. Ibid.
9. 1 I. B. 668.
10. 25 Gen. 29.
11. 25 Gen. 34.
12. 25 Gen. 30.
13. 25 Gen. 31.
14. 25 Gen. 32.

Jacob" for a mess of pottage and took an oath to that effect.[15] Jacob then handed a bowl full of lentils to Esau who satisfied has ravenous appetite. Parenthetically, you may wish to consider for a moment the probability that Jacob often partook of the venison Esau supplied over the years and, if so, whether Esau ever put an astronomical price tag on the meat. It is safe to assume from Esau's character that he gladly offered the food to his brother. While biblical scholars are not entirely in accord as to the precise nature of the birthright allegedly "sold" to Jacob, all agree that it included a greater share of the inheritance.[16]

The clergy both condemn and condone Esau and Jacob for their parts in the transaction.[17] The consensus is well stated by Dr. Hastings. "But in truth neither Esau nor Jacob can be called an ideal character. Esau is frank, straightforward, generous, but without depth of character or farsightedness of aim: he is governed by the impulses and desires of the moment; a 'profane' person . . . i.e., unspiritual, a man without love or appreciation of worthier possessions, and heedless of what he is throwing away. Jacob is selfish, scheming, and clutches at every advantage; but he looks beyond the immediate moment; he has ambition and perseverance."[18]

It has also been said that there "is something revolting in the whole transaction. Jacob takes advantage of his brother's distress to *rob* him of that which was dear as life itself to an Eastern patriarch."[19] The word "rob" in this quotation is underscored to emphasize the erroneous belief of several scholars

---

15. 25 Gen. 33. "The brief narrative of the sale of Esau's birthright for a meal does not tell how the exchange was confirmed or whether it was recorded officially." Douglas 594.
16. Cf. 1 Gray 115; Skinner 362; 1 Jamieson 30; Alleman 193; 1 Clarke 167; 3 McClintock 285; Tuck 209, 210; Piercy 111; Jerome 26.
17. Cf. Tuck 210; 1 Hastings (2) 203; 1 Gray 105, 106; Skinner 362; 1 Jamieson 30; 1 I.B. 666; 1 Cook 157; 1 Clarke 167; 3 McClintock 285.
18. 1 Hastings (2) 203.
19. 1 Smith 982, emphasis added.

that the transaction between Esau and Jacob was larcenous.[20]
They are mistaken. There was nothing criminal about the deal.
Jacob did not rob Esau of anything. However, in civil law the
transaction was illegal from its inception and could have been
set aside by Isaac, the family chancellor, for two reasons.

In the first place, the contract of sale was devoid of a consideration. It is fundamental that, to be valid, the "sale" of
the birthright would have to be supported by a consideration
or *quid pro quo* (what for what; something for something).
This rule dates back to biblical times, since transactions of that
age appear to have been based on some consideration.[21] Here
there was no consideration, no *quid pro quo*. Nothing belong-
ing to Jacob passed to Esau to support the so-called sale[22] of
the birthright. Jacob did not have any pottage to sell. It was
not his. The pottage belonged to Isaac, for in biblical times,
the father owned all of the family property and exercised complete dominion over it as well as over the wives and children.[23]
"The authority of a father was thus very great in patriarchial
times; . . . the more real powers of parental character were not
only left unimpaired, but were made in a great degree the basis
of the judicial polity which the law established. The children,
and even the grandchildren, continued under the roof of the
father and grandfather; they labored on his account, and were
the most submissive of his servants. *The property of the soil,
the power of judgment, the civil rights, belonged to him only,*

---

20. Cf. 1 I.B. 668 where it is said that Rebekah schemed for "Jacob to
    steal the birthright." Dr. Clarke also calls the deal as a "species of
    robbery." I Clarke 177, Drs. McClintock and Strong agree also using
    language comparable to that which appears in 1 Smith 982. 3
    McClintock 285.
21. Cf. 33 Gen. 19; 2 McClintock 493. Consideration is defined as the
    reason or cause of a contract; a benefit to the promisor or a detri-
    ment to the promisee by which the former gains or profits by the
    loss or prejudice of the latter. Cf. Black 379.
22. Though the Bible refers to the deal as a sale, it would properly be
    regarded as an exchange in this day and age.
23. Cf. 2 Cheyne 1504; 5 Singer 338; Miller 186.

and his sons were merely his instruments and assistants."[24] The pottage, therefore, belonged to Isaac and was not saleable by his son Jacob.

Nor can it be said that Isaac had made a gift of the pottage to Jacob, thus transferring title. Nothing in the Bible indicates donative intent on Isaac's part. Providing Jacob with pottage was merely the fulfillment of a parental obligation to feed him; not to merchandise or deal in produce. As it was in biblical times, so it appears to be today, namely, the necessaries of life, such as food, shelter, clothing, furnished to the child by the parent, remain the property of the parent and do not belong to the child.[25]

Because the sons in biblical times labored for the account of the father, he, as just noted, had the reciprocal duty to provide them with food and shelter, just as it is today. It follows *a fortiori* that Esau was not obliged to pay for the pottage. He had as much right to eat the food as did Jacob. Hence Esau got no benefit whatever when he received something in which he shared equal rights with Jacob. Esau could have taken his share of the mess by force. Probably he never thought of resorting to force or, if he did, he was too exhausted from the hunt to resort to violence.

No stretch of the imagination is needed to predict how Isaac would have settled the matter had Esau presented his side of the case seasonably and asked for relief. It is reasonable to assume that Isaac would have granted Esau's request and restored the birthright to its rightful owner since he, as the family arbitrator, had the power to do so.[26] At the same time, he probably would have censured Jacob for his greed and heartlessness even though Dr. Skinner maintains that the "ordinary Israelite would see nothing immoral in a transaction like this, where the advantage is pressed to the uttermost."[27] But Esau was neither a whiner nor a telltale.

---

24. 3 McClintock 496, emphasis added.
25. 67 C.J.S. 764; 59 Am. Jur. 2d ed. 135, 136.
26. Piercy 111, cf. also Payne 166.
27. Skinner 361.

The purported sale of the birthright was illegal for another reason. The deal was voidable for lack of valid consent on Esau's part. It is elementary that the consent of the parties to every transaction must be free and voluntary. If consent is acquired through duress or undue influence, the deal is voidable at the option of the party whose consent was wrongfully obtained.[28] Hence, it was a question of fact, to be determined by Isaac, acting in his capacity as the family judge, whether Esau had been subjected to duress or undue influence.

Undue influence includes any wrongful control exercised by one person over another so as to substitute his will for the volition of the victim.[29] Contracts have been set aside on the ground of undue influence where the party who benefited was a brother of the person who was duped or cheated.[30] On the other hand, duress includes oppression of any kind by which an unfair advantage is taken of the weakness or necessities of another resulting in a material loss to the oppressed person.[31] Of course these rules of jurisprudence had not been laid down in texts or case law for the guidance of either Isaac or Esau. But they are so basic that anyone with a sense of justice and fair play can comprehend and apply them. So could Isaac.

The oath Esau uttered does not remedy the situation either. It was mere surplusage, and it could not cure the defects of the transaction. Superfluity does not legalize.

Years later, Jacob again took unfair advantage of his twin brother. On this occasion Rebekah hatched a plot against Esau and her blind husband in an attempt to deprive Esau of his father's blessing to which he was entitled as the oldest son. Jacob was a willing participant in the nefarious scheme and, prodded by his mother, committed prevarication, fraud, filial

---

28. 17 Am. Jur. 2d ed. 551 et seq.; 17 C.J.S. 942 et seq.

29. 17 C.J.S. 969 et seq.

30. 17 C.J.S. 973, 974.

31. 17 C.J.S. 942 et seq. Clarke believes Essau was so exhausted from the hunt that he would "have perished had he not obtained some immediate refreshment." 1 Clarke 166. In this condition Esau could have been acting under duress.

impiety, and blasphemy. Some of the biblical commentators suggest that Jacob was guilty of theft on this occasion also, because he purloined the parental blessing from Esau.[32] Again they are in error. The only crime Jacob committed was blasphemy, denounced as such by one of the Seven Commandments of Noah.[33] The sordid affair came about in this way.

In the last years of his life when Isaac was blind and tottering,[34] he called Esau to him. "Behold now, I am old, I know not the day of my death:

"Now therefore take, I pray thee, thy weapons, thy quiver and thy bow, and go out to the field, and take me some venison;

"And make me savoury meat, such as I love, and bring it to me, that I may eat; that my soul may bless thee before I die."[35]

Esau lost no time in complying with his father's request. "If Isaac had a wish for something special to eat, it was Esau who would go and get it."[36]

Rebekah overheard the conversation and whipped into action. She summoned Jacob and said to him, "Behold, I heard thy father speak unto Esau thy brother, saying,

"Bring me venison, and make me savoury meat, that I may eat, and bless thee before the Lord before my death.

"Now therefore, my son, obey my voice according to that which I command thee.

"Go now to the flock, and fetch me from thence two good kids of the goats; and I will make them savoury meat for thy father, such as he loveth:

"And thou shalt bring it to thy father, that he may eat, and that he may bless thee before his death."[37]

---

32. Cf. 1 Gray 115; 1 Clarke 179; Fausset 321; Payne 166.
33. 8 Jackson 184; cf. also Cain Reconsidered, supra.
34. 27 Gen. 1.
35. 27 Gen. 2, 3, 4.
36. 1 I.B. 666.
37. 27 Gen. 6-10. "The mother's jealousy for her favourite son ... is aroused by what she has overheard; and she instantly devises a scheme whose daring and ingenuity illustrate the Hebrew notion of capable and quick-witted womanhood." Skinner 370.

Jacob did not need much coaxing. He fell in with his mother's scheme at once. Deceiving his father and cheating his brother was all right as long as he landed on top of the heap. The only thing he feared was the possibility of detection and parental punishment in the form of a curse.[38]

"Behold," he said to his mother, "Esau my brother is a hairy man, and I am a smooth man:

"My father peradventure will feel me, and I shall seem to him as a deceiver; and I shall bring a curse upon me, and not a blessing."[39]

Rebekah had a ready answer. "Upon me be thy curse, my son: only obey my voice, and go fetch me them."[40]

That satisfied Jacob, though one expositor expresses the idea it "is strange that he should agree to his mother's incurring so grave a responsibility."[41]

Jacob went to the field, rounded up two young goats and brought them home. While cooking the meat Rebekah took Esau's best clothes and put them on Jacob.[42] She tied or glued the goat skins upon his hands and the back of his neck.[43] When the "savoury meat" was ready, she served it on a plate with some bread and handed the meal to Jacob.[44] Thus fortified and rigged to impersonate his older brother, Jacob approached his blind father.

"Here am I," he said to the old man.[45]

"Who art thou, my son?" Isaac asked.[46]

---

38. 1 Gray 112. "It is remarkable that his scruples were founded not on the evil of the act; but the risk and consequences of detection." 1 Jamieson 31. Cf. also 1 Clarke 174 to the same effect.

39. 27 Gen. 11, 12. "The objection shows just enough shrewdness on Jacob's part to throw his mother's resourcefulness into bolder relief." Skinner 370. Cf. also 27 Deut. 18 where it is said: "Cursed be he that maketh the blind to wander out of the way."

40. 27 Gen. 13.

41. 1 Gray 112.

42. 27 Gen. 15.

43. 27 Gen. 16.

44. 27 Gen. 17.

45. 27 Gen. 18.

46. Ibid.

"I am Esau thy firstborn," Jacob lied. "I have done according as thou badest me: arise, I pray thee, sit and eat of my venison, that thy soul may bless me."[47]

Old Isaac was skeptical. He did not understand how Esau could return from the hunt in such a short time.

"How is it that thou has found it so quickly, my son?"[48]

"Because the Lord thy God brought it to me," Jacob lied again.[49]

This was blasphemy and a violation of one of the Seven Commandments of Noah. But Isaac was still not convinced even though Jacob had taken a oath.

"Come near, I pray thee, that I may feel thee, my son, whether thou be my very son Esau or not."[50]

The impersonator obeyed his father's command.

"The voice is Jacob's voice, but the hands are the hands of Esau," the blind father said as he passed his hands over the goat skins covering Jacob to satisfy himself the pretender was Esau.[51]

"Art thou my very son Esau?" Isaac asked with lingering doubt.[52]

"I am," Jacob lied for the third time.

"Bring (the savoury meat) near to me," Isaac ordered, "And I will eat of my son's venison, that my soul may bless thee."[53]

After the old man finished the meal, he bestowed the parental blessing.

---

47. 27 Gen. 19. "It is pitiable to note the efforts of critics to explain and excuse here. Who can make less than a lie of this?" 1 Gray 113.
48. 27 Gen. 20. "... blasphemy added to falsehood: this, the worst feature in the whole infamous transaction.' 1 Gray 113. Cf. also 1 Cook 162 for comparable comment.
49. Ibid.
50. 27 Gen. 21.
51. 27 Gen. 22.
52. 27 Gen. 24.
53. 27 Gen. 25, parenthesis added. Communication of the blessing called for appropriate ceremonies like eating or drinking. 1 Clarke 174.

"See," he said, "the smell of my son is as the smell of the field which the Lord hath blessed."[54]

This makes it clear that Isaac believed he was addressing Esau. "The smelling of the garments . . . is a final test of Esau's identity."[55]

The blessing was of the nature of a divine right, conferring dominion over the rest of the family, in addition to bestowing political supremacy and prophetic power.[56] Biblical scholars agree that, once given, it could not be revoked.[57] Some also say that Isaac's blessing carried with it the distinction of being the progenitor of the Saviour.[58]

A short while later Esau returned with real venison. He stewed a portion of the "savoury meat" and brought it to his father.

"Let my father arise, and eat of his son's venison, that thy soul may bless me," he said.[59]

Isaac was dumbfounded.

"Who art thou?" he cried.[60]

"I am thy son, thy firstborn Esau," was the reply.[61]

Here was drama in the raw which should have been filmed for posterity. Esau was rocked with anger and grief when his father told him that Jacob "came with subtlety, and hath taken away thy blessing."[62] Esau wanted his father's blessing more than anything else in the world. He threatened to kill his brother after Isaac's death.[63] The old father was so disgusted and angry he "trembled very exceedingly," but sub-

---

54. 27 Gen. 27.
55. Skinner 371.
56. Cf. Skinner 373; 1 Jamieson 31; Alleman 194; 1 Gray 114-116; Piercy 112.
57. Cf. 1 Gray 114-116; Skinner 372; Piercy 112, 113; 1 I.B. 684.
58. Cf. 1 Clarke 176, 177; 3 McClintock 284 et seq.
59. 27 Gen. 31.
60. 27 Gen. 32.
61. Ibid.
62. 27 Gen. 35.
63. 27 Gen. 41. "If Esau was careless about the particular advantages of the birthright, he was not careless about his father's blessing. He wanted that, whatever else was lost." 1 I.B. 666.

mitted to the idea that the blessing had been irrevocably conferred upon Jacob.[64] Rebekah and Jacob were conspicuous by their absence, but when told of Esau's threat to kill the darling of her heart, the lady warned Jacob to "flee ... to Haran[65] ... until thy brother's fury turn away."[66] Jacob needed no further admonition. He took off like a frightened jackrabbit, and Rebekah never saw him again.[67]

Clerical comment on the morals of the story is voluminous. It is only of passing interest here since this text is chiefly concerned with the legal aspects of the case. Some excuse Jacob and figuratively crucify Esau. Some imply that the means justify the end because of a divine plan that Jacob should have both the blessing and the birthright. The Reverend Cook even considers Jacob "an upright man, a man of steady, domestic, moral habits."[68] Do you? Esau, in turn, is classified as a profane man, incapable of appreciating his birthright because he sold it for a pittance. For this reason and also because he married a Canaanite, it is contended Esau forfeited his right to the parental blessing.[69]

Clarke makes a good point. He says that all the apologies advanced for Jacob serve a "system" rather than the cause of God. "To attempt to palliate or find excuses for such (Jacob's) conduct, instead of *serving, disserves* the cause of religion and truth. Men have laboured, not only to excuse all this conduct of Rebekah and Jacob, but even to show that it was *consistent,* and that the whole was according to the *mind* and *will of God.* ... The cause of God and truth is under no obligation to such defenders. ... With some people, on the most ungrounded assumption, Esau is a *reprobate,* and the type and figure of all

---

64. 27 Gen. 33. "The emotions of Isaac, as well as Esau, may easily be imagined—the astonishment, alarm and sorrow of the one—the disappointment and indignation of the other." 1 Jamieson 31.

65. 27 Gen. 43. Haran is in Mesopotamia about three hundred miles northeast of Jerusalem.

66. 27 Gen. 44.

67. 1 Jamieson 31; 1 I.B. 686; Lofts 28.

68. 1 Cook 156.

69. Cf. Skinner 373, 374; 1 Jamieson 30, 31; Alleman 193, 194.

reprobates, and therefore he *must be* every thing that is *bad*.
This serves a *system*; but, whether true or false in itself, it has
neither countenance nor support from the character and conduct of Esau."[70]

It is hard to find anyone who has a good word for Rebekah.
According to Dr. Jamieson, she "acted in the sincerity of faith;
but in a crooked policy—with unenlightened zeal; on the false
principle that the end would sanctify the means."[71] The beautiful story of the courtship of Isaac and Rebekah in chapters 24
and 25 of Genesis, portraying the lady as a standard of perfection, of beauty, and of moral excellence, hits a stone wall in
chapter 27 and scatters her reputation on the ground like the
pieces of a shattered idol. "It was the uncomfortable realization
of this that made the revisers of the *American Book of Common Prayer* omit in the 1920s the reference to the mutual faith-
fulness of Isaac and Rebekah which had been in the inherited
book for centuries."[72]

The idea has also been advanced that the entire story is
a myth or folklore to illustrate fulfillment of a prophesy that
the elder son would serve the younger[73] in that Israel (Jacob's
progeny) gained temporary supremacy over Edom (Esau's
descendents). This is the only way the prophesy could have
materialized because Esau never served Jacob for a moment,
even though his father said he should.[74] Poor old Isaac was
too blind to see into a crystal ball.

The belief is unanimous that Jacob got his father's blessing. Isaac thought so. He even said so after he learned of Jacob's
deception.[75] Rebekah thought so, too. Esau and Jacob shared
the same opinion.[76] And every clergyman, commentator, exe-

---

70. 1 Clarke 175, 212; parenthesis added. To the contrary it has been
     said that Jacob's conduct is part of a "divine plan." Jerome 26.
71. 1 Jamieson 31.
72. 1 I.B. 667.
73. Cf. 25 Gen. 23; 27 Gen. 40; Skinner 361.
74. 27 Gen. 40.
75. 27 Gen. 33, 35.
76. 27 Gen. 33-46.

gete, expositor, and biblical scholar whose works have been examined is similarly minded.

But from a legal standpoint they are all mistaken. Esau got the blessing. Jacob did not. He was merely a self-appointed proxy for Esau. More to the point, he was a trustee *ex maleficio* or constructive trustee, holding the blessing in trust for Esau as the actual beneficiary. A constructive trustee is defined as a person who, being guilty of wrongful of fraudulent conduct, is held to the duty and liability of a trustee in relation to the subject matter of the trust so as to prevent him from profiting by his own wrong.[77] Stated another way, a "constructive thrust, otherwise known as a trust *ex maleficio* . . . is a trust . . . which arises, contrary to intention . . . against one who, by fraud . . . or by any form of unconscionable conduct . . . either has obtained or holds the legal title to property which he ought not, in equity and good conscience, hold and enjoy."[78]

These two definitions are applicable to Jacob and the blessing. Jacob was a constructive trustee, and the blessing was the *corpus* (body) of the constructive trust. Isaac fully intended to bestow the blessing on Esau. He thought he was doing so at the time he conferred it. By unconscionable conduct Jacob impersonated Esau, deceived his father, and became the depositary of something to which he was not entitled. Hence the blessing was Esau's, held by Jacob in trust for his brother's benefit.

Pronouncement of the blessing severed the family ties. The four of them never met again as a group. Jacob fled to Haran, and the subsequent history of his life shows that while he acquired wealth, he did not gain in moral stature.[79] Evidently he did not fare as well as Esau who "made himself supreme in the surrounding country of Idumaea."[80] Jacob's

---

77. Black 1685.
78. 76 Am. Jur. 2d ed. 446; 167, 168; cf. also St. Louis, etc. Co. v. Spiller, 274 U.S. 304, 309.
79. Cf. Dinah and Shechem, supra.
80. 3 McClintock 286.

life was speckled with tribulations, disappointments, and calamities. "He who was destined to rule, had to serve. The cheat was cheated year after year—by Laban (Rebekah's brother), by his wives, by his children. He had to present himself, a supplicant for life, before the brother he had wronged. He had to witness his daughter's irremediable shame. He was made 'to stink' in the nostrils of his neighbours by the craft and ferocity of his sons. His own children repaid on Joseph, his darling, the very wrongs which he himself had inflicted on Esau."[81]

Thirty or forty years went by before the twin brothers met again. When Jacob learned of his brother's proximity and power, he was "greatly afraid and distressed."[82] He still feared Esau would kill him. Pricked by his own conscience, he made extravagant plans to placate his brother's anger and resentment which he believed still blazed or smouldered. He thought a shower of valuable gifts would have a hypnotic effect on Esau. As a defense he divided his people, livestock, and other chattels into two groups so that "if Esau come to the one company, and smite it, then the other company which is left shall escape."[83]

With considerable trepidation Jacob approached the rendezvous with Esau, trailing behind the skirts of his womenfolk who, apparently, comprised a vanguard to blunt Esau's wrath.[84] If Esau killed them, Jacob was in a good tactical position to beat a hasty retreat. When he finally came within sight of his brother, he "bowed himself to the ground seven times."[85] And what did Esau do? Indifferent to all the gift offerings[86] and without sign of malice, resentment, or rancor in his heart, Esau "ran to meet (Jacob), and embraced him, and fell on his neck, and kissed him."[87]

---

81. 1 Hastings (2) 210, parenthesis added. Cf. Concise 355.
82. 32 Gen. 6, 7.
83. 32 Gen. 7, 8.
84. Cf. 33 Gen. 1, 2, and Edman 34.
85. 33 Gen. 3.
86. 1 I.B. 730.
87. 33 Gen. 4, parenthesis added.

"How sincere and genuine is this conduct of Esau, and at the same time how magnanimous! He had buried all his resentment, and forgotten all his injuries; and receives his brother with the strongest demonstrations, not only of forgiveness, but of fraternal affection."[88]

Who do you think was the blessed man?

---

88. 1 Clarke 212.

18
Susanna and the Elders

THE NARRATIVE OF Susanna and the elders is not accepted ecumenically as the Word of God. It does not appear in all Bibles. The Protestants have omitted it from their King James and Revised Standard versions. They regard the tale as an apocryphal addition to the Book of Daniel, that is, as a legend of questionable origin and of doubtful religious significance. But at the Councils of Hippo (393 A.D.) and Trent (1546 A.D. the Roman Catholic church accepted the Susanna story and added it to Daniel as Chapter 13.[1]

The preceding chapters of this text have been limited to a discussion of those biblical stories, the facts of which are accepted ecumenically. An exception is made here because the Susanna story brings into bold relief:

1. the virtue and chastity of Hebrew womanhood,
2. the brilliance of Daniel as a lawyer and trial tactician,
3. the birth of the art of cross-examination,

---

1. Cf. 10 McClintock 38, 39; 2 McClintock 671, 672; Miller 24, 25; 1 Smith 707; 4 Cath. Encyc. 621-626; Cath. Comm. 642; 11 Singer 602; 1 Jackson 212-218; Piercy 198, 199; 1 Fallows 496; Fausset 43.

4. the intervention of divine help on the right side of the case for a change,

5. the injustice of mass hysteria and mob rule, and

6. the advancement of criminal law and procedure over the ages.

Susanna was a beautiful, virtuous, and God-fearing Jewess, well-schooled in the law of Moses.[2] She was the wife of Joakim, a rich Semitic[3] merchant of Babylon during the exile of the Jews.[4] Joakim, in turn, was a highly regarded, personable chap, to whom his compatriots showed great respect by the frequency of their visits to his home.[5]

Among the callers were the two elders of the story. They are described as "ancients of the people appointed judges that year."[6] They were rascals at heart, "of whom the Lord said: Iniquity came out from Babylon from the ancient judges, that seemed to govern the people."[7]

The two old judges used to see Susanna walking in her garden every day and, as time went on, became "inflamed with lust towards her."[8] Just as Amnon was lovesick for Tamar,[9] the elders "were both wounded with the love of her."[10] But each man kept his feelings to himself and did not reveal to the other the cause of his emotional unrest. For, we are told, "they were ashamed to declare to one another their lust, being desirous to have to do with her."[11] They saw the woman many times and felt a passion for her. They wilfully indulged in their sensual desires, forgetful of the law of God and unmindful of

---

2. 13 Dan. 1, 2, 3.

3. Ibid.

4. Sixth century B.C. Cf. footnote in Rheims-Douay Version to chapter 13 of the Book of Daniel.

5. 13 Dan. 4-6. "Her husband was one of the most distinguished Jews, and it was in his house that the exiles met for the purpose of administering justice and teaching the law." Cath. Comm. 642.

6. 13 Dan. 5.

7. Ibid.

8. 13 Dan. 8.

9. Cf. The Rape of Tamar, supra.

10. 13 Dan. 10.

11. 13 Dan. 11.

the punishment for such sexual offenses. Fully conscious of the impropriety of their desires, they tried to conceal them from one another."[12]

After leaving Joakim's home one day, the pair were about to separate when one said to the other, "Let us now go home, for it is dinner time."[13]

Instead of going home, each man returned to Joakim's garden to get another good look at Susanna. They met face to face and, with or without embarrassment, "acknowledged their lust; and then ... agreed upon a time, when they might find (Susanna) alone."[14] This chance meeting "strengthened their passion, and together they planned how to satisfy their desires."[15]

Shortly thereafter, the two elders again sneaked back to Joakim's home and secreted themselves in his garden without being observed.[16] Susanna entered with two maids and announced her intention to take a bath because of the hot weather.[17]

"Bring me oil, and washing balls," she told the maids, "and shut the doors of the orchard, that I may wash me."[18]

Without realizing the two old reprobates were hidden in the garden, the servants closed the orchard gate and went to fetch Susanna the oil and washing balls.[19] As soon as they were gone, the elders approached Susanna who, by that time, may have been scantily attired.

"Behold," they said to her, "the doors of the orchard are shut, and nobody seeth us, and we are in love with thee: wherefore consent to us, and lie with us.

"But if thou wilt not, we will bear witness against thee,

---

12. Cath. Comm. 642.
13. 13 Dan. 13.
14. 13 Dan. 14, parenthesis added.
15. Cath. Comm. 643.
16. Cf. 13 Dan. 15, 16.
17. Ibid.
18. 13 Dan. 17.
19. 13 Dan. 18.

that a young man was with thee, and therefore thou didst send away thy maids from thee."[20]

While the biblical account only tells us that Susanna "sighed,"[21] it is more likely she was a thoroughly frightened woman when she realized her precarious position.

"I am straitened on every side," she replied to the expectant old men, "for if I do this thing, it is death to me: and if I do it not, I shall not escape your hands.

"But it is better for me to fall into your hands without doing it, than to sin in the sight of the Lord."[22]

With these words she cried for help, preferring death to disgrace. The elders also "cried out . . . against her."[23] One of them rushed to the orchard door and opened it. The servants immediately assembled in response to the commotion and heard the story of the two old men. Nobody would listen to the lady of the house. Everybody was "greatly ashamed: for never had there been any such word said of Susanna."[24]

The next day she was summoned before the two elders and the other judges constituting the court,[25] although the final decision rested with the people who acted as a mob jury. The case attracted widespread attention and interest just as it would today. A beautiful woman charged with adultery always has been and probably always will be a public drawing card. With her head high and with a firm conviction in the right, the lovely lady faced her accusers, the court, and the multitude.

At the start of the trial the wicked elders told Susanna to uncover her face in order that they might feast their eyes upon her beauty.[26] This custom of unveiling a suspected adulteress "was prescribed in Num. 5:18, though in later times

---

20. 13 Dan. 20, 21.
21. 13 Dan. 22.
22. 12 Dan. 22, 23.
23. 13 Dan. 24.
24. 13 Dan. 27.
25. Cf. Cath. Comm. 643.
26. 13 Dan. 32.

the Mishna, tr. *Sota* 1, 5, forbade the uncovering of a handsome woman."[27] The two elders then rose up "in the midst of the people, laid their hands upon her head."[28] By doing this they stepped down from the bench, so to speak, and into the role of complaining witnesses,[29] because under Jewish juridical procedure a witness could not be a judge.[30] They then addressed the people.

"As we walked in the orchard alone, this woman came in with two maids, and shut the doors of the orchard, and sent the maids away from her.

"Then a young man that was there hid came to her, and lay with her.

"But we that were in a corner of the orchard, seeing the wickedness, ran up to them, and we saw them lie together.

"And him indeed we could not take, because he was stronger than us, and opening the doors he leaped out:

"But having taken this woman, we asked who the young man was, but she would not tell us: of this thing we are witnesses."[31]

This speech worked the multitude into a frenzy. Nobody even considered the possibility that the elders might be lying. Nobody thought to ask them how they happened to be loitering in the lady's private garden at the time. Nobody asked for a description of the young man or how he was dressed. Without so much as giving Susanna a chance to refute the charge and tell her version of the affair, the assemblage condemned her to death.[32] On hearing the sentence, Susanna was distraught. Raising her arms in supplication, she cried out to the Lord.

"O eternal God, who knowest hidden things, who knowest all things before they come to pass,

---

27. Cath. Comm. 643.
28. 13 Dan. 34.
29. Cf. 24 Lev. 14; Cath. Comm. 643.
30. Cath. Comm. 643.
31. 13 Dan. 36-40.
32. 13 Dan. 41.

"Thou knowest that they have borne false witness against me: and behold I must die, whereas I have done none of these things, which these men have maliciously forged against me."[33]

The Lord heard her plaintive voice and prompted Daniel, a "young boy," to intervene in her behalf."[34] He immediately took an appeal from the adverse decision of the mob jury.

"Are ye so foolish," he told the people, "ye children of Israel, that without examination or knowledge of the truth, you have condemned a daughter of Israel.

"Return to judgment, for they have borne false witness against her."[35]

In accordance with established juridical procedure of those times, an appeal from a conviction of a capital offense stayed execution of the judgment until fresh evidence was asked for and received.[36] That reopened the case and afforded Daniel the oportunity to cross-examine the two old scoundrels. Before doing so, he asked to have them separated so that neither man would know how the other had testified. Daniel then addressed the first elder. Eliminating his explosive prefatory remarks berating the witness, Daniel's only question pertained to the kind of a tree under which Susanna and the fictitious "young man" were alleged to have been seen in an intimate embrace.

"Now then, if thou sawest her, tell me under what tree thou sawest them conversing together."[37]

"Under a mastic tree," the first elder replied without hesitation.[38]

---

33. 13 Dan. 42, 43.
34. 13 Dan. 45.
35. 13 Dan. 48, 49.
36. Cath. Comm. 643, citing Mishna, tr. *Sanhedrin* 6, 1.2.
37. 13 Dan. 54; cf. 13 Dan. 37. "The way in which Daniel addressed the elders, recalling their past misdeeds and his denuciation of the first evidence before proving its inconsistency with the other, shows clearly that divine inspiration was the source of his knowledge." Cath. Comm. 643.
38. 13 Dan. 54.

Daniel dismissed him from the witness stand, summoned
the other elder, and propounded the same question. This time
the reluctant witness answered,

"Under a holm tree."[39]

With that Daniel concluded his cross-examination, and
wisely so because even the dullest clod in the assemblage
could see that the story of the elders was discrepant. Again
the multitude took snap judgment. They made short work of
the two old rakes. "To fulfill the law of Moses . . . they put
them to death, and innocent blood was saved in that day."[40]

Susanna's name was cleared, and the story ends with the
usual fairy tale presumption that she and her husband lived
happily ever after.[41] Justice prevailed, right mastered might,
innocence gained a complete victory over guile, mass hysteria
was channeled to the cause of righteousness, and the wicked
got what was coming to them.

Several aspects of the story are of more than passing
interest.

Where was Joakim during the trial? Why wasn't he ac-
tively engaged in his wife's defense? Did he desert Susanna in
her hour of greatest need? Is it possible that he too was swayed
by the trumped-up story of the elders? Did he have lingering
doubts as to Susanna's virtue? The only plausible answer to
these questions lies in the fact that the story is part of the
Book of Daniel, and that had Joakim taken a leading role at
the trial there would have been no room for Daniel. Joakim
is entitled to the benefit of the doubt and, most likely, exerted
himself behind the scenes in his wife's behalf.

That Daniel displayed remarkable mental dexterity in his
cross-examination of the elders is universally acknowledged,
and the fact that he was a "young boy" at the time supports
the theory of help from Heaven. The story records the birth
of the art of cross-examination. The contradictory answers of

---

39. 13 Dan. 58.
40. 13 Dan. 62.
41. Cf. 13 Dan. 63.

the elders played into Daniel's hands and inured to the lady's benefit.[42] However, Daniel gambled with Susanna's life by limiting his examination of the first elder to a single question. Seasoned trial tacticians of today would probably criticize him for doing so, because he did not know at the time the first elder testified what the answer of the second witness would be when asked the same question. Other discrepancies might have been shown in respect to her alleged lover's clothing, appearance, and utterances. Through sheer luck or happenstance, the two elders might have named the same tree. In that event Daniel would have been obliged to question the last witness in greater detail and then recall the first to the witness stand in the hope of establishing a conflict in other aspects of their stories. Thus the overall effect on the populace, the initial punch as it were, would have been lost. But thanks to the intervention of the Lord on the right side of the case, Daniel took and kept the lead throughout the entire proceedings.

According to the history of the affair, Susanna was as innocent as a newborn babe. Yet an inflamed and misguided mob jury found her guilty. This phase of ancient juridical procedure shows how easily people are swayed by inflammatory remarks, slanted news, and persuasion. The same is true today. Initially the people were mesmerized by the pomposity and rhetoric of the elders. Daniel turned the tide and swung the mob like a pendulum to the other side of the case. Thus, public sympathy could make or break a criminal case in Susanna's time, just as it can today, depending on how the facts are colored. Courts today recognize that extensive and con-

---

42. "The paronomasias in Daniel's examination of the elders ... only prove that the Greek is an elaboration of an old Hebrew story, but not that it originated with the Alexandrine translator of Daniel. The Song of Solomon may have suggested material to the author. The opinion of Eusebius, Apollinarius, and Jerome, that the prophet Habakkuk is the author of the History of Susanna is evidently derived from the Greek inscription of the History of Bel and the Dragon." 10 McClintock 39.

tinuing adverse local publicity may prevent the accused from having a fair trial.[43]

All these things highlight the progress made by mankind in the field of criminal law and procedure for the preservation of the fundamental rights of a person accused. When compared with the crude, swift, but erratic administration of justice by the ancients, you may well speculate on the question of whether the polishing and refinements of the centuries have been good or bad.

---

43. Sheppard v. Maxwell, 384 U.S. 333; Cf. 22 C.J.S. 521 et seq.

Bibliography

ABBREVIATION	TEXTS, AUTHORS, PUBLISHERS
Ala.	Alabama Reports.
Alleman	*Old Testament Commentary,* Herbert C. Alleman and Elmer E. Flack (The Muhlenberg Press, 1948).
Am. Jur.	*American Jurisprudence,* 1st and 2nd eds., (Bancroft Whitney Co. and The Lawyers' Co-operative Publishing Co., 1936 et seq.).
Black	*Black's Law Dictionary,* 4th ed., Henry C. Black, M.A. (West Publishing Co., 1968).
Boling	*The Anchor Bible-Judges,* Robert G. Boling, (Doubleday & Co., Inc., 1975).
Cath. Bib. Encyc.	*Catholic Biblical Encyclopedia,* John E. Steinmueller, S.T.D., S. Scr. L. and Kathryn Sullivan, R.S.C.J., Ph.D. (John F. Wagner, Inc, 1950-1956).
Cath. Comm.	*A Catholic Commentary on Holy Scripture,* Dom Bernard Orchard, M.A. et al. (Thomas Nelson & Sons, 1953).
Cath. Dict.	*The Catholic Encyclopedia Dictionary,* editors of The Catholic Encyclopedia (The Gilmary Society, 1941).
Cath. Encyc.	*The Catholic Encyclopedia,* Charles G. Hebermann, Ph.D., LL.D. et al. (Robert Appleton Company, 1907).
Chase	*Readings from the Bible,* Mary Ellen Chase (The Macmillan Company, 1952).
Cheyne	*Encyclopedia Biblica* Rev. T. K. Cheyne, M.A., D.D. and J. Sutherland Black, M.A., LL.D. (The Macmillan Company, 1899).

C.J.S.   *Corpus Juris Secundum* (The American Law Book Co.,
                    1936 et seq.) .

Clarke   *The Holy Bible Containing the Old and New Testa-
                    ments with a Commentary and Critical Notes,* Adam
                    Clarke, LL.D., F.A.S. (William Tegg, London, no pub-
                    lication date) .

Concise   *Concise Bible Commentary,* Rev. W. K. Lowther
                    Clarke (The Macmillan Company, 1953) .

Cook   *Holy Bible, Commentary by Bishops and Other Clergy,*
                    F. C .Cook, M.A., Canon of Exeter (John Murray,
                    London, 1871) .

Deane   *Abraham: His Life and Times,* Rev. William J. Deane,
                    M.A. (James Nisbet and Co., London, no publication
                    date) .

Douglas   *The New Bible Dictionary,* J. D. Douglas, M.A., S.T.M.,
                    Ph.D. (Wm. B. Eerdmans Publishing Co., 1962) .

Dummelow   *A Commentary on the Holy Bible,* Rev. J. D. Dumme-
                    low, M.A. (The Macmillan Company, 1908) .

Edman   *Of Wise Men and Fools,* David Edman (Doubleday &
                    Co., Inc., 1972) .

Encyc. Amer.   *Encyclopedia Americana,* Int. Ed. (Americana Cor-
                    poration, 1971) .

Encyc. Brit.   *Encyclopaedia Britannia,* 11th and succeeding editions
                    as noted (The Encyclopaedia Britannia Co. Ltd. and
                    Encyclopaedia Britannia Inc., 1910 et seq.) .

Exp. Bible   *The Expositor's Bible*
                    vol. 1 (Genesis) Marcus Dods, D.D.;
                    vol. 2 (Numbers) Robert A. Watson, D.D.;
                    vol. 4 (Judges) Robert A. Watson, D.D.;
                    vol. 5 (Samuel) W. G. Blaikie, D.D., LL.D.;
                    vol. 6 (Kings) F. W. Farrar, D.D., F.R.S.;
                    vol. 7 (Esther) Walter F. Adeney, professor of New
                          Testament Exegesis and Church History, New
                          College, London (A. C. Armstrong & Son, 1893
                          et seq.) ;
                    vol. 13 (Daniel) F. W. Farrar, D.D., F.R.S. (Hodder &
                          Stoughton, London, and George H. Doran Co., no
                          publication date) .

Fallows   *Popular and Critical Bible Encyclopaedia and Spiritual
                    Dictionary,* Samuel Fallows, D.D., LL.D. et al. (How-
                    ard-Severance Co., 1909) .

Fausset   *Bible Cyclopaedia Critical and Expository,* Rev. A. R.
                    Fausset, M.A. (George H. Doran Co., no publication
                    date) .

Forlong	*Faiths of Man: A Cyclopedia of Religions,* Maj. Gen. J. G. R. Forlong (Barnard Quaritch, London, 1906 and University Books, Inc. 1964).
Fosdick (1)	*The Modern Use of the Bible,* Harry Emerson Fosdick, D.D. (The Macmillan Company, 1925).
Fosdick (2)	*A Guide to Understanding the Bible,* Harry Emerson Fosdick, D.D. (Harper & Bros., 1938).
Gore	*A New Commentary on Holy Scripture,* Charles Gore, D.C.L., LL.D. et al. (The Macmillan Company, 1928).
Gray	*The Biblical Museum,* James Comper Gray (Anson D. F. Randolph & Co., 1871).
Harrison	*Old Testament Times,* R. K. Harrison (Wm. B. Eerdmans Publishing Co., 1970).
Hastings (1)	*Dictionary of the Bible,* James Hastings, M.A., D.D. (Chas. Scribner's Sons, 1905).
Hastings (2)	*The Great Texts of the Bible,* James Hastings, M.A., D.D. (Chas. Scribner's Sons, 1911).
I.B.	*The Interpreter's Bible,* George Arthur Buttrick, et al. (Abington-Cokesbury Press, 1952 et seq.).
Islam	*The Encyclopaedia of Islam,* M. Th. Houtsma et al. (Late E. J. Brill, Ltd. and Luzac & Co., London, 1927).
Jackson	*The New Schaff-Herzog Encyclopedia of Religious Knowledge,* Samuel Macauley Jackson, D.D., et al. (Baker Book House, 1960).
Jacobus	*A New Standard Bible Dictionary,* Melancthon W. Jacobus D.D., et al. (Funk and Wagnalls Co., 1936).
Jamieson	*A Commentary, Critical and Explanatory, on the Old and New Testaments,* Robert Jamieson, D.D., et al. (S. S. Scranton & Co., no publication date).
Jenks	*The Comprehensive Commentary on the Holy Bible,* William Jenks, D.D. and Joseph A. Warne, A.M. (Fessenden and Co., 1835).
Jerome	*The Jerome Biblical Commentary,* Raymond E. Brown, S.S. et al. (Prentice-Hall, Inc., 1968).
Kaufman	*Man and Sex,* Joseph J. Kaufman, M.D. and Griffith Borgeson (Simon & Schuster, Inc., 1961).
Kitto	*The Cyclopaedia of Biblical Literature,* John Kitto, D.D., F.S.A. (Newman and Ivison, 1853).
Lamb	*Dear Doctor: It's About Sex,* Lawrence E. Lamb, M.D. (Walker & Company, 1973).
Lange	*A Commentary on the Holy Scriptures: Critical, Doctrinal and Homiletical,* Johann Peter Lange, D.D. (Chas. Scribner's Sons, 1902).

Lofts   *Women in the Old Testament,* Norah Lofts (The Mac-
                             millan Company, 1949).

Maly   *The World of David and Solomon,* Eugene H. Maly
                             (Prentice-Hall, Inc., 1966).

Masters   *Human Sexual Response,* William H. Masters, M.D.
                             and Virginia E. Johnson (Little, Brown & Co., 1966).

McCary   *Human Sexuality,* James L. McCary, Ph.D. (Van Nos-
                             trand Reinhold Co., 1967).

McClintock   *Cyclopaedia of Biblical, Theological and Ecclesiastical
                             Literature,* John McClintock, D.D. and James Strong,
                             S.T.D. (Harper & Bros., 1894 et seq.).

Miller   *Harper's Bible Dictionary,* Madeleine S. Miller and J.
                             Lane Miller (Harper & Bros., 1952).

Montgomery   *The International Critical Commentary-Daniel,* James
                             A. Montgomery, Ph.D., S.T.D. (Chas. Scribner's Sons,
                             1927).

Moore   *The International Critical Commentary-Judges,* George
                             Foot Moore, professor, Andover Theological Seminary
                             (Chas. Scribner's Sons, 1906).

Morton   *Women of the Bible,* H. V. Morton (Dodd, Mead &
                             Co., 1941).

New Cath. Encyc.   *New Catholic Encyclopedia,* The Catholic University of
                             America (McGraw-Hill Book Co., 1967).

Paton   *International Critical Commentary-Esther,* Lewis B.
                             Paton, D.D., Ph.D. (T & T Clark; Chas. Scribner's
                             Sons, 1908).

Patrick   *A Critical Commentary and Paraphrase on the Old
                             and New Testaments and the Apocrypha,* Rt. Rev. Dr.
                             Symon Patrick, Lord Bishop of Ely, et al. (J. Harden,
                             London, 1842; Wiley & Putnam, 1844).

Payne   *Encyclopedia of Biblical Prophesy,* J. Barton Payne
                             (Harper & Row, Inc., 1973).

Piercy   *Bible Dictionary,* Rev. William C. Piercy, M.A. (E. P.
                             Dutton & Co., 1908).

Robertson   *Notes on Genesis,* Frederick W. Robertson, M.A. (E. P.
                             Dutton & Co., 1877).

Scott   *The Holy Bible Containing the Old And New Testa-
                             ments According to the Authorized Version, etc.,*
                             Thomas Scott, rector of Aston Sanford, Bucks (J. B.
                             Lippincott Co., 1866).

Singer   *The Jewish Encyclopedia,* Isidore Singer, Ph.D., et al.
                             (Funk and Wagnalls Co., 1906).

Skinner   *The International Critical Commentary-Genesis,* John
                             Skinner, D.D. (Chas. Scribner's Sons, 1910).

Smith   *A Dictionary of the Bible,* Sir William Smith, D.C.L., LL.D. J. M. Fuller, M.A. co-authored volume 1 (John Murray, London, 1893).

H. P. Smith   *The International Critical Commentary-Samuel,* Henry P. Smith, professor of Biblical History and Interpretation, Amherst College (Chas. Scribner's Sons, 1899 et seq.).

Tuck   *A Handbook of Biblical Difficulties,* Rev. Robert A. Tuck, B.A. (Thomas Whittaker, Bible House, London, 1891).

U.S.   *United States Reports* (Supreme Court).

Vincent   *A New Self-Interpreting Bible Library,* John H. Vincent, D.D., LL.D. et al. (The Bible Educational Society, 1913).

Wharton   *Medical Jurisprudence,* Francis Wharton and Moreton Stilles (The Lawyers' Co-operative Publishing Co., 1905).

Winthrop   *Military Law and Precedents,* William Winthrop, Col. U.S.A., Judge Advocate Department (Little, Brown & Co., 1896).

Wood   *The Distressing Days of the Judges,* Leon Wood, Ph.D. (Zondervan Corporation, 1975).

Index

Abel, 3–6
Abelbeth, 82
Abiathar, 83, 84
Abijah, 93
Abimelch, 78, 115, 116, 118
Abishag, 82, 83
Abner, 79, 85, 86
Abraham, 13, 101, 111–20
Absalom, 80–82, 86, 122, 136–39
Accessory, principal and, 46
    49, 147
Achan, 64
Achish, 70–72
Adonijah, 83, 84, 122
Adultery, 61, 62, 80, 81,
    121–23, 131, 137
Agag, 14–21, 34
Agency, 96
Ahab, 26, 47–50, 94, 96
Ahasuerus, King, 30–46, 141
Ahaziah, 93–95, 97
Ai, 64, 65, 145
Amalek (Amalekites), 14–21, 54
Amasa, 81, 82, 85, 86, 88
Amaziah, 98

Ambrose, Saint, 109
Ammon (Ammonites), 8, 9, 17,
    54, 74–76, 103, 121
Amnon, 80, 122, 133–39
Amon, 98
Amorites, 17, 60
Ark, 171, 173, 175
Asa, 93
Assyrians, 90, 98
Athaliah, 97
Augustine, Saint, 105

Baal (Baalism), 26, 27, 47,
    61, 94, 95
Baasha, 92
Babylon (Babylonians), 90, 122,
    163–65, 168
Balaam, 59, 61
Barak, 51, 52, 66
Bathsheba, 75, 81, 83, 121–27,
    130–32, 137
Belshazzar, 165
Benaiah, 85
Benammi, 103
Ben-hadad, 24

Benjamin (Benjamites) 81, 142, 144–149
Bethel, 22–24
Bethlehem, 141
Bightan, 34, 39
Blasphemy, 185

Cain, 3–6
Canaan (Canaanites), 11, 51, 52, 60, 66, 111, 156, 170, 172–75
Captivity, Jewish, 90, 122
Castration, 170, 173
Christ, Jesus, 25, 27
Chrysostom, Saint, 109
Circumcision, 154, 155
Concubine, Levite's, 141–44, 147, 149
Consideration (*Quid pro quo*), 178–80
Conspiracy, 60, 61
Cowardice: Abraham, 112, 115; Isaac, 118, 119; Jacob, 156–58, 190; Jephthah, 7; the Levite, 143
Crime: act plus intent, 103; defense of incapacity, 107, 108; defined, 3, 5, 15; Mordecai's offense, 36; murder, 15
Cross-examination, 192, 197–99

Daniel, 163–69, 197–99
Darius, 165, 167, 168
David, 20, 69–76, 79–90, 121–32, 133–35, 137–39
Dead Sea, 14
Deborah, 52, 66, 141
Deluge, the, 6, 103, 171, 172
Derision, 170
Dinah, 151–54, 156–59
Diplomacy, 38, 39, 44
Discrimination, 4, 169
Divine protection, 113, 115, 117, 164, 166, 168, 169
Divorce, 131

Duress, 182

Edersheim, 10
Eglon, 54–57
Egypt (Egyptians), 16, 17, 35, 61, 90, 111, 113–15
Ehud, 55–57
Elah, 92
Elijah, 22, 24–29, 47, 49, 50, 95
Elisha, 22–25, 28, 50, 93, 94, 96
Enoch, 5
Equity (restoration of rights), 181, 182, 189
Esau, 20, 151, 177–91
Escheat, 49
Esther, 30, 32–34, 37–46, 141
Ethopians, 173
Evidence, 4, 17–19, 103, 123, 167, 197
Ex post facto, 6
Expressio unius est exclusio alterius, 60

Fornication (incest), 61, 62, 80, 101–3
Fraud (deceit, falsehood, etc.) 51, 70–72, 112–20, 134, 135, 154–57, 183–88

Gath, 70, 79
Gehazi, 24
Geneva convention, 58
Gerar, 115, 116
Geshurites, 138
Gibeah, 144, 145, 147–49
Gibeon (Gibeonites), 66
Gideon, 66–69, 78
Gilboa, 73
Gilead, 8
Gilgal, 14–16, 18, 20
Goliath, 69
Gunkel, 105

Ham (Cham), 170–75
Haman, 34–37, 39–43

Haman act, 36–38, 41, 45
Hamor, 153, 155, 156
Hanum, 74
Haran, 111, 189
Hazael, 24, 93, 98
Hebron, 79, 80
Hegai, 34
Helam, 74
Herod, 98
Hittites, 60
Hivites, 60
Holy Family, 98
Homicide, 3, 4, 9, 15, 23, 27,
    28, 40, 42–46, 48, 50, 51,
    55, 60, 64, 66, 68–70, 73,
    78–98, 126, 127, 138, 143,
    144, 156, 166
Hosea, 96
Hoshea, 98
Hospitality, 51, 52, 70, 109
Hypocrisy, 70–72, 74, 75, 124, 128

Idumaea, 189
Incest, 74, 101–3, 135
Interpretation (vows, statutes,
    dreams, etc.) 12, 13, 18,
    20, 43, 45, 131, 132, 164, 165
Intoxication, 102, 106–9, 170–76
Irenaeus, 105
Isaac, 13, 117–20, 177, 180–89
Ishboseth, 79, 80, 86
Israel (Israelites) , 15–17, 25,
    26, 37, 47, 48, 50–56,
    59–62, 66, 67, 70, 73, 79, 80,
    90–94, 96, 98, 141, 144,
    145, 148, 164

Jabesh-gilead, 146–49
Jacob, 151–59, 177–90
Jael, 51–53
Jebusites, 60
Jehoiada, 97
Jehoram, 93
Jehosaphat, 93
Jehu, 24, 50, 94–97
Jephthah, 7–13

Jerahmeelites, 70
Jericho, 22, 63
Jeroboam, 92, 96
Jerusalem, 70, 75, 80, 82, 94,
    121, 122, 124, 138, 164
Jether, 68, 85
Jezebel, 26, 46–51, 96, 141
Jezreel, 47, 48, 51, 67, 94
Joab, 74, 75, 79, 81–89, 121,
    125–27, 131
Joash, 25, 97
Jonadab, 134
Jonathan, 86
Joram, 50, 93, 94
Jordan, River, 55, 67
Joseph, 35, 164, 190
Joshua, 16, 63–66
Jotham, 78
Judah, 50, 54, 70, 73, 79, 80,
    85, 90, 92–94, 97, 98

Kenites, 70
Kidnap, 147, 149
Kimchi, 10
Konig, 10

Laban, 190
Laws, 13, 15–17, 21, 50, 59,
    60, 63, 65, 67, 73, 76, 123,
    124, 129, 134, 138, 140;
    Seven Commandments of
    Noah, 6, 103, 185; Talmudic,
    131; Ten Commandments,
    6, 10, 20, 21, 24, 25, 29,
    45, 53, 63, 76, 95, 140.
    See also Lex Talionis; War,
    laws of
Leah, 151
Levi, 151–59
Levite, The, 141–44, 147–49
Lex Talionis, 4, 59, 63
Lot, 74, 101–9
Love, 109, 130, 134, 136, 152,
    153, 193

Maonites, 17

Megiddo, 51
Menahem, 98
Mercy, 74, 128, 129, 166
Mesopotania, 54
Micah, 13
Midian (Midianites) , 59–62
Mizpeth, 15, 144
Moab (Moabites) , 54, 55, 61,
    73–75, 103
Mohar, 110, 140
Mordecai, 33–46
Mordecai Act, 41–46
Moreh, 111
Moses, 15, 16, 18, 20, 25,
    59–62
Mt. Carmel, 26, 67
Mt. Sinai, 63
Murder, defined, 15

Naaman, 24
Naboth, 47–50
Nadab, 92
Nathan, 74, 83, 128, 129, 132
Nebuchadnezzar, 90, 164, 165
Nimrod, 5
Nob, 70
Nod, land of, 5

Old age, cure for, 82, 83
Omri, 93
Ophrah, 78
Oreb, 67
Othniel, 54
Ownership, 180, 181

Palestine, 14, 51, 66, 91, 164
Pekah, 98
Pekahiah, 98
Penuel, 68, 69
Perizzites, 60, 156
Perjury, 147
Pharaoh, 111–15
Philistines, 15, 17, 20, 69,
    71–74
Phinehas, 62
Phoenicia, 26, 47

Pirke Rabbi Eliezar, 176
Primogenitive rights
    (Birthright) , 177–79, 186
Psalms, authors of, 89
Punishment, 4, 23, 40, 41, 49, 64,
    65, 67–69, 79, 84, 85,
    113, 123, 124, 128, 129,
    137–39, 148, 157, 158,
    165, 170, 173
Purification, 32, 33, 111, 113
Purim, Feast of, 43

Rabbah, 75, 121, 127, 132
Rachel, 141
Rahab, 63, 64
Ramoth-Gilead, 50, 94
Rape, 135, 136, 141–50, 152,
    153, 157
Rebekah, 117–19, 141, 177, 178,
    182–84, 187, 188
Rehoboam, 91–93
Rephidim, 16
Rizpah, 79
Rock Rimmon, 145, 146, 150

Samaria, 50
Samuel, 14–21, 34
Sarah (Sarai) , 111–13, 115–17,
    119, 141
Saul, 14–16, 18–20, 69–71, 73
Self-Defense, 41, 45, 52, 53,
    77, 148
Sennacherib, 98
Seven Commandments of
    Noah. See Laws
Sexual impulse, 103–5, 122, 123,
    125, 126, 133, 134
Sexual potency, 106–8
Shallum, 98
Sheba, 81, 82, 86
Shechem (Shechemites) , 78,
    151–59
Shemei, 88
Shiloh, 146–49
Shushan, 37, 38, 42, 43
Sichem, 111

Simeon, 151–59
Sisera, 51, 52
Sodom, 101, 104, 107, 109
Sodomy, 109, 142, 143, 170, 172, 173
Solomon, 80, 83–91, 122, 130
Succoth, 68, 69
Syria (Syrians), 50, 74, 93

Tabernacle, 13
Tables, 63
Tamar, 80, 133–39
Taxation, 91, 92
Ten Commandments. *See* Laws
Teresh, 34, 39
Thebez, 78
Theft, 64, 156, 157, 159
Theodoret, 105
Tirzah, 93
Tob, 8
Torture, 7–9, 68, 69, 74–76, 78, 89, 132
Transfiguration of Christ, 25
Treachery, 70–72, 86, 96, 126, 155–58
Trustee, constructive, 189
Tyrannicide, 56

Undue influence, 182
Uriah, 74, 122–27, 131, 132

Vashti, 31, 32, 34
Versions of Bible: Aramaic (Targums), 8, 12, 31; Greek (Septuagint), 4, 8, 12, 37; King James, 8, 31, 89; Latin (Vulgate), 8, 12, 37; Revised Standard, 8, 12, 31; Rheims-Douay, 12, 14, 31, 154, 193
Viticulture, 170, 171
Vows, 7, 9, 12, 13, 145, 146

War, laws of, 58, 59, 63–65, 67, 76
Wisdom of Solomon, 90
Witness (false), 48, 196
Women, status of, 31, 110, 111, 133, 134, 140, 141, 143

Zachariah, 98
Zalmunna, 67, 68
Zebah, 67, 68
Zechariah, 97, 98
Zeeb, 67
Zeruiah, 88
Zidonians, 17
Ziklag, 70
Zimri, 50, 62, 92, 93
Zoar, 102, 104, 107